Failure, A Writer's Life

Failure,
A Writer's Life

Joe Milutis

zero books

Winchester, UK
Washington, USA

First published by Zero Books, 2013
Zero Books is an imprint of John Hunt Publishing Ltd., Laurel House, Station Approach,
Alresford, Hants, SO24 9JH, UK
office1@jhpbooks.net
www.johnhuntpublishing.com
www.zero-books.net

For distributor details and how to order please visit the 'Ordering' section on our website.

ISBN: 978 1 78099 704 9

A CIP catalogue record for this book is available from the British Library.

Design: Stuart Davies

Printed and bound by CPI Group (UK) Ltd, Croydon, CR0 4YY

Keep reminding yourself that literature is one of the saddest roads that leads to everything.

— *André Breton*

CONTENTS

Ungreat Books

William Gold

"William Gold has earned only 50 cents after 18 years of unceasing labor."

Any child who read the Guinness Books between 1976 and 1982 has reflected on these words. In 1976, William Gold first appeared as the world's "Least Successful Author," a record which he held, tenuously, until 1982. He was not included in 1980, returned in 1981, and by 1982 only remained as perhaps a cautionary image, no longer with an official record entry. He appeared alone, a superstar of failure, in the early years, but had the privilege (or indignity) of later sharing his space with, alternately, Agatha Christie and Jacqueline Susann, as if to exemplify the extremes of literary destiny, one of those little cosmic jokes the McWhirter twins liked to play, here at Mr. Gold's expense.[1]

For a long time, this image was a haunting one for me, as perhaps it still is. It now strikes me there is something saintly about Gold. Maybe it's the head cradled over his typewriter in lotus petal hands, his ringed Svengali eyes daring you to fail more, fail better than he. But as a young adult, it was another matter entirely. Here was someone who had every semblance of having the role of "writer," not to mention "human being," under his control; he owned a suit and seemed to reside in some kind of office. Particularly shaming to me was the fact that he had the energy and time to have completed eight books and seven novels. Why was Gold more "Least Successful" than I? Hadn't I put in long, undocumentable hours, months, and years into writing that was unpaid, unpublished, and unbindable even by my own stapler?

This category no longer exists, and for good reason. All of our failures are incalculable.[2] Many of them compete handsomely with Gold's failure, although these failures might not submit easily to Guinness metrics. Thc literary world is haunted by the unpublished, and in fact may productively be generated only by the existence of the vastness of the unreadable. But can we say that Gold's fifteen books have impacted the literary world in any way? How different are they from, say, Jacqueline Susann's unreadable *The Love Machine*, for which she garnered a $500,000 advance, after submitting to the publisher merely seven pages, handwritten on pink paper?[3] While still a freelance writer, Nora Ephron wrote in 1969 that "The publication of 'The Love Machine' should not be confused with a literary event. Not at all. There is nothing literary about Miss Susann—a former actress who became somewhat successful in the fifties doing Schiffli embroidery commercials with her poodle Josephine—or her writing."[4]

The literary world is also haunted by metrics, the math—many times computer modeled—out of which literary value has been erected in the age of the publishing conglomerate. The Guinness book, dealing only in numerical extremes, transforming otherwise anonymous personalities and invisible oddballs into momentary spectacles merely on account of their numeric prodigy, is perhaps the purest example of this. In fact, it would, in the years when it cannibalized the failure of William Gold, become the world's "Most Successful" publication.

In another, perhaps more cruelly organized world, William Gold's dubious achievement would be placed next to that of Mrs. Marva Drew, whose claim to fame is the seemingly more wholesome, cheerfully troglodytic activity of typing the numbers one to one million, for which she took six years out of her life. However, the indefatigable Drew's stunt is separated from "Arts and Entertainment" by over two hundred pages. In "Endurance."

Marguerite Duras

Another saint? Or perhaps here is an allegorical figure of "endurance," "duration," and a sense of the hard materials of life: Marguerite Duras. Is she the inverse of Gold? She is fearless towards the negative pull of the unpublished, the unprofitable, delighting in things unrepresentable because of the ravishment of time. There was a destructive force that was foundational to her work, not a product of despair after the fact. In the words of Maurice Blanchot, she was "one who could destroy by a pure movement of love . . . bestowing an infinite emptiness where the word destroy becomes a non-privative, non-positive, neutral word."[5] When she took the soundtrack of her film *India Song,* and created a sequel by merely adding new images, completely devoid of any sense of contemporary human activity, she said, "If you must define me, I think it is there that you must look. In this wager, in this wager that I make against myself, to undo what I did . . . I call that progress. To destroy what I have done."[6]

Even in the original film that she "destroyed,"she was already playing out the creative destruction of non-representational art by composing it without clear action, locatable dialog, or discernable tempo. *India Song* is a film of memory, evanescences, absence, heat, with a horrible cry of pain at its core. We are not given any framework by which to hold these elements (even the actual frame of the film is complexified by a large mirror in the *mise-en-scène*), and in fact, it is hard to remember anything about the film even immediately after the film is finished. It leaves no moments for us that we can take as souvenirs, no "things." In this way, one plays out the ruin of one's own art, not merely thematizing but embodying death and forgetting, operating through despair and absence, while motivated by, as Duras says, love: "If *India Song* is successful in any way, it can only be in that it documents a failed project. A result that fills me with hope. . . . The only possible setting for the story is the incessant swing of our despair *between this love and its body*: the very obstacle to any narration."[7]

In 1957, Duras defined what she called "virtual literature." She couldn't have known anything about hypertext, caves, and data gloves. The reference occurs in the introduction to a short piece entitled "One out of a Hundred Novels Makes it to Publication," where she defines virtual literature not as the electronicized dream-world of floating words, but rather, as that which is *not* literature. She says, "Published literature represents only one percent of what is written in the world. It seems worthwhile to talk about the rest, an abyss, a black night out of which comes that 'bizarre thing,' literature, and into which almost all of it disappears again without a trace."[8] As such, "virtual literature" becomes a useful term providing a link between works that accidentally find themselves in the void of the unpublished, such as Gold's and those that, for whatever reason, find that the failure of their work is not only preordained, but also is the condition for its creativity (and, in a sense, its lovability).

Duras' "one percent" may seem quaint to us now, too fat an integer. It may be that published literature now forms a mere infinitesimal speck on the spume of great oceans of data. If it seemed worthwhile for Duras to talk about "the rest," this would now include not merely the weekend novelist who is not published, but the multifarious forms of self-publishing, as well as those modes of writing that are para- or sub-literary, which could include, among other things, the data fall-out of Web 2.0. This "remainder"—although it is too much in the majority to really call it that—assails us everyday in the noise of the web, and we are already virtual when we navigate this vast metacategory of "what is not literature."

We can make our own literature out of this non-literary realm, and it is perhaps no longer such a dark realm when we can so easily activate a lost memory, or frame some data detritus for enjoyment and wonder, connecting each new fragment in a total system of sympathies. Duras' more terrible virtual still exists, but one wonders whether we are distracted enough by digital positivism not to see at the heart of any database her pure destructive nothing, whether we can see, as in the almost featureless face of her early photographs, time nullified, but duration (unperceived, unrecorded) sustained.

André Breton

To blacken some paper. This is how Breton describes the surrealist writing experiments he conducted with Phillipe Souppault, which lead to his formulations in the "Surrealist Manifesto." *Write quickly, without any preconceived subject . . . put yourself in as passive, or receptive, a state of mind as you can . . . do not be tempted to reread what you've written . . . with every passing second there is a sentence unknown to our consciousness which is only crying out to be heard . . . Put your trust in the inexhaustible nature of the murmur . . . Keep reminding yourself that literature is one of the saddest roads that leads to everything.* His confidence that he could externalize thought—which for him could be not faster than the pen, but which still could be held up at the customs of the mind—was bolstered by the belief that its formless, uncensored contents were more marvelous than those shaped by literature.

Instead, he wishes to become a passive recording mechanism. If the pen drives thought rather than the opposite, then our thought is only limited by the speed of our machines. But how can a machine poetics *be thought*? Why should our productions submit to thinkability? Why should *we*? Indeed, as Gilles Deleuze will later assert, it is the image of thought itself that blocks some of the more exciting assemblages of which we are capable, including the experience of virtuality in its purest state.[9] Breton stood at a golden time where he could imagine a harmonic alignment between the typewriter, the radio, the dreamer and the poet, and so his unliterary assemblages did not seem so far outside of literature or the thinking being's constitution; one could still feel like a swim in the black sea of data was salubrious for the writer, especially if that black sea was the repressed contents of one's very self.

For Breton, literature was merely a type of filter, and the Surrealists "we, who have made no effort whatsoever to filter."[10] Today, this filterless experience may strike us as an outright impossibility, since we have access not only to our own unedited, unconscious contents but potentially to those of millions. And their cat photos. But the filter—whether implicated in the structure of the mind, narrative or the computer—always determines the borderlands between actual literary practice and its virtual backdrop, between what gets read and the wilderness of the unreadable.

If we were to create some sort of spectrum of artistic attitudes towards this virtual realm of the unpublished, where would we put Breton?[11] On each end are the impossible attitudes towards the virtual: either full emersion in the filterless (a kind of death) or totally filtered experience (a kind of idiocy). As with Duras, Breton espouses a loving nihilism, with his particular form of anti-literature framed (or unframed) as an initiation into death that one must undertake. Yet his anti-literary gestures are precisely those that, in turning attention to the unframed contents of existence, affirm life, and create a new literature. In *Nadja*, the main character—only approached by various feints and oblique indications (she is not even mentioned until halfway through the book)—asks Breton to bring her some of his books, to which he replies "Life is other than what one writes."[12] But Breton's surrealist paradox is that his new combinations and attentions make for a better capture or experience of life. The act of continuous passive recording becomes a form of action-art, with energies reawakened by the virtual, approaching life more willingly than do the deadly impositions of generic forms.

Warren Motte describes Breton's supposed antagonism between literature and life as a game where the terms constantly mutate, so that the anti-literary becomes the heart of the literary, and the non-book secretly congeals into a book, while "the potentiality of writing is . . . the primary concern of *Nadja*."[13] As we will see, "potentiality" is one of many synonyms for the virtuality of the text in this, my bestiary of the unpublished and unpublishable. The word implies an openness into which literature renews itself, primarily through the presumed anti-literary—process, duration, archive, junkpile. Thus, in *Nadja*, the flea market is a central engine of this potentiality, where one can access "objects that can be found nowhere else: old fashioned, broken, useless, almost incomprehensible, even perverse."[14] Its picked-over jumble stands to outdo the order of the library. There Breton finds an object that I feel is meant stand for a competing writing machine, a perverse dream-image through which he can imagine a future poetics emanating. He describes it as an "irregular, white, shellacked half-cylinder covered with reliefs and depressions that are meaningless to me, streaked with horizontal and vertical reds and greens, preciously nestled in a case under a legend in Italian, which I brought home and which after careful examination I have finally identified as some kind of statistical device, operating three-dimensionally and recording the population of a city in such and such a year, though all this makes it no more comprehensible to me."[15] Next to a volume of Rimbaud's complete works "lost in a tiny, wretched bin of rags, yellowed nineteenth-century photographs, worthless books and iron spoons,"[16] this abandoned statistical machine is a hieroglyph of future writing—attuned to the minute data of life in the city—and all the more useful for literature since it seems, here in the flea market, to come from a future that has failed.

Breton did, after all, finish this book, as well as others. There is a photograph of him at the end of *Nadja*, plate 44, with the caption "I envy (in a manner of speaking) any man who has the time to prepare something like a book . . . "[17]. He wants to believe, however, that having finished the book, one could still give it up. If we imagined *Nadja* to actually be given up in some way—that what we have just read was not a finished book, but rather something loosely grouped like a box of flea market nick-knacks—then the photo of Breton becomes merely one discard among others. I can even imagine this picture of Breton hanging in the foyer of a dilapidated mansion in a pulp novel for sale in a box with playbills, broken telephones, and rosaries with missing prayers. In this imagined potboiler, a plucky ingénue has been dispossessed of an enormous fortune by some wily and litigious relation. However, it turns out that the eyes in the portrait direct her towards an even bigger booty—the location of a hidden treasure chest, filled with wooden chips painted to look like pirate doubloons (but in the world of this novel, they are coin of the realm!) I think Breton would rather have us read his book in this way, and, in fact, Breton's eyes in the photo of plate 44 direct us to the following passage: "The sudden intervals between words in even a printed sentence, the line which we speak, we draw beneath a certain number of propositions whose total is out of the question, the complete elision of events which, from one day to the next or to another, quite upsets the data of a problem we thought we could solve."[18] It is in-between the words where we are invited to give up the book, the blind spot where Breton urges our attention, and the source of his anti-literary gold.

Can these intervals between words be calculated by a better machine—for instance, the inoperative Italian white cylinders with the three-dimensional statistical grid? Or perhaps even photography itself, with its speed of capture and minute detailings of the real, poses itself as a competing mechanism to literature. Breton does not address this issue directly, although he does note that he took many of the photos for the book so that we could be brought to "the places to which this narrative happens to lead . . . at a special angle from which I myself had looked at them."[19]

The photo of Breton was, however, not taken by Breton, but by Henri Manuel. Manuel, working for the French government, took over one million photos during Breton's lifetime.

(photography)

Throughout this book, we will find many who will compete with Surrealism's privileged claim to the unliterary, but the photographic itself quietly tops any artistic attempts. In fact, according to Susan Sontag, photography "is the one art that has managed to carry out the grandiose, century-old threats of a Surrealist takeover of the modern sensibility. . . [It is] the only art that is natively surreal,"[20] surpassing, even in its most banal manifestations (or rather, precisely then) official Surrealist photographic experiments.[21] If literature is nothing more than a filter, a kind of metadata ordering consciousness, the photo promises a mechanical capture of the world without this interposition of the conscious mind. According to Cortázar in "Blow Up,"—his story of the competing regimes of photographic, typewritten, and standard human perception—the photo "reconstitutes things in their true stupidity."[22]

The wild popularity of photography makes me hesitant to add it to this catalogue of failure—a catalogue, which, after all, is quasi-photographic in its organization of singular entries with loose connections, snap-shots of failure to reflect upon, then put aside. Photography's failure is only "second rate." Yet, while the photographic industry is quite profitable, any melancholy box of cast-away family photos in a junk store will attest that photography as a practice is, for most of its users, a dead end—literally. The presence of these once intimate photos *en masse* in the junk shop announces death, diaspora, divorce, releasing the photograph from its narrative bindings, or at the very least its physical photo album, returning it to its proper place—an unassimilable fragment of lost time. It will now only attain value again by way of the armchair ethnographer, drawn to the image by a perverse detail, a trace of history, a shock of recognition. Even then, this rescue merely prolongs its inevitable fate.

Some photos do not get the privilege of warming themselves

in a welcoming home for maybe a generation or two, but are shot on the brink of oblivion. The street photography vendor of yore worked to trace every grimace and blur and pose that the avenue offered, yet these photos were not taken with much care or choice, but were perfunctorily framed, and in most cases weren't even developed if they didn't find an immediate buyer. There is an archive of a million such images in the Visual Studies Workshop at Rochester, taken by Joseph Selle for Fox Movie Flash between 1950-70 at 942 Market Street in San Francisco. As Andrew Eskind describes

> The business strategy for this all-but-forgotten photographic genre demanded certain skills, but was largely speculative. The photographers working for Joseph Selle on the streets of San Francisco shot hundreds of pedestrians daily – engaging with them, handing out numbered tickets as they worked – hoping that some percentage – inevitably small – would pay a small fee to receive a post-card souvenir photo – without guarantee of its quality – by return mail. So it was speculative in both directions – on any given day, the photographers had no way of predicting how many pedestrians might be tempted to spend 50 cents (or later $1) on a souvenir photo of their outing in downtown San Francisco.[23]

Artists from the Visual Studies Center have attempted to navigate this unmanageable archive, creating artist books as stop-gap organizing principles (e.g. Elizabeth Tonnard's *Two of Us*), or media artifacts which animate each isolated frame shot from the ever-static position of the professional street photographer (David Mount's *17523 Pictures*).[24] The sidewalk was Selle's assembly-line, nothing more, nothing less. To make anything of this activity, we would, again according to the anti-human logic of Cortázar's "Blow Up," be "guilty of making literature."[25] Of course, the amount of data collected for this extensive undertaking seems quaint next to photographic projects such as those undertaken by Google Maps, the implicit surrealism of which is mined in books such as Jonathan Rafman's *Google Street Views*.

Charles Fort

If I were to characterize the prose of Charles Fort as well-nigh unreadable, yet strangely exhilarating, the same characterization might serve for many of the writers in this book of literary monstrosities. However, for Fort the unreadability is by design. Here was someone whose inclusive embrace of the real was so cosmic that it would shame, and perhaps embarrass, Whitman. Perhaps "reality" is the wrong word, since his subject was the supernatural, or rather—dogged "Intermediatist" that he was—something in-between supernatural and real.[26] He thus had to engineer a method whereby one could intuit other worlds without allowing for the conscious mind to project its prejudice on the data, which he collected with an intensity somewhere between angelic and idiotic.

It is uncertain whether he could actually remember what was in his personal archive of scribbled notes, or even how big this archive was. Ordered pell-mell in card board boxes, the number in one account is 28,000,[27] in another one 48,000,[28] in another 60,000.[29] An internet site says that he burned 40,000 of his notes in 1920, but there still remain thirty boxes in the New York Public Library (graced with such headings as #18 Accidents-Sheep, #20 Eclipse-Pollen, #21 Potential-Zones, #22 O-Stigmatic; Art, science, errors and personal) and others at the University of Pennsylvania. In all, it is a vast dispersion of potentially legendary events that have instead been forgotten, deemed *un-noteworthy*—if such a heading can be said to have any bearing on Fort's oeuvre; it may be that where our notes end is where the supernatural truly picks up. His texts give the impression that he was reluctant to turn his horded scraps of outlandish research into anything but scraps. However, it was not through any laziness that his texts only loosely cohere—the proliferation of these notes themselves should disabuse that notion. Rather because his overall practice was to resist any kind of sense-making, he did not want to explain away the inexplicable events recorded on these pieces of paper via narrative or scientific authority. We espouse a form of bad faith towards mystery when we try to make sense of his research fragments; his pataphysical anti-method, then, is to just let them be. The goal was not an aestheticization of a fragment, but a more humble stance in the face of a cosmic whole that we can only discern fragments of, but cannot understand, and *should not* understand, *in toto*: "Every science is a mutilated octopus."

The main substance of his books are these notes, culled from newspapers, scientific journals, museum archives and libraries. They are laid end to end for our delectation and wonder. He is perhaps also going for the overall affect of boredom, *intentionally,* since one of his overarching theses is that the ubiquity of supernatural-seeming events points to their ultimate banality. He interrupts what are nothing more than obsessive compulsive lists with the random moment of authorial pique or comic aperçu. His collected books—*The Book of the Damned, Lo!, Wild Talents,* and *New Lands*—are so uniform in their method and content that they could very well be the same book, running to over a thousand pages—a hulking monotone of the fantastic.[30] I could only get through about half without coming to the conclusion that to finish would be a monumental waste of time. Yet to "finish" may be another kind of "mutilating the octopus" if Fort's goal is to detail "A heterogeneity so great that it amounts to infinite dispersion of indistinguishability."[31]

Fort's works enact rather than aestheticize the surrealist love of unfiltered data, what Fort calls "the data of the damned." He has a whole book dedicated to things reported to have fallen from the sky, like blood, fish, charred remains, frogs, and thunder-axes. These prodigies he explains through the agency of a Super Sargasso Sea, a major topic of interest for his proposed science of "Super-Geography." This ethereal sea is a sidereal flea market where float

> Derelicts, rubbish, old cargoes from inter-planetary wrecks; things cast out into what is called space by convulsions of other planets, things from the times of the Alexanders, Caesars and Napoleons of Mars and Jupiter and Neptune; things raised by this earth's cyclones: horses and barns and elephants and flies and dodoes, moas, and pterodactyls; leaves from modern trees and leaves of the carboniferous era—all, however, tending to disintegrate into homogeneous-looking muds or dusts, red or black or yellow—treasure-troves for the palaeontologists and for the archeologists—accumulations of centuries—cyclones of Egypt, Greece, and Assyria—fishes dried and hard, there a short time: others there long enough to putrify—
>
> But the omnipresence of Heterogeneity—[32].

Ultimately, he admits that "in our own expressions we are limited, by the oneness of quasiness, to the very same methods by which orthodoxy established and maintains its now sleek, suave preposterousnesses."[33] Consequently, he quickly throws the Sargasso Sea hypothesis out the window and simply says:

> Here are the data.
> Make what you will, yourself, of them.[34]

"We visualize them in an environment of blankness,"[35] he says of these tales of hailing stones, blood, and frogs; women who have burnt to death on unscorched beds; pictures falling from the wall at coincidental moments; and the like. He says that "vast holes of ignorance always will be bridged by very slender pedantries,"[36] and so, for instance, when he ruminates on the possibility of telepathic phenomena as the cause of all coincidence, he ultimately opts for no explanation. Although the analogy verges on the very kind of glibness Fort challenges, it may be productive for our meager purposes to compare his methods and intent to those of today's database artist: "Sometimes I am a collector of data, and only a collector, and am likely to be gross and miserly, piling up notes, pleased with merely numerically adding to my stores"[37]; or "I am impelled to arrange my materials under headings—quite as a wind arranges fallen leaves, of various sizes, into groups—as a magnet makes selections from a pile of various things."[38] Even though the data he collects are stories that can't *but* engage the imagination that turns strange coincidences, uncanny repetitions, and telepathic correspondence into narrative sense, he's ultimately more interested in the terrible immensity of unfiltered experience out of which these events come, and thru which they attain meaning. "A field—the dismembered body of a child—a farmhouse near by. . . . But I can pick up no knowledge of relation with environment. Friendly neighbors—or a neighbor with a grudge—all around is vacancy. . . . [T]he surroundings are blankness: in the usual way the story was told, as an unrelated thing."[39]

For Fort, the supernatural is just a case of decontextualized data: elements floating without connective material. And only fools try to explain. But because he is no moralist, he engages in foolishness as well, embracing his own stupidity, and stupefaction, in the face of his overwhelming archive of outré occurrences. We could say that Fort is one of the first poets of data overload, if it weren't for the fact that he's more of a comedian of data overload than anything else. At one moment he says:

> I now have a theory that our existence, as a whole, is an organism that is very old—a globular thing within a starry shell, afloat in a super-existence in which there may be countless other organisms—and that we, as cells in its composition, partake of, and are ruled by, its permeating senility. The theologians have recognized that the ideal is the imitation of God. If we be a part of such an organic thing, this thing is God to us, as I am God to the cells that compose me. . . . [W]hat is

> ennobling us is senility. . . . Year after year I am becoming nobler and nobler. If I can live to be decrepit enough, I shall be a saint.[40]

He then continues on with his catalogue of sensational data about vampire bats, poltergeist girls and cattle mutilation.

Charles Fort was not globular in stature, but was a small pudgy man, who liked to write while wearing one of those green celluloid eyeshades we associate with card sharps, but which, in the day were standard issue for those whose job was to continuously monitor flows of finely detailed, minute information. It is particularly interesting to think about the ways, like the ameliorative green visor, specific bodies are connected up and acclimated to these flows of incessant, unpretty textual noise. Indeed the body itself is an integral part of each memory machine we are positing as a literary failure or virtual genius. One becomes virtual, one dwells in virtuality, by nature of having a body that resists the will; it is the fleshy filter between the things you can do and the things you can't. To a certain extent, the gravity of bigger body expands the territory of the things it can't act upon, but consequently expands its virtuality. Fort makes an explicit analogy between fatness, the unruliness of his tomes, and spiritual enlightenment when he says

> wideness is an aspect of the Universal. We go on widely. According to us the fat man is nearer godliness than is the thin man. Eat, drink, and approximate to the Positive Absolute. Beware of negativeness, by which we mean indigestion.[41]

I'm reminded of Orson Welles, early in his career, introducing his radio version of G. K. Chesterton's *The Man Who Was Thursday,* where he felt it necessary to describe Chesterton as "the fat man —the fabulously fat, the fantastic, the famous fat man" as a prelude to setting up the metaphysical unruliness of Chesterton's thin book, turned into a thinner radio half-hour, but posing an unfathomable mystery linking anarchists and police in a cabal that strains explication. We know that as Welles started to alienate himself from Hollywood's studio system and his films became harder and harder to make—some only existing even now as fragments, potentials, virtualities—that his body became larger and larger. Again, we might frame this weight-gain within a moralistic narrative about failure, or we can say that, for him, even in his younger, thinner days, literally and figuratively becoming "bigger than life" was an enticing prospect. Welles was left to endure moments of self-irony, as when he has Marlene Dietrich in *Touch of Evil* tell him, "You're a mess, honey. You ought to lay off those candy bars," or when, *yes*, he posed as the gourmand philosopher of the Paul Masson wine ads, an *imitatio* of Chesterton. But is there an avant-garde or even spiritual dimension to this becoming larger, this unwillingness to make one's world and even one's very self submit to shallow formal concerns, on the road to a fully virtual being?[42] How would we critically assess this art of unmaking oneself?

In Chesterton's essay on Tolstoy's legendary attempt to relinquish worldly power and return to the state of a rustic, he says that to simplify is absurd, evidence of a "small and noisy moralist" striving for "obscene purity" within the great man.[43] Tolstoy—the vegetarian writer of fat, well-read novels—chose to "fail" by returning to the status of the common man, only to find himself abused by his subordinates. But while, for Chesterton, this quest for simplicity is obscene and impossible, the source of all violent fundamentalisms, it is for all that no less admirable: "The simplification of anything is always sensational. Thus monotheism is the most sensational of things: it is as if we gazed long at a design full of disconnected objects, and, suddenly, with a stunning thrill, they came together into a huge and staring face."[44] Is this all just a question of data management, from indigestion to enlightenment, the disconnected to the networked? We are in a time when literature, film, painting, music can be reduced to the same data stream—thrown in with stock averages, status updates, and spam emails—making questions of media specificity moot. But further, if existential input is reduced to this data stream as well, between the body, its representations, and God, there is an intermingling and indiscernability, with God either a Big Filter allowing for sense-making or one data point among the rest.

Charles Fort explained God as merely an organizational convenience, albeit an important one. It allowed for the communal focus needed to enter into "intense mental states" that ultimately power the world. But for Fort, anything could fulfill this role of linchpin for our telepathic light industrials, and he accordingly proposed thought-booths where distracted people could go and focus their mental energies so as to provide power to cities.

Monsters of the Memorious

Jill Price

"I remember him (I have no right to utter this sacred verb, only one man on earth had that right and he is dead)."[1] That our memory fails, falsifies and ultimately forecloses any ability to accurately represent the past is a boon to all memoirists: "remember" a sacred verb, perhaps only available truly to the angelic or the damned. Borges' fantastic creature of total recall, Funes the Memorious—himself a relic remembered, or half-remembered, from a time just before the advent of recording technologies—embodies both the promise and the nightmare of ubiquitous media and unlimited memory. This "vernacular Zarathrustra" was able, after a horsing accident in his youth, to remember everything not merely in the manner of the prodigious mnemonicians of the ancient world—Cyrus, Mithridates Eupator, Simonides, Metrodorus (a list he rattles off only to be "amazed that such cases be considered amazing"). Instead, his "garbage heap" memory

> knew by heart the forms of the southern clouds at dawn on the 30th of April, 1882, and could compare them in his memory with the mottled streaks on a book in Spanish binding he had only seen once and with the outlines of the foam raised by an oar in the Rio Negro the night before the Quebracho uprising. . . . [E]ach visual image was linked to muscular sensations, thermal sensations, etc. He could reconstruct all his dreams, all his half-dreams. Two or three times he had reconstructed a whole day; he never hesitated, but each reconstruction had required a whole day.

He is frustrated by the generality of language, and desires other systems to represent his "intolerably precise world."[3] This other system, to truly represent memory without "wasting time"—what would it be? The fictional author of this reminiscence on the life of Funes claims his may be the poorest and shortest account of this legendary Argentine prodigy. But does his poverty of representation point to a richness that is only possible through the abstractions of selective memory? This unnamed author comes to the realization that Funes "was not very capable of thought,"[4] and in the end, does not envy him; the accumulation of impressions of even a sleepy South American hamlet makes it difficult for Ireneo Funes to sleep.

At one point in this short story—the shortness an intentional formal impoverishment in the face of Funes' less fully representable *ars memoria*—there is a description of a Latin book the author leant to Funes, Pliny's *Naturalis historia*. When the author, about to leave town, goes to Funes to collect his books, he hears Funes reciting from chapter 24 of *Naturalis historia*: "The subject of that chapter is memory; the last words were *ut nihil non iisdem verbis redderetur auditum*, [So that, nothing that has been heard can be retold in the same words]."[5] Funes is perhaps unable to understand what this phrase implies to his obsessive retellings—that there is no "retelling" only "telling," that time moves without repetition, that the past conforms to the dictates of the present. He is reading the words that would make his very self impossibly fantastic, like a centaur reading aloud "centaurs don't exist." Yet, because Funes' tone when he reads this passage is "mocking" he could very well be reading out this truism only condescendingly; any inability to recall the past is based not on the limits of his genius, nor even the impossibility of his existence, but instead the function of our impoverished language, which he would like to reinvent, heaven help him.

In 2008, Jill Price of Los Angeles, California came forward as "the woman who remembers everything." Triggered by trauma related to her family's relocation from New York to Los Angeles when she was eight, her extreme "autobiographical memory" kicked in fully in her teens. "She described her life as like a split-screen television, with one side showing what she is doing in the present, and the other showing the memories which she cannot hold back."[6] Indeed, her television metaphor is not an innocent one. Just as the myth of Funes is a metacommentary on the culture of the book, so Price's existence is a commentary on the memory machines of electronic, televisual world—here in the heart of their functioning (her father was a talent agent no less).

In her appearances and interviews after she broke her anonymity, most of her interrogators, who themselves are television personalities, ask her about particular television events and their dates. She is more than once asked the date of the "Who Shot JR" episode of *Dallas*—at which point the viewer may become cynical that she has memorized this particular memory stunt; however, she is equally able to identify more arcane TV lore on-the-spot, like the theme song to the short-lived *Happy Days* spin-off *Banksy's Beauties*. Listening to these interviews, I get the feeling that I would like more significant autobiographical detail from Price—and at times it seems that she too would like to talk about herself and her own memory, rather than celebrate televisual memory. But, in fact, the network of her memory is deeply tied to the specific patterns and rhythms of the televisual, and so television *is* her memory. The data points of her reminiscences read as "what I'm watching—what I'm doing—what I'm watching—what I'm doing." Television is a crucial tool in her voracious mnemotechnic arsenal, which includes "every stuffed animal she's ever gotten. . . . 2,000 videotapes and countless audiotapes, not to mention more than 50,000 pages of diary entries in idiosyncratic handwriting—so dense that it's almost unreadable. Until recently she owned a copy of every TV Guide since summer 1989."[7] A writer for *Wired* concludes that her memory is no "natural" prodigy, but a strange variation on obsessive-compulsive disorder.

But rather than turn Jill Price's gift into soft pathology, or categorize it by the scientism of "hyperthymestic syndrome" (a term invented just for her), or even Oedipalize it (an angle the journalists and scientists surprisingly never brought into play), why not say this: that her memory is the function of her writing technique, that she is a genius of virtual literature, that she has much to say about the future of literary experimentation? She has had the skill, privilege, energy, and "foresight," to amass an archive through which she can contemplate a vast and minutely detailed alternative landscape, and she has catalogued this archive in a way that is instantly searchable. She has reinvented writing to be commensurate with her particular needs. As she describes in her "autobiography" (the one you can buy and read as opposed to the one that flaunts readability):

> For the single five-year period of January 1987 to December 1991, for example, my journal entries cover 350 double-sided 8 1/2 x 11 inch pages, each side divided into 32 boxes of written text measuring 1.5 x 1 inch and containing roughly 60 to 70 words each. That means each side contains over 2,100 words, the equivalent of 9 typed manuscript pages per side, so my journals for just those years alone number more than 6,300 "typed" pages. The total number of pages in my journals written during all the years I've kept them is over 50,000.[8]

The actual quality of the writing on these pages is beside the point. They would be nothing anyone would "enjoy reading," at least *en masse*. Yet the impoverished data that comprises these entries—the fact that everything is *not* included, that, contrary to her sobriquet's claim, everything is *not* recalled, that she is, in effect, a bad writer but a virtuoso data manager—is precisely what enables her "trick." Literature is a verb: how better to exemplify its activity than such an irrepressible and existentially dire practice?

Jill Price, as well as the world, does not recognize the true nature of her work. She comments on the paradoxical nature of "the woman who remembers everything" needing this massive diary; it is only paradoxical if we attempt to unlink the operations of memory and the creation of a written artifact. And we *could* unlink them, but only if we assert that memory consists of neither her journal *nor her articulate recall of past events*. Price describes that, "If I didn't write things down, I would get a swimming feeling in my head and would become emotionally overwhelmed."[9] Could we say rather that this "swimming feeling" is closer to the virtual substance of memory, closer to her true experience of time, than her rapid-fire recall of a historical event, a TV show, a trip to the mall and a talk with a friend?

To paraphrase Deleuze, a truly virtual image would only emerge with the failure of her aesthetic activity.[10] While Marguerite Duras's "virtual literature" was coterminous with merely "the unpublished"—under which Price's journaling activity would undoubtedly fall—because the unpublished is still *written*, it does not obtain the status of the virtual for a variety of thinkers, including Deleuze, who would place virtuality outside of representation itself, and outside our ability to act. This ultimate exteriority of the virtual has been nuanced so that it is not a completely metaphysical concept, although it can be mistaken for such.[11] In Deleuze, the cinema allows us to perceive the virtual, although it is not available in any shot before us, but rather is the whole that moves. The extent to which we can even talk about a virtual literature—an art which engages in the paradoxical marking of the unmarkable or unremarkable—depends on whether this whole can be apprehended, and if so, are there strategies for heightening this apprehension.

Between an impossible, inaccessible virtual and a virtual accessed through a more dogged, redirected processing, lies the distinction between the mythically impossible Funes and the incontrovertibly real Price. Yet perhaps neither of these poles of the virtual experience are adequate for a future literature, and as such, they remain merely monsters of the memorious.

Henri Bergson

Anyone, like myself, who examines literary failure redeemed as "virtuality," who looks past market liability to examine how unreadable work more deeply impacts our lives—or at the very least our notions of "life"—than do the Great Books, would have to embrace the philosophical framework of Henri Bergson. As would befit the formal constraints of this catalogue, however, I would have to present him as just another emblem of failure, equivalent to the others rather than master of them. As Bergson himself might say, his image is only one in an image-universe, which we can choose to act upon, or instead let slip into the virtual. In the Bergsonian cosmos, this virtual is roughly equivalent to memory, however not memory as we "know" it—the stored snapshots and locatable recollections that we can call upon with more or less ease—but something radically outside recollection, yet accessible through intuition. It is time in its purest state—duration, the unrepresentable—thus deeply fated to fail the literary impulse. "Inextensive and powerless,"[12] this virtual aspect of time is commensurable neither with our sensations, nor the devices that extend and record these sensations.[13]

You may not be satisfied that here we are "philosophizing failure," rather than encountering it head-on, that it is not exactly playing fair to muscle into these entries an intellectual giant whose success "could only be compared to the vogue Sartre enjoyed in the late 40s and early 50s."[14] However, Bergson was largely forgotten, or at least ignored in the latter half of the twentieth century by the academic world. The Kantian and materialist philosophies that he critiqued held triumphant sway, and even though he created a sophisticated rapprochement between these two modes of thought, there was little patience with his work. It could have been some residual anti-Semitism, but most likely, since Bergson's spiritualism was more universalist, it was his interest in spirit *generally* which contributed to his marginalization. He could be easily written off as a mystic by people who've neither read any mystical work, nor any Bergson for that matter. (There are certain readers for whom the idea of mysticism will always be equated with a vague, rhapsodic effeteness obscuring sinister subtexts, which Bergson certainly was without).

The simplest way to talk about the Bergsonian virtual (as well as how we reflect upon failure) is to be reminded of these basic facts: we do one thing, not another; we perceive one slice of space-time, not another. We stumble over words. We think. As a human being, we are caught between action and reflections—Bergson's "two jets"[15] (or Price's split-screen television) that each moment splits into. Bergson describes the universe as a data stream of images, with the brain as a network router that does not store anything. If the past doesn't exist *out there*, it exists even less *in your head*. Even our own self-image, seemingly privileged because our location obliges us to return to it, is only one piece of data in this data cosmos, which we must learn to filter effectively if we are to live healthy lives, according to Bergson. Perhaps Bergson's insistence upon "health" or "normalcy" is, understandably, one more reason why he fell out of favor, since he highlighted the importance of educating a healthy, common-sense, action-oriented relation to data overload. It is the most square thing about his work, given that contemporary artists have embraced, and even bragged about their unhealthy data processing habits; as once schizophrenic and aphasic were transformed into aesthetically positive terms, so now OCD and autistic tendencies are bellwethers of artistic genius. While at one point, Bergson affirms that "we must have the power to value the useless,"[16] he also paints a picture of what would constitute a more wholesome relation to our data than that espoused by the other examples I've proffered so far in this gallery:

The characteristic of the man of action is the promptitude

> with which he summons to the help of a given situation all the memories which have reference to it; but it is also the insurmountable barrier which encounter, when they present themselves on the threshold of his consciousness, memories that are useless or indifferent. To live only in the present, to respond to a stimulus by the immediate reaction which prolongs it, is the mark of the lower animals: the man who proceeds in this way is a man of *impulse*. But he who lives in the past for the mere pleasure of living there, and in whom recollections emerge into the light of consciousness without any advantage for the present situation, is hardly better fitted for action: here we have no man of impulse, but a *dreamer*. Between these two extremes lies the happy disposition of a memory docile enough to follow with precision all the outlines of the present situation, but energetic enough to resist all other appeal. Good sense, or practical sense, is probably nothing but this.[17]

We can imagine that the younger Marcel Proust—one of literary history's great inaction heroes, and a page-boy at Bergson's wedding—rebelled against his elder acquaintance's veritably Texan assessment of the practical uses of memory. Proust's cork-lined room, in which he cut himself off from the world to pursue a dream of the past recaptured, is a machine with which he flaunted uncommon sense with a more experimental relation to one's memory, words, and body.

Bergson was ultimately pessimistic about the active machines of memory that later avant-gardes would take up as devices to shape, however obliquely, our sense of virtuality in explicit challenges to common sense. He says that "You have gained nothing by depositing the memories in matter,"[18] a sentiment that may be as germane to writing as it is to cinema (the virtual is as old as language itself), although the emerging cinematic perception was his main concern. His theory of the *élan vitale* depends on its clear distinction from cinematic, quantified, frame-by-frame consciousness, although he had not many cinematic exemplars to reflect upon. His *Creative Evolution* appeared the same year as Griffith's early work *The Lonedale Operator* and Méliès' *Les hallucinations du Baron de Münchausen,* but he was probably thinking about much earlier scientific films, such as the time-work etudes of Étienne Jules-Marey.

However, as memory machines proliferate, engendering new actions as well as inactions, our common sense relation to data mutates, for better or worse. The surrealists would begin to appreciate the alliances between machinic, human, and cosmic perception, even if the implication was that human sensibility would be dwarfed, and common sense unrecooperable in the face of the absurd virtualities of the unreadable. But even mainstream film would begin to proliferate "useless" images—what Deleuze calls pure optical and sound situations, "deliberately weak connections and floating events"[19]—logical consequences of even the most generic film conventions, which contribute to a loosening of the filmic from the sensory-motor dictates of action and narrative. Film, for Deleuze, shows us how the "virtual, for its part, detaches itself from its actualizations, starts to be valid for itself."[20]

Deleuze's insight into Bergson is that Bergson was correct on all counts except in his pessimism towards the media. Deleuze is typically open to the future and the new assemblages it offers—without ascribing to any corporate or linear notion of "future," "evolution," or "progress"—and, for him, Bergson failed to see that cinema, for example, was an ally in thinking the virtual.[21] Particularly, while Bergson conceived of cinema as ontologically immobile, Deleuze was able to appreciate how cinema acclimated itself, both through technology and technique, to more improvisational, creative rhythms, breaking through immobilized perception and instead creating new lines of flight:

> The cinema cannot avoid the 'detour through the direct'. There is always a moment when the cinema meets the unforeseeable or the improvisation, the irreducibility of a present living under the present of narration, and the camera cannot even begin its work without engendering its own improvisations, both as obstacles and as indispensable means. These two themes, the open totality and the event in the course of happening, are part of the profound Bergsonianism of the cinema in general.[22]

Both theorists, however, would have been opposed to merely equating the virtual with data recording and processing machines themselves, especially those which have been more closely associated with the "virtual" given their relation to digital immersive experiences. Deleuze has many synonyms for the virtual: the whole, spirit, thought, potential, the open, relation, thirdness, interval, encompasser, plane of immanence, the absolute, the out-of-field, sound, the non-divisible (yet difference itself), the mental. The digital is not one.

Even though his theories are uniquely fitted to understanding many digital practices, leading Deleuzean theorist Brian Massumi has said, "Nothing is more destructive for the thinking of the virtual than equating it with the digital,"[23] and this sentiment is echoed by Keith Ansell Pearson and Aden Evens, among other Deleuzean scholars.[24] Aden Evens goes as far as to add that if the digital is not the virtual, correspondingly, the digital is not creative; while I agree with the spirit of this essay, it doesn't take into account the various ways in which artists have negotiated the virtual, but who also happen to use digital technology, in their work.[25] As Claire Colebrook points out, the only way we could possibly start to conceive of the durational substance of Bergson's virtual is with "a perceptual machine that was liberated from sensory motor apparatus,"[26] and as such the digital, hyperextending the abstractions of a cinematic pulse, should provide even more tools, but also more pitfalls, for such a project. In the end, however, it is the inventiveness and puissance of *our own* machines—real or imagined—the pure positivity of their "creative destruction," that will determine the quality of virtual experimentation, and be the benchmark of its failure.

(film)

Momentarily, we will assess how these theories that are explicitly geared towards the cinema might be applicable to literary productions; it is only by conceiving image, text, and other data on the same register that we can fully assess how the virtual operates today. Yet, film has been attuned to these issues of virtual literature well before literature proper, and in fact uniquely inspired literature towards these dimensions, since it can potentially record data without the intervention of human consciousness. The problem of the relation between the overwhelming data of the real and our organization of it has been the crux of many of the debates around film's capacity for approaching the inhuman. The primal argument concerning the status of cinematic humanism seems to have been between Eisenstein and Vertov, the latter of whom Lev Manovich posits as a precursor to a database aesthetic. Just think about Eisenstein complaining that Vertov merely played around with the data of film, rather than organizing sequences to deliver "a *maximum of emotion and stimulating power.*"[27] Vertov, in contrast, started a kind of data or database realism that exposes the aspect of data that at times is inassimilable to singular human sense.

But we need not muck around in the avant-garde for clear examples of how this database realism proliferates in the heart of some of the most well-known films. Vertovian potentiality is implicit when any director, faced with the unedited contents of a film about-to-be, must invent its organizing principle.[28] Orson Welles famously kept his production style open-ended, so as to be more receptive to the chance encounters and unexpected combinations that film can offer those who choose to be alert to these potentialities. Most film histories will posit his style in contradistinction to that of Hitchcock, whose mastery of the continuity script—with every shot meticulously mapped out and priced-out *in advance*—made him ultimately bored with the process of actual shooting and editing, but insured his success in the studio system. Welles could be just as exacting in his earlier films, starting with a shooting style which tried to incorporate as much as possible into one shot, so that there were limited choices to be made in post-production: yet he was ultimately reduced to more "tricky" filmmaking, piecing together, as in his European films, various incommensurable space-times because he "had to fake things, and learn how to cut in order to cover troubles I was in."[29] Where better, then, to discuss the alienation of machinic data from common sense than in Welles' masterpiece, one of the few films he retained control over throughout, but which thematized the failure of its protagonist to make sense of his past and synthesize virtualities proliferating out of his control?

Citizen Kane is a crucial film in Deleuze's discussion of the virtual, as it brings to the fore the seemingly simple question "What happens when we search for a recollection,"[30] while inviting readings that decenter the human protagonist of such a search, suggesting an inhuman, crystalline assemblage of sheets of time. In *Kane*, a newsreel reporter, Thompson—himself an avatar of the very industry that Kane created—elicits the stories of various narrators who also, in some sense, were "created" by Kane. As such, the newsman's search for the meaning of Kane's last word—"Rosebud"—is less epiphanic (although the film does deliver on such a climactic revelation) than fractalized. After all, the veritably Vertovian newsreel that opens the film—coming after moody expressionistic dissolves of the ruins of Kane's Xanadu palace (Venetian gondolas and golf courses, empty tiger cages and Moorish turrets) tells "the whole story." The "sheet[s] of virtual past" which this "News on the March" reporter goes on to explore "are all coexistent, each containing the whole of Kane's life in one form or another. Each has what Bergson calls 'shining points', singularities, but each collects around these points the totality of Kane or his life as a whole as a 'vague nebulosity.'"[31] Rosebud is merely a convenient search term, impelling action, within a virtual cloud of purely cinematic time.

But while Rosebud impels the actual, it is what Deleuze calls a "virtual secret,"[32] since it falls outside the scope of the actual (quite literally, it does not make it into the "actualities" of the newsreel). Here is an example of the virtual's tendency to chase after the actual, and vice-versa, without any closure. The oscillation of virtual and actual always circuits through Kane, described in the film as the man who "never finished anything" but who, as such, had his hand in everything, creating a cosmos in which there may be infinite intersections (including a real newspaper tycoon, Hearst, who insured that the film would languish in the art house circuits, owing to its *film à clef* status). But the film's ultimate duplicity is that while it provides such keys to reading—Rosebud and Hearst as privileged poles of biographical knowledge—it ultimately plays fast and loose with them. As we will see, this duplicity is part of the double nature of the shot, and the virtuality implicit in any film or literary production.

The narrative sheets of *Citizen Kane* have as their backdrop an alternate reality with its competing and intersecting rhythms, networks, machinery: the newspaper. The anti-novelistic rhythms of the everyday, of speed, of history as it happens, are at the heart of Kane's world, but prove inadequate for telling his "story"; in the opening newsreel, he is literally described as if he is time itself. It is precisely in Kane's spontaneity, his ability to engage the "powers of life" through this writing machine, that Kane becomes Kane, or rather that he experiences multiple becomings that make it impossible to extricate a story from any singular aspect of his life (since it is there, at all points). In a moral sense, we could simply say "he lost himself." Welles has called his character "an empty box," thus as much of a virtual cipher, a stop-gap organizing principle to the flows of life, as is "Rosebud."[33] But Kane is, in the "end," a "media" man, if we take "media" to imply that which exists in the middle; for Deleuze "It is never the beginning or the end which are interesting; the beginning and end are points. What is interesting is the middle."[34] Again, we might conceive *Citizen Kane* as a Bergsonian moral tale about how best to use memory: because Kane hooked himself up to the inhuman temporalities of the news, he was unable to recover what he loved most; he then buried himself amidst European art treasures, as if trying to buy back the past, and died alone and misunderstood by those closest to him.

But what is more interesting is that, as Deleuze points out, Rosebud exists precisely for no one, and thus is unavailable for such interpretation. It calls into question all accounts of Kane's life, rather than positing a master meaning. It exists, as the opening newsreel tells us, in a "collection of everything, so big it can never be catalogued or appraised." Thus, within the diegesis it is an example of images that are "quite useless because they can no longer be inserted into a present which would extend them into action."[35] Such images will become more noticeably austere and politically fraught in post-war neorealism, which for Deleuze marks the point in cinema history in which characters as well as the filmmakers themselves are placed in historical situations which have no precedent, and for which there is no ready-made "common-sense" response, in which unthinkability is as much an ethical stance as it is the state of things. Thus emerges a visionary cinema, or a cinema in which vision eludes interpretation, floats without destiny, and becomes the pure composition. "Time as primary matter, immense and terrifying, like universal becoming,"[36] as in the improvisations of Rossellini.

For now, though, Rosebud exists within a space where these pure visionary powers are not nakedly manifest. There are two points in the film in which it has the potential to be connected with the action of the plot, to be used by the narrative, rather than remain hovering outside the film, in a shot no one but the audience will see. The first is in Colorado, in 1871, at the boyhood home of Kane. That we are perhaps, as viewers, closest to Rosebud in this scene is belied by way in which it is delivered to us. That is, Thompson is lead into an archival space that is treated as laughable—a self-important memorial to the over scrupulous Thatcher; it is the only space where the news reporter expresses frustration, because he's high-hatted by its officious keeper, and generally put off by its air of dubious, finicky grandeur. But it is precisely because of the attitude of the archivists and Thompson himself towards this data—muscular as well as psychic, infrastructural as well as spatial—that none are able to access the secret. But what do *we* see? There is of course a difference between what is available to the action of the characters, and the mental relations created by the film itself (legible perhaps only through multiple viewings), and this split between the audience's versus the character's ability to apprehend the secret of Rosebud is, however modestly, a harbinger of the virtual. If Rosebud exists for no one, it is because it exists only for the film.

The first text we read is the underscored name *Charles Foster Kane*, and (if we see it at all, since it is not signaled as significant by the camera framing or the soundtrack) the words "when these lines appear in print"—something that, we are lead to believe, will never happen. It is implied that the memoir and the whole library operation into which Thompson has found himself is nothing but a wealthy man's vanity project. Then, as the handwritten text of Thatcher's unpublished memoirs pans across the screen, the white of the page dissolves into the snow of Colorado, and we are delivered from the unpublished to the space of memory, two virtualities that collide to form quite literally a crystalline form. The snow, as soon as it is materialized, however, returns to a virtuality; with its white abstract intensity, it is no less than the consciousness cloud of Kane, the white negative space in which his success with the black letter is activated.

What is the attitude, the combination of cinematic effects that makes it possible to have this flashback, to make time crystallize in a way that, while immediately perceptible, forks off into various other realms—creating emotional and intellectual intervals across various sections of the film, carrying in its wake various "useless" images? The narrative convention of music linked to a dissolve signaling the activation of memory allows for us to bring this new image of Kane's childhood back into our common-sense, rather than floating as pure paratactical jump. However, this music is immediately interrupted by the young Kane's snowball thrown up against another text—the sign for his mother's boarding house, white letters on black, instead of black on white (the snowball adds to, rather than obliterates his mother's word). The pure energy of Kane, his movement forward in time, will constantly distract from the memorializing impulse, so it is even here, with his snowball's imposition on the formal niceties of memory, that we are again made aware of the "two jets" of memory; related to what Deleuze describes as the dual nature of the shot,[37] these two jets include not only "action" and "reflection," but in the frame and out-of-field, what we see and what sight is implied by the composition—and the latter can be an absence that is merely a compositional convenience, or can intersect with something mental or purely filmic. Welles great innovation is this: instead of tacking back and forth between one reality and another, he contains both in the same shot. The camera tracks from the "virtual cloud" of Kane's snow world into the more acculturated space of the boarding house, where a legal decision regarding Kane's fate is about to be finalized by his mother. Throughout, the supposed historical "subject" of memory—the transfer of guardianship of the boy to the alien banker from the East—is simultaneously accompanied by Kane playing in the snow, and yelling "The Union forever!" in the background.

Here is Welles' deep-focus at its formal and philosophical

finest, combined with his contrapuntal "musical" compositions of dialogue. We are able to perceive this dual nature of the shot in one, and it should not be underestimated how this innovation "gives rise to all kinds of adventures in memory,"[38] rather than moving us through a singular, and perhaps dubious, recollection. That is, depth of field and overlapping dialog allow us to see the choreography of competing temporalities, inviting exploration of different "virtual zones of the past,"[39] here as embodied in the disruption of the child, the steely fore-sight of the mother, the bumbling resistance of the father, the banker more at ease with the dictates of his fortune than the unpredictabilities of his new ward, the inhuman rhythms of the weather, the geologic fickleness of the earth (indeed the whole story, devolves from the unforeseen payload of an abandoned mine, the ownership of which is discussed in this scene). When these intensities are contracted into a more spatially unified shot, interrupting Kane's play, Rosebud becomes a tool for fighting off the banker, rather than a sentimental memory. Beyond this point, Rosebud is technically useless—inaccessible, virtual. It will only enter partially into the diegesis once more, when Kane is diverted from exploring the contents of his mother's belongings in storage, by a combination of splattered mud—it is here raining, rather than snowing—and a stranger's toothache—a crucial forking path that, however, can only be seen as such within the structure of the film, but not by any of its *dramatis personae*.

Is it possible, or even desirable, to avoid the interpretative and narrative pull that the structuring principle of *Citizen Kane* creates for *us* rather than for its characters? How do we benefit from this knowledge, and the pleasure that it gives, or does the interpretive framework of the film block a perception of its "real" subject—the virtual life of data, and the immensity of time? If we think about film as data, it might be instructive to think of a singular film as a type of website. On the web, metadata such as keywords, lists, and tags have guided us thru its oceanic content, making it less virtual along the way. In a similar way, captions, voice-overs, visual analogies, and plot conventions negotiate and organize the data of the film. While it is nearly impossible to avoid these conventions, we can still assess strategies for, however obliquely, heightening our perception of data, and releasing its energies in ways that challenge our own consistency, while creating new assemblages.

Take a more recent popular film like *Magnolia*, a film which seems to update *Citizen Kane*'s data realism, but is less heroically centered on the life of one man. Structurally, the film first comes off as a collection of vignettes—a term which, when used to describe stories, implies an overcoming of narrative by the forces of the photographic. The vignette has over the years enabled a form of storytelling dramatizing the everyday, perhaps best exemplified in the fiction of Renata Adler, or the filmmaking of Robert Altman, in works where there is a loose relation between the data presented and its means of organization. On first glance, beyond the shop-worn "everything is connected" ploy that usually reins in the fragments of such works, we sense that the metadata of *Magnolia* turns out to be conservative . . . that all the film's disparate data traces a dispersed familial relationship, with Earl Partridge—dying television magnate—as the patriarch.

Considered merely within the walls of his house, Earl's family includes a much younger wife, a menagerie of show dogs, his nurse, and eventually his estranged son. But, through the more inhuman system of "Earl Partridge Enterprises," he becomes the common connective material for a much more dispersed family, both created by and deterritorialized thru the televisual (and TV, in this case anachronistically "live," serves as a nostalgic signifier for a lost era of electronic community). As an organizing principle, a seductive ordering force, Earl is failing . . . and the system he has created seems to be on the verge of imploding as he nears death. In one of the film's many sequences that cut between various levels of action, Earl begins to mumble and rage about love and regret; soon his incoherent speech accompanies unrelated vignettes of action, asking us to interpret these images by way of his disintegrating voice-over. But just as that sequence ends, another sequence—and another connective principle—is introduced, as all the characters separately sing to one of the film's many songs.

Throughout *Magnolia* such montage sequences trot out different potential ways to organize the sense of the film, as if anxiously looking for a way to narrate (or sing) the flux of life, after the patriarch leaves the scene. The voice-over is the most denigrated or parodied form of filmic metadata, performed not only by the delirious Earl, but by Jimmy, the cop, who, in his failed attempts at authority, turns the god-voice on its head, even as he tries to make a connection to God through his prayers. Other modes of organization include the arrow of time itself—the temporality of live TV which everybody watches, the weather which happens to everyone, and the prodigy of the film's finale, all of which unite place and time and character in a fashion less peremptory than a moralizing voice-over or song. Certain visual analogies and similarities across cuts—the continuity of red-heads, the two men named Jim, a generally "incestuous" editing style that approximates the play of floating pronouns in Robert Coover's "The Babysitter"—forms another connective strategy; is Oedipus as false a lead as the ghetto kid's rap riddle? While leading us to some partly correct insinuations, these hints may serve merely to prove our complicity in a familial metaphor that the film strains against. Additionally, there is a plenitude of clues meant for rewind hermenauts—referencing Freemasonry, Alan Thicke, *The Life of Samuel Johnson*, Exodus 8:2 and Charles Fort—held out as an interconnective hyle, networking a mystery of the everyday.

Of the above levels of organization and interpretation, no one level holds priority. In fact, one of the themes of the film is precisely the problem at hand: how to organize and use useless knowledge. At the end of the movie, quiz kid Donnie Smith says

"I don't know where to put things. I have love to give and I don't know where to put it." It's a sweet line that nevertheless holds within it a tasteless and perhaps homophobic pun; given the movie's obsession with masculine anxiety (especially via the Frank T. J. Mackie character) we might as well also say that another interpretative master key—the film's purloined letter—is the cock. The thematic mis-use of the cock, as well as the possible interpretation of the film's end as divine retribution for these sins, suggests that we need instead turn to God. Indeed references to Exodus 8:2—foretelling the finale's *deus ex machina* by way of Moses' threat to Pharaoh of a plague of frogs—would suggest, Pat Robertson-style, that our fancy postmodernism is in for some angry snark from Jehovah. However, another presaging of the final frogs is instigated through the film's covert references to Charles Fort, cataloguer of such prodigies.

The tension between the Fortean explanation and the Biblical one, then, if anything, forms the crux of the film's struggle against all forms of data management. If one follows the Exodus key, it points to divine retribution: thus, *Magnolia* becomes a moral tale in which sinners will be punished, or at the very least, forewarned. The Fort key, instead, points to the very problem of interpretive keys for events that do not have a "why." For Exodus, God is the ultimate guarantor of meaning (kind of like DVD extras, which these filmmakers, perhaps calculatedly, have made utterly useless); Charles Fort, as we have seen, constantly plays against this desire for meaning by enumerating events that challenge the sense-making of our habitually distracted minds (some of which, culled directly from his book *Wild Talents*, appear in *Magnolia*'s prologue).

In France, these sensationalistic bits of everyday oddness are called "*fait-divers*" which, while a denigrated popular form, have been taken seriously by writers Félix Fénéon and Roland Barthes. Collected as *Novels in Three Lines*, Fénéon's haiku-esque forays into the lives of the anonymous combine laconic futurist violence, understated dark comedy, and pathetic tableaux that challenge our ability to synthesize the everyday.[40] Some examples:

> Louis Lamarre had neither job nor home, but he did possess a few coins. At a grocery store in Saint-Denis he bought a liter of kerosene and drank it.[41]
>
> Before jumping into the Seine, where he died, M. Doucrain had written in his notebook, "Forgive me Dad. I like you."[42]
>
> Too young to be mothers, Mlle Meuzeret, of Saint-Barthélémy, Seine-et-Marne, and Mlle Garnier, of Chassagne, S.-et-L., killed their sons.[43]
>
> Fearless boys of 13 and 11, Deligne and Julien were going off "to hunt in the desert." They were brought back to Paris from Le Havre.[44]
>
> Harold Bauer and Casals will give a concert today in San Sebastian. Besides that, they may fight a duel.[45]
>
> On the bowling lawn a stroke leveled M. André, 75 of Levallois. While his ball was still rolling he was no more.[46]
>
> Three is the age of Odette Hautoy, of Roissy. Nevertheless, L. Marc, who is 30, did not consider her too young.[47]
>
> "To die like Joan of Arc!" cried Terbaud from the top of a pyre made of his furniture. The firemen of Saint-Ouen stifled his ambition.[48]
>
> Mme Fournier, M. Vouin, M. Septeuil, of Sucy, Tripleval, Septeuil, hanged themselves: neurasthenia, cancer, unemployment.[49]

> God in the schools of the Belfort district: the city council of Chaix has reinstated him; the mayor of Méziré has fastened him to the wall.[50]

As a form of virtual literature, the *fait-divers* present us what Barthes' calls "the unorganized discard of news; . . . [which] would begin to exist only where the world stops being named, subject to a known catalogue . . .; in a word, it would be a monstrous item, analogous to all the exceptional or insignificant, i.e., anomic phenomena classified under the modest rubric *Varia*, like the platypus which gave poor Linnaeus so much trouble."[51] Through a quirk of coincidence, these phenomena enter the news from out of the flow of everyday life, forsaking their virtuality in becoming significant. Through the *fait-divers* things emerge into the light of day from out of what Fort calls "event-jungles."[52] They "happen" (or at least enter the journalistic flow of official "happening") when an otherwise ahistorical event fits into a dramatic, rhetorical, or poetic trope. So, in effect, the *fait-divers* does not merely point to a chance encounter, but highlights how *language* is the chance of the encounter. An apt conjunction of words and concept makes things retrievable from the archive of human experience. This definition would be, you might say, equally fitting for what is called the *literary*. However, because it exists on the cusp between a vast, anonymous archive and momentary, fleeting intelligibility, the *fait-divers* tends to direct our attention to the void from whence it came. As a vignette, fading to white at the edges, the *fait-divers* disrupts our ability to make connections and give a why to things. Like the duplicitous film shot, one half of it is in the world we know. However, the blank of the unknown is the direction that our minds follow . . .

Richard Owen Cambridge

Richard Owen Cambridge, author of the *Scribleriad: An Heroic Poem in Six Books*: 'Memba him? If the hero of the *Scribleriad*—Martin Scriblerus, "Antiquary, Pedant, and Alchymist"—had as his mortal enemy Time itself (personified as Saturn), then too Cambridge might have engaged the same foe, and presumably lost. The *Scribleriad* may strike some as second-rate doggerel, nearly four hundred years old; as such, for our can-do attitudes it is utterly useless, the epitome of the unreadable, or at the very least, no longer connected to our literary appetites and intellectual needs. Yet, what saves the *Scribleriad* for future literature, why it may have lost the battle but won the war, is that the very theme of this epic adventure is the drama of unreadability and the comedy of useless knowledge. Thus, for it to truly to speak to us on its own terms, the *Scribleriad* would have to undergo a period where it enacts its own failure, and "the mazy paths of wisdom trace."[53] Like its hero who dons beggar's clothes during his darker years, it might even aspire to invisibility, so that it may rise again if only to chide us in our vanity.

When we read epic poetry—if we read it at all—we don't usually think that for every Virgil there's someone who didn't make the cut.[54] That's because while competition between poets has always existed (see for example the lyric rivalries of shepherds in pastoral poetry), the epic exerts a monoculture around a singular, shared text. The *Scriblerad* emerges out of an environment of the eighteenth-century London coffeehouse, the literary conviviality and exchange, the manic *scribbling* of which are the antithesis of arts germinated through state or royal patronage. It was also a promiscuous publishing culture in which the "mock-epic" proliferated—e.g. Pope's *Rape of the Lock* and the *Dunciad*, Swift's *Gulliver's Travels*—although the satire of the mock-epic was ambiguous, and was not necessarily a ridicule of the epic itself. Instead its target much of the time was the cultural values threatening a more gentlemanly appreciation of the classics. While haunted by the bad writing that proliferated when men of commerce, lacking proper education in Latin and Greek, took to the pen, the energy of this literary scene was undoubtedly the product of a loosening of the strictures regarding who could write and be read. Perhaps as a bulwark against the rising tide of published work, Pope, Swift, and other illustrious writers formed a coterie that went by the name of "The Scriblerus Club." In 1714, they embarked on a collaborative writing project called *The Memoirs of Martin Scriblerus*, which they abandoned a year later.

The hero of Cambridge's 1751 *Scribleriad*, then, is a shamelessly recycled one. Forty years after the notable failure of the first Scriblerian episodes, Cambridge finds that it is no crime to take him up again, and in fact, admits to doing so in his preface:

> I consider'd that taking up a Character which had been already explained would be a great advantage in an Epic poem, which . . . should always hasten into the midst of things. . . . I chose rather that [the reader] should get an idea of this ethusiastick character from a work already printed, than to repeat the description and clog my book with it. . . . I might as well have had a new character of my own invention, with a new name: But what advantage would have resulted from that? And what Objection to the Character and name of *Scriblerus*? Do not all these idle travels, all these frivolous investigations and useless pursuits end in *Scribling*, to the unreasonable increase of that wordy lumber, which provokes the humorous *Fajardo* to cry out, *O! Jupiter, if thou hast any compassion for poor mortals, send us, once in a century, an army of* Goths *and* Vandals *to redress the calamity of this inundation of authors.*[55]

Alas, at heart, the Scribelerian is difficult to paraphrase.

Nevertheless, he goes on to call for a different kind of scholarship, one that does not labor over mastering oeuvres and periods. Rather, like a one-man Evelyn Wood Speed Reading Institute for white-wigs, he insists that only by reading *less* can one read more effectively. He quite literally calls for a networked type of reading. There is no need for computers, although the faintly anachronistic words "real information" appear at the end of the above-cited paragraph, so much so that I wonder whether there has been any tampering with my digitally accessed copy.

What, then, counts as "real information" for Martin Scriblerus in his many adventures? Early on in the epic, he arrives at the Island of Poetry, and confused by the various warlike arrays he finds there, is immediately thrown into battle with "bold Acrosticks . . . High o'er the rest," "Bout-rimeès [who] bring up the lagging rear," "looser Chronograms," "uncouth Anagrams . . . Shifting, in double mazes, o'er the plain," "the Centos . . . with borrow'd, patcht, and motley ensigns proud," "Riddle, and Rebus, Riddle's dearest son;/And false conundrum, and insidious Pun."[56] Even a "wanton Lipogrammatist" is there, taking up the rear, among quibble, antithesis, "doggrel-rhyme" and echo.[57] Scriblerus slays the "leader of th' Acrostick crew"[58] and immediately flees the island. The first letters of each line in this section read "ta ta coward,"[59] an acrostic sentiment addressed to Scriblerus, since while these lesser constraints and poetic games do not seem suited to the high themes of epic poetry, it is really Scriblerus, in his misunderstanding of them and rash enmity, that is ill-suited as a hero who is *writing itself.*

The conflict here—not so much allegorical as it is, *ahem,* metrical—is between big time and small time. Scriblerus is on an epic journey, which by definition requires great actions, amenable to future, deep and historically meaningful reflection. Yet the poetic forms of which he makes unnecessary enemies are *pastimes,* suitable for more frenetic, aimless, idle literary activity. His heroic "virtue"—a cognate of "virtual"—is seemingly lessened because of his missteps on this island. Prophesy alerts Scriblerus to the fact that his bad luck after leaving the island can only be reversed by returning, in order to "make atonement [for the] murder of the Acrostick . . . and celebrate games in his memory."[60] While the ubiquity of prophesy and the importance of memorializing characterize the deep temporalities of epic consciousness, subsuming action in the larger context of one's *arete*, both are here brought into play so that Scriblerus can return to the "small time." Once back on the Island of Poetry, he goes one step further than any epic hero would by submitting himself wholly—not to the words of an immortal bard, but rather to the industry of this lower verse. In effect, he comes into his own as the embodiment of all things scribbled:

> The great Scriblerous comes your dearest friend.
> A copious subject for your labour'd song,
> To tire each hand, and weary ev'ry tongue:
> Th' extensive theme his glorious deeds afford,
> Shall sweat six well-breath'd poets to record.[61]

This poem is still an epic, however, and not an indie movie. Instead of learning about life, love, and happiness in this literary backwater, his path remains the virtuous (or virtual) one. The last two books of the *Scribleriad* put him in search for no less than the Philosopher's Stone and the Elixir of Life

> The grand elixir art thou doom'd to know:
> But first must roam a mendicant in show;
> Naked and pennyless thro' distant lands,
> And eat thy bread the alms of stranger hands.[62]

It would seem that this path, since it is predicted by a seer named Morosoph, is ultimately under ridicule, as well. Nevertheless, his companions are conversely fated to have a more tangibly industrious career, plying the arts of "Saxon wisdom,"[63] i.e. the kind of useful, nationalistic scholarship that would include an active curation of historical relics and ancient knowledge. But this literal splitting between the active life and the reflective life, embodying Bergson's two jets in two distinctly different types of character, is belied by the more hectic oscillation of action and reflection that imbues this whole Scriblerian project.

Take, for example, a telling couplet in the midst of Scriblerus' perhaps obligatory voyage into exotic non-Christian realms, where "barb'rous rage the sainted form devours,/Foe to the chizzel's consecrating pow'rs."[64] The very jazzily spelled "chizzel" next to "consecrating" heightens the sense of the action that *goes into* memory, and as well, how that action *goes*, somewhat akin to the word "fizzel"—it is as momentary, and suited to immediate appetites, as is the action of "devouring." One can't help but think of Walter Benjamin's line, "There is no document of civilization which is not at the same time a document of barbarism,"[65] and, if we are to subscribe to the terms of Scriblerus's cosmos, we could also say that there is no "virtue" (diachronically mapped, most likely after the fact) without the "actual" (getting one's hands dirty), or consequently that there is no virtual without the actual. But at least Walter Benjamin would still hold out for virtue, if only by approximating it with fragments and patchwork, rather than falling into the cynicism of the neoclassicist.

As we will find, trying to discern a literature of action from a literature of reflection, a "virtual literature" from Literature proper is fraught with paradoxes and impossibilities, a failed project, perhaps, from the get-go. Literature is either, as theorists like Foucault and Barthes would imply, all virtual, or, since there is a radical indiscernability between actual and virtual (as Deleuze would assert in his final text on the virtual), a virtual literature would be quite hard to name. Virtual literature, if isomorphic with Kristeva's notion of "poetic language," is indeed ethical, framing what has been "screened out by ordinary language, i.e. *social constraint*"[66] but also cannot be defined by a duality which would place the virtual as absolute outside: rather, the doubleness that comprises and compromises actuality holds the virtual *within* the word.[67] As such, the continuous, causal images that lead to the apotheosis at the end of Cambridge's epic are one side, the seemingly secondary episodes on the Island of Poetry form the other side—what Kristeva, following Bakhtin, identifies as monological and dialogical—of a machine to break free of social constraints, asserting a "defiant productivity."[68] While Scriblerus enters a timeless state at the end of the epic, "Monarch of th' Hermetic State,"[69] his virtual journey is one that engages history, not only because it is "in constant dialogue with the preceding literary corpus, a perpetual challenge of past writing"[70] but also because, history and society come to be "texts read by the writer, and into which he inserts himself by rewriting them."[71] Thus Scriblerus/Cambridge creates a future through a form of virtual industriousness, and irreverence towards fixed abstractions. Cambridge would seem to foreclose this state of constant, polyphonic writing about Scriblerus by an undoubtedly comic prose epilogue that forbids all future writers from continuing his story, since it ended so happily with Scriblerus transcending earthly concerns.[72] He cites as "fruitless endeavours" various paralipomena of the classical epic and sequels to *Don Quixote* and *Jerusalem Delivered*, forbidding such activity on his own output and urging silence, "representing the Secrecy with which all those who are possest of the Philosopher's Stone conceal, not only those minute actions of their lives which constitute their history, but even their very persons themselves."[73]Although, by keeping his mouth shut (in so undoubtedly paradoxical a way) he silently reminds us that he is failing to mention (even though he mentioned it in the introduction), that of course his work is itself a paralipomena of an earlier abandoned project.[74] In his very last words, however, he admits that the real reason why the epic ended was merely that he had run out of ink, one surefire way to represent a concealed Secrecy.

Oulipo

You may be beginning to doubt the ultimate usefulness of the term "virtual literature." A whole horizon of weird virtualities are seeping up through the once solid form you called the literary. What to do with them all? Supernatural literature—with its narrativizing of the unspoken or the unspeakable: isn't that virtual through and through? Coincidence in Dickens, O. Henry's surprise endings, the idea of "France" in Dostoyevsky: aren't these all virtualities that twist their ways into the fabric of everyday incident? And in the oceanic expanse of unliterary data looms Moby Dick, the most virtual literary character there is . . . an immeasurable white blank on which is homed the mad desire of a whaling captain. For the moment, though, we are after smaller fry.

It would seem, on its surface, that the Oulipo group is the antithesis of the virtual. Their emphasis on mathematics, exactness, and constraint, in pursuit of a vocally anti-surrealist agenda, puts them at clear odds with the lyrical potentialities of untamed data, their self-definition intending "to eliminate obscure or vague authors, hermetics and literary madmen."[75] Disdainful of what they call "eructative" or "shriek" literature, they have set themselves up decidedly *against* any notion of free-play that might subsist outside of strict literary form. Their alliance with mid-century computational rationalism would seem to reinforce the idea that they were allergic to failure, or at the very least to aleatoric explorations of the unconscious, and were enamored instead of the idea of literary experimentation progressing as would advances in the telephone. Their status as a group seems more NASA than Beatles, and surely expresses contempt of more isolated poetic failure, and other ill-fated tilts at windmills.

Yet, if their name—"Ouvroir de littérature potentielle" or "workshop for potential literature"—is any indication, and if we are right in saying that, at least in France, there are various subterranean linkages between the words "potential" and "virtual," then the activity of this group would warrant a closer look for our purposes.[76] "Their final goal," says Marcel Bénabou, author of *Dump This Book While You Still Can!* and manufacturer of *locutions introuvables,* "is not a mere exhibition of virtuosity but rather an exploration of virtualities," to which he adds, "it is not only the virtualities of language that are revealed by constraint, but also the virtualities of him who accepts to submit himself to constraint."[77] As well, the notion of a continual "workshop" implies the "defiant productivity" of collaborative work that does not fetishize a finished product. Instead, what Oulipo values is the collective "craftmanship" of their work, spurning inspiration-dependent practices more associated with the independent author-creator. They find ways to dispense with saintly waiting, fickle muses, ephemeral sparks, and the like. *"The goal of potential literature is to furnish future writers with new techniques which can dismiss inspiration from their affectivity."*[78] For Oulipo, *"The truly inspired person is never inspired, but always inspired."*[79]

By unleashing encyclopedic arrays of what Perec calls "paraliterary monsters" (of the kind that could be found on the *Scribleriad's* "Island of Poetry") or innovating aberrant amalgamation techniques for the word (Queneau's *Hundred Thousand Billion Poems,* a recombinatorial sonnet, unreadable in its entirety by a human operator), the Oulipo reveals the discontents of composition, but nevertheless composes more insistently in their midst. Enamored of an "active" stance towards literary production, this activity is nonetheless underwritten by a strong sense of both the virtuality and the failure implicit in these compositional gymnastics. For example, a mathematical sublime is obviously inherent in Queneau's limitless sonnet, while Perec has conveyed a strong philosophical sense of absence or the "void" behind seemingly innocuous lipogrammatic tricks. Such experiments create a virtual panorama of the unreadable behind easily accessible, but exacting techniques. "The prodigious labors of Oulipo are not meant to balk reading but to place it firmly against a cosmic (or computationally stupefying) panorama."[80] As well, there is a sense that these at-hand techniques, many drawn from centuries of cast-aside word games, are themselves virtualities that the triumph of free verse has erased from communal memory, and which need to be rescued.

But these constraints are not merely forgotten substance, but literally function as tools of memory themselves—hence actualities for accessing the virtual. The politics of memory behind these deceptively playful games runs deep, directly influenced as the movement was by the Holocaust and the Resistance, historical traumas language will always fail to approximate, yet forming the despondent void that these practices articulate. The choice of conscious craft over unconscious explorations, ironic exactitude over vague rhapsody, brings the literary project closer to the sciences, while nevertheless preserving the night-side of language. As Peter Consenstein points out, "Not to do so is to allow unconscious memory to determine the shape of the present, past, and future. . . . [Oulipo's] emphasis on consciousness ignites memory and plunges both text and writer deeper into the structure and the workings of literature."[81] If the Oulipo focuses on mathematical "grams" of language—their conscious structuring and computational generation—it is not falling into the trap of an unsupple, grasping creativity that thinks, as Bergson might say, in film stills rather than holistic intuition. Instead, these stills or units of language are incarnated by history and time, making a perfect constraint ultimately impossible. Oulipo is fully aware of the unattainable ideality of their formalist purities. The imperfection or insufficiency of language to mathematics or other poetic order testifies to the importance, in the Oulipo cosmology, of the ancient concept of *clinamen*—that creative swerve that instigates the birth of the cosmos out of the void, a movement immanent to atomic exactitude, rather than transcendent of a fixed order.[82]

The split between highly controlled language and the mess of the virtual, and the attempt to keep this split within consciousness, in *swerve* at all times is part of the *duplicity* of Oulipo writing, what Kristeva points out is the productive "doubleness" inherent to poetic language, related to Deleuze's crystalline circuitry of language mirroring itself to infinity.[83] For veteran Oulipo writer Jacques Roubaud, this doubleness is what he calls "*mêmeté*," or twinness, "the relationship between an actual event and the image the mind creates of that event . . . which is one of the origins of rhythm."[84] This rhythm—productive of an oscillation rather than a strict temporality—is what generates the swarms of conceptual doubles that overcome his self-consciously failed novel *The Great Fire of London*, not least of which are the various versions—written, imagined, or forgotten—of the original dream that inspired this project (even though *The Great Fire of London* is the title, we are never quite sure we are reading it). *The Great Fire of London* is unique in Oulipo literature, because the constraints are not obvious, but rather existential.[85] Presented as an alternative to suicide, the writing of this novel—characterized as a failed project from its inception—is not merely one that puts suicide in the background, but rather in abeyance—less an alternative, writing is, in fact, *the other side of suicide*. He keeps himself to strict writing habits—tight black script written continuously "without deletions, without regrets, and without impatience, always at the same times, as close as possible to the myopic continuity of the irreversible and hated present,"[86] as if to literalize Bergson's notion that while the past is *idea*, the present is *ideo-motor*. What accumulates every morning in a Clairfontaine notebook is a blind motor accretion, around the "center of indetermination" called a life, a project, a dream.

The purpose of this pure present, according to Roubaud, is to extirpate memory. He's not repressing the past, per se, but rather amassing an irrepressible archive of a new present.

> Once set down on paper, each *fragment of memory* . . . becomes, in fact, inaccessible to me. No doubt this doesn't mean that the record of memory, located under my skull, in the neurons, has disappeared, but everything happens as if a transference has been made, something in the nature of translation, with the result that ever since, the words composing the black lines of my transcription interpose themselves between memory and myself, and in the long run completely supplant it.
>
> At the same time, the light of my recollections grows dull. . . . The recollection's emotion has disappeared. . . . [A] second induced emotion, whose origin is the lines themselves, in their minute black succession—their visible thinness—procures for me something like a simulacrum of the original emotion, now grown remote, unapproachable. But this original emotion does not recur, even weakened.
>
> For all practical purposes this process involves, in fact, a destruction. I've devoted myself to the enterprise of destroying my *memory*.[87]

What makes this writing paradoxically double is not merely the notion that he is creating memory as a method for its very destruction. In a second step in this dogged act of writing-as-destruction, he moves on to another translation—not, as stated above, one from unwritten to the written memory. Rather, he still must transform this destructive mnemonic trace into literary artifact. The handwritten script, illegible even to himself, is consequently transferred to an electronic Brother CE50—which he calls Miss Bosanquet (after Henry James' secretary)—in order to create the imaginary consistency that he is calling "a novel." In this secondary revision, as he shapes what was previously a pure motor capture of the present, virtualities start to invade the scene, crystals form around the seeds of the present. In the process of transforming his language so that it is mechanically standardized (so as to be not only readable by *another* but also by himself, now another), he has to assess the lie of the sensory-motor, and reflect on the impossibility of eliminating memory and reflection from the literary. His solipsism, which once wound itself tenaciously around the seed of the present, becomes what he calls a "biipsism,"[88] caught between language and the polymorphous situations that created the language, deflecting the presumed unity of his meditation into the multiplicities of time.

The whole structure of his book becomes evocative of Deleuze's crystal-image, a structure of time itself, revealing inhuman multiplicities of the virtual behind each seemingly coherent moment. Extensive "insertions" and "bifurcations" for which one must leap to the back of the book, immediately detour the forward motion of the prose. These forking paths perform the ambivalence of making one decision or one word over another, showing up "those places of hesitation where no 'right way' perhaps exists."[89] Irrepressible pluralities, "mutually contending modes of the present," start to dramatize the impossibility of locating the present as a singular entity:[90] "the condition of presentness coupled with the *conditions of truthfulness* . . . means that my book is necessarily located in a plurality of worlds . . . my 'detailed description' of the room is *not* the room, but a sampling of viewed fragments made of words."[91]

Thus Roubaud is able to combine the Oulipan interest in what Perec calls the *infraordinaire*—that difficult, almost invisible substance of everyday banalities—with an intensely methodical approach to the infinity within the infraordinaire. As he unfurls descriptions in which "two halves of the room [are] joined seamlessly in time in its future state"[92] the procedure ultimately seems more filmic than mathematic, even though Roubaud talks much of the significance of numbers to his work, and the role of his career as a mathematician. There is a sense that the date of the real "Great Fire of London"—1666— when cabalistically permutated, has significance to some of the intervals and insertions that cross his book, or that narily undetectable misprints of the number 1 when the word I is meant are intentional, or even that Riemann Spaces impact the design of the prose. Nevertheless, the overall intent of the book is one of meticulous destruction—and if there remains mathematics, there is only the ruin of it.[93] The "melancholic orgy" of this book, related to the premature death of his wife, does not affect the reader as does, he points out, the *danse macabre*, an emblem of death that nevertheless alleviates terror by "imposing an imaginary order upon the filthy amalgam of the inert, shapeless, threatening entanglement of Reality"[94]—an obvious reference not only to the control mechanisms of mathematics, but also to poetic constraints themselves. Instead, his Oulipo-styled approach to the abyss founders when he finds that "real, perverse, and polymorphous forgetfulness struggles against my attempt at reasonable destruction, at an orderly obliteration."[95] Consequently, he is able to make death—existing within the infinity of real failure subsisting in every line of tight black script he writes—even more palpable.

Why not silence, the virtuous path of meditation? Wouldn't that be the appropriate virtual stance towards the deep despondency Roubaud expresses? In a telling passage near the beginning of the book, he talks about interviewing his parents with a tape recorder, and notes that their relative silence about the past stemmed not from any loss of memory, but rather from the "uncurious attitudes" of an older generation.[96] Even though pure memory is radically exterior to our ability to write it, there is a sense that the assemblage that Roubaud has invented, intersecting with tape-recorders, jelly-making, shaving, and walks along the Mississippi, is precisely calibrated so as to pick up on its vibrations a little more insistently: "I have inherited a double tradition, of silence and bereavement, where the dead, after twenty, thirty, or fifty years, though still present all around, appear only in empty silences, maintaining violent existences in the black holes skirted by speech, but thereby made manifest, highlighted by a timbre of sorts, some vibration, some displacement in the movement of a story."[97]

If pure memory is that unpublishable substance that can only make it into consciousness if it meets the requirements of clear forward action (and even then, compromising itself in the translation), then when one changes the terms of what constitutes "clear forward action," new virtualities form. Think for a moment, not of Deleuze's crystal-image, but of the new age crystal, on which one can focus active energies in order to visualize a *vita nuova*. Or how meditation *techniques* do not necessarily get rid of the virtual—those various distractions calling us to act from a space outside that of the meditation—but rather bring us to the stunning realization that the body itself has been virtualized in everyday life, and thus must be re-membered via active techniques. Compare, if you will, the function of writers who highlight the *"materiality of the signifier"* in pursuit of a hyperconscious poetics, reacting against writing in which the word itself has been forgotten. Roubaud's trick is to materialize the asignifying substance of non-being, which nevertheless holds the whole together: "The *Project*, itself, was a collection of scattered, disjointed fragments, whose subtly perceptible incompleteness would allow a few readers to surmise, perhaps (Oh, those *happy few*, so similar to oneself!), the absence of something grandiose, and intentionally plundered from the text: an absent God, issuing from a decisive *delectatio morosa*, how marvelous!"[98]

To remember, according to Bergson, we must make a concerted leap into the past, not because memory is at a far remove, but because it is different *in kind* from the present. A completely autonomous being unto itself, memory, conceived as the virtual, is nevertheless available in its totality at any point. This whole—which is time itself—is conceptualized by Deleuze as a crystal, or a system of mirrors in which we can see ourselves, but which gives lie to the self-similarity of our singular image, in an ongoing multiplication of surfaces. A sense of time and the inorganic overcomes a sense of self and presence, as we can see, for example, in the Enantiomorphic Structures and geologic concretisms of Robert Smithson. According to Ansell-Pearson, "The crystal-image removes time from the realm of presence by complexifying it into regions, sheets and strata of time past and time to come."[99] Time becomes geological, it has its own being and logic so that our past time is just as unavailable (but no less present) than the cosmic time of continental drift and galaxy formation.

While Roubaud manifests this crystal image in his textual assemblage, a text like Christian Bök's *Crystallography* would be ready made to take this crystal-image further into the literary, or rather unliterary non-being. At one point, Bök writes "crystals are atlases of nothingness"[100]; as such, crystals are both records and guides that nonetheless articulate a void; in another place, he gives a veritably gnostic definition of the crystal, redolent of an Oulipo game or two (what follows is an almost exact anagrammatic line—"virtually" anagrammatic—announcing cubic acrostics on the facing page): "crystals are acrostics generated by the stochastics of a cage."[101] In Christian Bök's Oulipo-inspired *Crystallography*, we see, on multiple levels, the attempt to manifest the exactitude of what might be a crystalline language, down to the very atoms. Attending to the shape and permutation of each letter, magnifying letters to reveal their crystalline structures, or graphing the "meteorological conditions necessary for the crystallization of poetic forms,"[102] Bök concretizes a crystalline reality, while taking the Oulipo interest in exact form to the nth-degree. If Verlaine described the art of poetry as "the tipsy song/where the Undefined and Exact combine,"[103] in Bök's interplay of textual surfaces, we have the encounter of the Exact and Exact. Elsewhere, he even calls for a complete elimination of the poet:

> Has not the poet already become a virtually vestigial, if not defective, component in the relay of aesthetic discourse? Are we not already predisposed to extract this vacuum tube from its motherboard in order to replace it with a much faster node? The irony here is that, while the witless machine knows much less about poetics than even the most artless amateur knows, falderal written by the mechanism invariably outclasses doggerel written by the rhymester.[104]

It would seem again that failure is not an option and the virtual is elusive here, even though he references the "virtual" in its more colloquial usage of "not really but just as well" by alluding to the author's "virtually vestigial" status.[105] Isn't this the cold, rational truth of science and technocratic order at work? As such, it would seem that the "powers of the false" implicit in Deleuze's crystal would have no play. But the notion of "virtual vestigiality" is more telling than it would at first seem, since the poet in such experiments will always have to be "virtually" vestigial—that is, almost, but not quite eliminated—in a system that proposes the overcoming of the literary author by the inhuman beauty of scientific truth. In *Crystallography,* while a post-human poetics manifests itself when the inhuman world speaks back and confounds the order of the poet, the effect may be merely Heisenbergian ventriloquism. The clinamen invades any pure attempt at scientific capture; after all, how can the poet approximate what the inhuman world requires and still remain a poet? Bök claims to want to exceed poetry by forging an alliance with the optics of technoscience, although, as in the following exhortation from the fractal world, his literary control and lineation would imply otherwise:

Fractals tell their raconteurs
to counteract at every point
the contours of what thought
recounts (a line, a plot): recant
the chronicle that cannot coil
into itself—let the story stray
off course, its countless details,
pointless detours, all en route
toward a tour de force, where
the here & now of nowhere is.[106]

The section of this poem "Fractal Geometry" ends with a typical Oulipan warning against the aleatory, hemmed in with anagrammatic recombinations:

Don't ramble—lest you dream
about about a random belt of words
brought to you by Mandelbrot.[107]

Needless to say, this poem does not mathematically model a fractal, although the attempt to give the impression of such tight mapping creates the illusion that the fractal has been grasped. Instead of instigating a form of scientific mimesis, in which poetry becomes a mirror for scientific reality (thus situating "science" as the transcendental measure of truth) science has entered the literary mirror and been transformed by it—by its powers of the false, its implicit virtuality in this "atlas of nothingness." Description in the crystal-image is *mêmetic* not mimetic: "a crystalline description stands for its object, replaces it, both creates and erases it . . . and constantly gives way to other descriptions which contradict, displace, or modify the preceding ones."[108]

Many, including Bergson, have philosophized on the failure of science to represent more intangible qualities of reality—

hence, the productive "swindle" implicit in any form of systemic thought, replacing a worldview in which god-granted *virtu* no longer gives meaning to things.[109] Here, though, the swindle is embedded in the text, rather than the product of something repressed by scientific positivism. As Bök says in the afterword, *Crystallography* is, from the get-go, a pataphysical "misreading."[110] The lapsus between the scientific order and the poetics that attempts to translate it create unequal exchanges, rather than equivalences, literalizing Deleuze's concept of the crystal-image "endlessly relaunching exchange which is dissymmetrical."[111]

So it is that a text fiercely without essence, anti-Platonic, and materialist at heart such as *Crystallography*, has as its central "flaw," a virtuality which marks the failure of *all* literary work. As such it demonstrates Kristeva's notion, not only that "Any sentence is both syntax and nonsentence, normative unicity and disorderly multiplicity"[112] but also, correspondingly, that "Literature is . . . the experience and proof of the negativity specific to the linguistic process: 'A writer is someone for whom language is a problem, who experiences its profundity, not its instrumentality nor its beauty.'"[113] This virtual limit of purely objective, positivist language is played out in Bök's "autobiographical" section on the diamond, which approaches a crystalline description of the patriarchal figure who makes a diamond, but which also attempts a perfectly self-enclosed poem-machine: made by the diamond, in the diamond, the poem thus becomes diamondness itself. The repeated refrain

MY FATHER
TAUGHT ME
PRECISION

mirrors the precision of the poem, formed out of concretic blocks of text (including the letters themselves, all in block caps), as if it maintains a one-to-one connection to the fabrication of the hardest material on earth. As well, the first line "C IS FOR DIAMOND,"[114] institutes a polysemic chain, not only connecting diamond to its elemental cognate (Carbon), but also to life (carbon as the element common to all living beings), writing (a graphite pencil), and the name Christian.

Yet, his pataphysical and anti-mimetic stance would require that this attempt to capture life and non-life, the biography of a diamond sawyer and the object of the sawyer's craft, all reigned in by the paternal requirement for precision, will have some slippage. It is a slippage that is even thematized in the poem—his father blinded by the stray chip of the diamond while cutting it, for example, "NERVES/SHOT BY THE THREAT/OF A SLIPPED RAZOR"[115]; but in proving to the reader that there is nothing that has eluded his control, creating literary value that is purely internal to his system, Bök succeeds in creating a diamondesque structure—each facet reflecting the other. It is not, of course, a diamond. It is not even cubic zirconia. However needless this assertion may seem, it is strikingly necessary, a conceptual forgetfulness crucial to Bök's illusion. Concretism in poetic language creates an undecidability between word, object, and image, intersecting textual surfaces that don't replicate the "thing itself" but rather dissolve the thing by bringing it into language.

But the profundity of the virtuality of this diamond, the "almost, but not quite" aspect of Bök's pataphysical, asymptotic approach to its reality, is that a diamond itself is not a diamond without a vast system of techniques, symbologies, and forces both geological and social that give it meaning, the "now you see it, now you don't" implicit in the creation of human value. Even real diamonds are never really diamonds. The words "VIOLENT WORDS UNDER MINING" accompanied by a list of historic mines provokes the types of aphanasis we are used to in the apperception of a poetic pun, and highlights the human rights abuses (which, of course, devolve upon questions of subjectivity, the "mining" and "yours-ing" that defines the parameters of the human) lurking behind this highly civilized object "TO ADORN/WEDDINGS/AND WARS."[116] But it also dramatizes how even the clearest perception of *the object itself* can undermine that object, how a double is not a replica, but rather the opposite of replica, an unsunderable quiddity.

Bruce Ivins

On February, 19 2010, the FBI released a 104-page report based on nearly 400,000 documents summarizing their case for identifying Army biodefense expert Dr. Bruce Ivins as responsible for the Anthrax attacks in 2001.[117] When the *The New York Times* subsequently released the unredacted report via their multimedia sidebar for the story announcing the end of the investigation, it provided a window—larger than is usually afforded by the news, but becoming more typical as news allows for "virtualized" content—onto what was the most expensive case of the FBI's history. Like all such bureaucratic documents, one would imagine it would be unreadable except by experts and fanatics—a hundred page document offends the cup-o-tea temporality of the typical *Times* readership. Yes, there are, justifiably, a large population of effected readers—demanding accountability, still parsing out the traumas of that September—who would indeed welcome such breaks in the pace of their news media consumption to reflect on the closure of this case. However, the significance of this text resides not so much in how such documents now virtually expand what the news can do, but rather expands for new audiences what the literary *is*. The *Amerithrax Investigative Summary* may in fact be the most significant document of literary criticism in the history of American letters.

Because if you look at these messages, they are, of course, poems:

THIS IS NEXT
TAKE PENACILIN NOW
DEATH TO AMERICA
DEATH TO ISRAEL
ALLAH IS GREAT

Lineated, incantatory, containing message, containing secrets, with suggestions for living the good life (or just plain living: "TAKE PENACILIN NOW"), metaphysical sparseness, and a little bit of langpo archness ("THIS IS NEXT"). *This* was not lost on the FBI. The American intelligence community has had a long history of mixing literary analysis with strategic defense, ever since the Black Chamber was created in the beginning of the twentieth century, staffed with Shakespeare and Poe scholars to decode possible secret messages in radio noise.[118] Stockhausen perhaps missed the boat with his comment that the 9/11 attacks on the World Trade Center were "the greatest work of art there has ever been." It begs the question of intentionality. The *Amerithrax Investigative Summary* released by the FBI sets out to prove that the letters from Ivins *were* intended *precisely* as art, and as such, provided a key leading the case to his doorstep (or, back to *their own doorstep* as it were).

Ivins, it turns out, in addition to being a leading government expert on this type of bioterror, was a failed writer. While the FBI makes no judgments upon his writing skills, it is noted as a significant part of the profile: "Dr. Ivins was a prolific writer—to friends and colleagues and strangers alike. He wrote e-mails; he wrote letters to members of Congress; he wrote letters to the editors of various publications; he wrote witty poems; he wrote songs; he even wrote a program proposal to ABC, NBC, and CBS about the life of Space Shuttle Challenger Astronaut Christa McAuliffe."[119] As well, the FBI quotes some of his poems, sent to colleagues. It is notable that while the investigators seem to define his writing (and perhaps *all writing*) as addressed "to" someone—siding with Lacan rather than Derrida on the purloined letter debate—the addressee of this poem is obviously more ambiguous:

> O, Healer! O devoter of your life to the lives of others! I can hurt/kill, and terrorize, but others place me with the vilest of

> the/ vile. . . . Go down low, low, low as you can go, then dig forever,/ and you'll find me, my psyche. I can kill none but myself. I can/ terrify none but myself, but I can love and hug and turn toward the/ good, all who are willing. Give[n] my long-distant and non/ productive past. Our pasts shape our futures, and mine was built/ on lies and craziness, and depression, and thievery, and things that/ make an honest man and woman cry. Alone. The farther I go, it's/ alone. The state smells its carniverous death-blood sacrifice. I/ look into the mirror and cry out who it is.[120]

The trope of the double or hidden life is continued in this one, sent in the fall of 2001:

> I made up some poems about having two people in one (me + the person in my dreams): . . .
> I'm a little dream-self, short and stout.
> I'm the other half of Bruce — when he lets me out
> When I get all steamed up, I don't pout.
> I push Bruce aside, then I'm Free to run about!
> Hickory dickory Doc — Doc Bruce ran up the clock.
> But something happened in very strange rhythm.
> His other self went and exchanged places with him.[121]

On the surface this would seem bargain-basement psychopath doggerel, the kind we've become accustomed to in various thrillers, where infantile sing-song is mixed with dark intention to maximum effect. This poetry is also the poetry that most Americans will gladly recognize as poetry, albeit reluctantly . . . it is devotional, it is soul-seeking, its references are not obscure, its symbology accessible, it is psychologizing, it rhymes. It is, it would seem, unremarkable.

However, the discovery of the Anthrax letters as literary *in-and-of-themselves* brought the FBI down the black hole of another type of poetry. These letters to Daschle, Brokaw, et al. are NOT the kind of artifacts Americans easily identify as literary. The deceptive simplicity of the letters reveals within the *letters* (a pun *en abyme* of which Ivins was surely aware) a hidden reference to genetic codon sequences ATGC, each codon scratched a little more intently into the paper, including the "A" in the tellingly misspelled "PENACILIN." Readers of conceptual and constraint-type poetry will probably be aware of such practices, now that Christian Bök is working on his *Xenotext* experiment, which proposes encoding of poem directly into the nucleotides of a strand of DNA. Bök's poem, however, engages the more aleatory potentiality of the posthuman, rather than encoding a predetermined message—a crucial aesthetic criterion delimiting an avant-garde exploration of freedom from human meaning from the more psychopathic assertion of self through a twenty-first-century infernal machine.

A loving destruction, à la Duras, would imply a different attitude towards representation itself, a failure encoded and embraced at the root of the project. Both Ivins and Bök are utilizing an immortal bacteria for their poems, but while for Ivins, anthrax is presumably just a deadly means to the ends of a message (and these messages turned out to be as bathetic as the e-mailed poems, referencing a lover who spurned him and his hatred of New York), Bök's approach is not as interested in imposing meaning as it is in discovering the virtualities between his scientific encoding and the inhuman organism's future activity. For Bök, the poem, when linked to the immortal substance of a bacterium, can become a *perpetuum mobile* of poetic creation: "the genome can now become a 'vector' for heretofore unimagined modes of artistic innovation and cultural expression. In the future, genetics might lend a possible, literary dimension to biology, granting every geneticist the power to become a poet in the medium of life."[122]

In a section of the *Amerithrax Investigative Summary* entitled

"Godel, Escher, Bach: the book that Dr. Ivins did not want investigators to find," the FBI establishes Ivins' fascination with the literary potential for genetic codes, and his fascination with code in general. In fact, Ivins' attempt to get rid of the book—an event the FBI designates as the "GEB trash run"—was a significant lynchpin in the case. A discussion of this bestselling, but largely unreadable book would be difficult to draw into a genre of document for which such literary-mathematical fol-de-rol would be mere distraction, and the FBI admits as much when attempting a summary. Nevertheless, they take its core premises seriously—at least seriously enough to provide a form of vernacular lit-crit in the service of closing the case. The author(s) of this FBI document tell us:

> The author of GEB discusses the concept of 'duality,' that messages can have multiple meanings. This is further evidence that the messages here related to both former colleagues. Similarly, it reflected the dichotomy between Dr. Ivins's intense love of and at times animosity for these women who were so integral to his mental state on any given day.[123]

It is remarkable that such a hamhanded literary reading should be the central corroborating evidence in so difficult a case (leading some to believe that Ivins' odd-ball profile made him merely a convenient patsy). The report flirts with the idea of duality in meaning, but forecloses the possibility that the case itself could be as complicated as the book which serves at its key. The whole affair is redolent of a culture in which *social constraints*—in writing as well as being—require clear, obvious signification of the self-same. If not, secret hidden meaning is tolerated, or at least expected, as long as it stays hidden; the literary analogy would be tolerance of difficult writing only if it hides secret symbology or cabalistic super-meaning. Such a culture of constraint without "clinamen" is productive of freaks who play by the rules enough to get hired by the government, but then are unable to assimilate their creative impulses, their "dark" pasts, their unacceptable desires—all difficult virtualities—into the fabric of their lives, or into the chaotic flow of life itself.

Nevertheless, while Stockhausen was heaped with opprobrium for even suggesting a link between the World Trade Center attack and a sublime avant-garde experience, it is precisely this link that would allow the FBI to identify Ivins as the chief suspect of the most notorious case of literary mail-art ever (although this case was never definitively closed; Ivins killed himself before there could be an indictment). But the literary-critical investigations of the FBI did not stop at the single letter and its possible double meanings. Rather, as is familiar territory for contemporary poets but perhaps more outré for Quantico folk, they sought out possible semantic meaning *in the envelope itself*. In what reads as the most beautiful aspect of the document, a conceptual poem that serves as an elegy to the use and making of these particular envelopes, the FBI author(s) detail their physical attributes and manufacturing process for approximately one and a half single-spaced pages. Here is a look into the ecstasy of military literary analysis, in which anything can be meaningful, but only in the service of a fantastic complicity of minutiae and masterplot, rather than a pure appreciation of the abyss of the unliterary. The section starts:

> The four envelopes used in the attacks were all 6 3/4 inch "Federal Eagle" pre-franked 34¢ envelopes. The "Federal Eagle" name was derived from the postage frank in the upper right-hand corner of the envelope, which consisted of an image of an eagle perched on a bar bearing the letters "USA." Underneath those letters was the number 34, which denoted the 34¢ postage. The eagle, lettering, and denomination are referred to hereinafter as "indicia."
>
> In addition to the printing on the front, on the backside of

> the envelope, underneath the flap, there was text which read: "© USPS 2000." Also on the back of the envelope, in the bottom center, there was text which read:
> "♻ THIS ENVELOPE IS RECYCLABLE AND MADE
> WITH 100% RECYCLED PAPER, 30% POST-
> CONSUMER CONTENT."[124]

"A thing of beauty is a joy forever:/ Its loveliness increases; it will never/ Pass into nothingness" Keats writes in the opening invocation of his reflection on immortality, *Endymion*.[125] Envelopes, in their blank, yet significant anonymity, form the substance of a postal *infraordinaire*—a kind of unrecollected memory and indecipherable backdrop to this high-stakes cloak-and-dagger plot, marking the daily rhythms of communicational affect rather than the terror of a deadly novelty. As such, they pass into nothingness *and* are eternal, in the same way that recycling is not "resurrection," but rather recirculation in another form.

But Keats, who could be marvelously petulant in the face of an indifferent readership, was just as vulnerable to the pathology of desiring attention as was Ivins. His struggle to insure immortality for his labors was accompanied by a sickening awareness that his craft could easily be undone by the inconvenient limitations of his life. He writes in the preface to the same work that there is "not a fiercer hell than failure in a great object"[126]; and in another, discarded preface, he even makes excuses:

> I fought under disadvantages. Before I began I had no inward feel of being able to finish; and as I proceeded my steps were all uncertain. So this Poem must rather be consider'd as an endeavour than a thing accomplish'd; a poor prologue to what, if I live, I humbly hope to do.[127]

It is precisely these types of potentially embarrassing admissions that must be rewritten into the narrative of life, rather than be excluded as undesirable virtualities, returning as violent actualities attempting an authoritarian reconciliation. This appreciation of poem as endeavor rather than a "thing accomplish'd," in a series of prologues and postlogues to an ambiguous consistency, is part of what would constitute an education in the virtual.

Cthulhu

Temple of the Spirit
No longer Bodies but
Pure aesthetic Images
Compared to which mere
Thought seems flesh,
Heavy and dim.

This verse is the only remaining text we have of Charles Lewington's oeuvre. He died young, before he was able to acquire a large audience. His fans consisted of admirers, mostly women, who copied out his poems for private delectation. Even if he had lived longer, he most likely would not have found a niche for his work. His poetry's metaphysical preciousness seemed at odds with postwar realist modes and conceptual experimentation; in fact, it seemed especially out of sync for someone who, as Lewington did, actually served in the military, having participated in the invasion of Anzio, and staying on in Italy after the liberation. An ungenerous reader might just chalk it up to aestheticized shell-schlock, but then it might be hyperbolic to assert that Lewington had enough of an audience to include the "ungenerous reader." Consequently, he has completely evaded any critical radar.

But if we wanted to establish a fragile structure for considering, indeed critiquing, this oeuvre that no longer exists, we'd have to bring in an earlier generation of forgotten poets cut down in their youth: Jacques Cégeste and Sebastian Venable. Lewington neither had Cégeste's prescient and fearless avant-gardism—eulogizing the unreadable expanse of nonbeing that he was soon to enter—nor Venable's queer gothic serialism. The most reliable critic of Venable's work, his mother (whose estate has made Venable's work unavailable to the public), has said,

> Most people's lives, what are they but trails of debris—each day more debris, more debris . . . long, long trails of debris, with nothing to clean it all up but death. My son, Sebastian and I constructed our days. Each day we would carve each day like a piece of sculpture, leaving behind us a trail of days like a gallery of sculpture until suddenly, last summer.

The Venable boy was known to use people like objects in this quest for an unbroken chain of aestheticized pleasures, and from what evidence we have, we can posit him as an example of what might be called a Bergsonian action-poet. Even his death, no matter how far it faded into the past would always be "suddenly." Yet this death, instigating an adventure in memory for those whom it immediately concerned, would cause all manner of virtualities to erupt and be contended—while his "Summer" long poems still remain unread.

Of course, Lewington, like Venable and Cégeste, are also fictional poets—from Rossellini's *Voyage in Italy*, Joseph Mankiewicz and Tennessee Williams' *Suddenly, Last Summer*, and Cocteau's *Orpheus* respectively. Lewington's memory haunts Katherine Joyce (Ingrid Bergman) and, like the memory of Venable in *Suddenly, Last Summer*, it warps the edges of the sexual, emotional, and aesthetic frameworks of the living. His spirit enters the images via subtle sonic intrusions—not supernatural, but not mere sound either. Rather when Bergman conveys distraction, her attention diverted by typical images and sounds from Neapolitan streetscapes, it reads on her face as a clear reminder of alternate realities that she has relinquished, and the unsupportability of her current mode of life (These alternate sheets of time are displayed more garishly in *Suddenly, Last Summer*). Unlike the Neapolitan street songs or sights of innumerable pregnant women that randomly impinge on her emotional states, however, Lewington's poem is directly invited, the invocation of a ghost.

We are lead to believe that Katherine's choice of the more urbane, yet cold and sarcastic Alex Joyce (George Sanders) over Lewington was partially the cause of Lewington's death—a familiar tale of a woman taking a more practical lover, sacrificing the idealist who cannot provide for her and thenceforth undergoing spiritual starvation in an otherwise well-fed milieu (a theme variously rejiggered in other Bergman marriage-of-convenience roles—Bergman's Ilsa in *Casablanca* and Karen in *Stromboli*; they would seem to contradict her real-life choice to marry for love, consequently signaling the end of her Hollywood career). While Lewington's poem-fragment pulls her into a virtual space outside of marriage, signaling her unhappiness, and reminding her of an alternative, it also brings her closer to death. After all, Lewington's quest for the "pure aesthetic image" is even colder than her husband's brutish neglect. Inspired by Lewington's love of the ruins of Naples, she fills her time somewhat miserably—although broken through by moments of wonder and awe—among the ruins of Naples and Pompeii. Like any neorealist hero, she is unexpectedly impacted by another kind of pure image—that which has the potential to undermine the human ability to interpret image and event according to the dictates of one's own desire and movement. In the unpredictable interstices along the way to each orchestrated tourist experience, she is shamed by the fecundity of sexual life that the natives display—in seeming ignorance of the memorials of death that surround them. It is not until estranged husband and wife are physically stopped on the way back from Pompeii to their villa—their car surrounded by a sea of people during a procession of the Madonna—that they are forced to recognize the unmanageable flow of life that they have thus far been unable to experience, forging a new, albeit temporary bond in counterpoint to it.[128]

Lewington's function as a ghost, then, is ambiguous, a potentially destructive virtuality that nevertheless instigates a new path. In later generations of fictional failed writers, we can see more uniform messages about the worthiness of bad writing. On the one hand there is the optimistic embrace of unwashed hackery, inspired by a culture of open-source and self-publishing, in which anyone can have a voice and become a star—so, for example, the multi-volume epic of the pompous pedophile janitor Henry Fool has the potential to open up new paths, inspire new expression, and in the end create new lives for the characters around him, regardless of the quality of his prose. On the other hand, there is always the terror of the unproductive—a life of passionate dedication to an art ending in disastrous blockage—we can think of Norma Desmond and Joe Gillis's *Salome*—or the perversely productive, which in the end might be the terror of the avant-garde invading our limited aesthetic consciousness—Jack Torrance's concrete masterpiece "All Work and No Play Makes Jack a Dull Boy" has more than once been taken up by contemporary poets as an important milestone in the history of conceptual writing. While Torrance's fate emphasizes the uncanny force of failed writing to destroy fragile family structures and place them on a larger cosmic panorama, such uncanny catastrophes point to virtual dysfunction. Lewington, however, is a type of literary ghost whose unsettling impact belies a more supple relation to the virtual; it holds within it the potential for a ghost to return in ways that are not patently destructive, serving as a reminder of the impoverished order that could not accommodate him in the first place, but conceivably salutary—forcing the creation of new linkages. While the *uncanny*, as a helpful concept for understanding such phenomena, thrives on the uncertain value of memory-effects impinging on the action of the living, the destructive side of the uncanny is the one that is usually most emphasized. Can we imagine an aesthetic of the uncanny that would enable a dark positivism that might free these writers from their other-worldly realm without returning them as vengeful angels?

That the uncanny is a category of the virtual there is no question. However, the uncanny tends to mark an attitude towards the virtual that has atrophied, one which is not constant and subtle, but is rather, as Freud says, a product of "psychical censorship."[129] One's superego splits off and becomes a persecutory double, one which embodies "all the possibilities which, had they been realized, might have shaped our destiny, and to which our imagination still clings, all the strivings of the ego that were frustrated by adverse circumstances, all the suppressed acts of volition that fostered the illusion of free will."[130] But, while this description seems to be useful for thinking about literary virtuality as the discarded, difficult, unpublished and unpublishable double of the more well-tended world of the readable, especially as it impacts the psychic consistency of characters and authors, I am ultimately suspicious of using Freud's account to understand the dynamics of literary virtuality.

My suspicion stems not merely from the fact that his readings of literary artifacts, while insightful, seem done only at arms length, as he makes claims for distinctions between the imaginative and the real that are above all *unimaginative*. Further, however, it seems that the "intellectual uncertainty" that accompanies his assessment of literary objects—whether performed by him as a way to bait the reader or unconsciously manifest as his own symptom—makes it clear that he is troubled by the literary itself. We can safely say that, instead of identifying uncanny moments in imaginative literature, he is revealing to his audience that, for all intents and purposes, all literary activity is the uncanny, repressed double of his psychoanalytic project. Thus, for him, the idea of "uncanny literature" is a tautology.

Freud's central literary object in his essay on the uncanny is E. T. A Hoffmann's "The Sandman," a story that shares the themes of countless later uncanny tales—the most iconic of which are

The Stepford Wives and *The Invasion of the Body Snatchers*—where presumed human beings turn out to be something else entirely. Hoffmann's genius is to give readers the sense that *narrative itself* is a machine that we attribute liveliness to, but that is only granted life in the same way Nathanael falls in love with the automaton Olympia, forgetting his childhood sweetheart Klara. Imagine if the makers of *The Stepford Wives* chose to let you in on the secret that *all* the characters displayed were only epiphenomena of the mechanical projector in the back of the auditorium, or, further, that even your own human substance was subject to interrogation, just another a viewing machine in the end; without any recourse to more obvious Brechtian techniques, Hoffmann was doing just that. In much the same way that Spalanzini scandalously inserts his automaton-daughter Olympia into polite society—a ruse that when discovered causes "a horrible distrust of human figures in general"[131]—so Hoffmann, by pointing to the problems implicit in creating a text that conveys an image of life, reveals behind his presumed fantastic tale a metafiction about how we create and process literary data.

The story is one—the narrator admits as much part way in—that doesn't *begin* as much as it is *instigated* by the "documentary" evidence of letters exchanged by the protagonists—a technique that he describes will help translate the complex affect of a shocking and implausible event into the "colorless, frigid, dead" world of speech.[132] All supernatural literature works in similar ways: a materialist or factual approach to the story at hand (here the pure documentary status of the letters) approaches a virtual secret threatening the consistency of the materialist world view itself. While most supernatural narratives start with the supposed superior framework of official science or vernacular rationalism, this narrator starts with what he admits are already impoverished means. Added to the narrator's doubts about his own storytelling powers, the protagonist Nathanael is also an author struggling to create readable work—a significant feature Freud fails to mention. "In truth, Nathanael's stories were really very boring,"[133] the narrator tells us and their lifelessness is the source of the story's main emotional dilemma. Nathanael can't find love with Klara, because she thinks his writing is tedious and grotesque—although there is the lingering sense that Klara as well as Nathanael are just more or less sophisticated reading machines programmed with different philosophical operating systems.[134] While Nathanael dwells in the abyss of memory-effects which thwart his romantic success (but feed his artistic soul, however unwholesomely), Klara is pragmatic and has no time for Nathanael's visionary self-flagellation.

No matter how much the reader may want to distance her/himself from Nathanael's self-defeating, and in the end homicidal vision, in order for the story to have power, you have to identify with Nathanael's "lacerated soul," and his literary struggle, not Klara's contempt for the fantastic. Here, Freud shows his hand by siding with Klara, who he describes as Nathanael's "wise and level-headed fiancée,"[135] seemingly breaking a crucial emotional contract of the story, and revealing a discomfort with any literary creation that does not point the way to procreation. An uncanny story does not work unless it brings you into difficult identifications, aligning your emotions with something best left unexpressed or forgotten; by its very nature it exudes an excess that cannot be contained or understood by official sanctioned frameworks for living, or even by the material surfaces of the story itself. Klara's "quiet, domestic happiness" that she ends up with is undoubtedly ironic, although Freud would imply that this ending is the happy one, rather than just an alibi for the play of fractalized perception within the text itself. If this story pointedly avoided a recognizable beginning, it can be safe to say that this end is also merely a convenience.

While Hoffmann can't *actually* give us the image of this

ending's alternative—an anti-Oedipal congress of inhuman data, with only our dreams to give it meaning—we can have a *virtual* sense of what that would constitute by taking the terrors of Nathanael's paranoiac hunches to their ultimate conclusions, in the mental space of reading and re-reading, between and across the lines, in the intervals between fragments and lacunae the author leaves for us to follow. In this way, we travel *within* rather that *through* a literary text; the experience can be very much like those in our well-known immersive virtual spaces, but, in the case of literature they are activated in the space between an author and reader, where there is enough play for the authorial composition to elicit the indeterminacy of the unliterary.[136] We are always thus in virtual literature *virtually* virtual. Never quite able to get there fully, intentionally, we approximate. The author sets out to explain something beyond the pale of human experience, claims that its publication would be an abomination, then sets out to write it anyway.[137]

The problem for virtual literature as a knowable category would rest in the creation of virtual effects—whether as a politicized ethical intervention, an embodiment of inexpressible duration, or a defamiliarization opening out onto the sublime—from within material form. It would be a literature that knows that it can't get at the inexpressible "it" of the virtual, but nevertheless does not play the tiresome game of artistic inarticulacy. We can think of the deep memory effects approached in the fiction of Arthur Machen, and how he gives us some sense of his strategy to frame or deframe them when he describes the nightly reading activities of Clarke—the witness-interpreter of *The Great God Pan* who "pined for the unseen." Clarke compiled, and read in different arrangements at each sitting, what he called his "Memoirs to prove the Existence of the Devil." Never intending to turn it into a book, he instead compulsively tended it so that it remained a suggestive archive of fragments:

> Clarke would find himself casting glances of warm desire in the direction of an old Japanese bureau, which stood at a pleasant distance from the hearth. . . . Its pigeon-holes and drawers teemed with documents on the most morbid subjects, and in the well reposed a large manuscript volume, in which he had painfully entered the gems of his collection. Clarke had a fine contempt for published literature; the most ghostly story ceased to interest him if it happened to be printed; his sole pleasure was in the reading, compiling, and rearranging . . . [138]

Which brings me to the archaic, cosmic monster Cthulhu, creation of H. P. Lovecraft—who idolized Machen's work. But whereas the imaginary of Machen's Pan comes from the vestiges of the pre-Christian civilization on the English landscape, Cthulhu is no merely culturally repressed, moral antiquity. Its horror is unprecedented in human consciousness, and stands as an ultimate sigil of a deep, unremembered virtuality impinging on the fate of the earth. The story of Cthulhu must convey this unthinkability without reference to anything we know. Consequently, "The Call of Cthulhu" is just that—a collection of fragments, accounts within accounts, of drawings, statuettes, and other semblances that call forth but do not give us the totality of Cthulhu—which we can assume would call us to our own madness or death. These representations already have the power to convey a reasonable amount of horror, yet are only human approximations of the inhuman, immaterial abomination of the *thing itself*. Yet even "thingness" would imply an accessibility via human consciousness that Cthulhu skirts. Existing "totally separate and apart" . . . the fragmented evidence of Cthulhu the Cthulhu *things* that are to be found in this tin box (for it is a "box" more than a story, a container rather than a monologue, added to by a variety of now-dead authors)—hints at "something horribly remote and distinct from mankind as we know it; something frightfully suggestive of old and unhallowed cycles of life in which our world and our conceptions have no part."[139]

Of course, Lovecraft has all sorts of this-worldly devices to facilitate the call of this immensely unperceivable no-thing, whether by referencing avant-garde aesthetics such as we find in Futurism (reader, if you thought Futurism was bad, this is even worse), or writhing out racist erethisms wrought by the spectacle of "diabolist Esquimaux"[140] and "mongrel celebrants"[141] in a Louisiana swamp ritual (which while expressing something "far deeper and older than negro fetichism"[142] nevertheless were peripheral to the horror calling out from the deepest swamp.) Lovecraft's narrator says, "The Thing cannot be described—there is no language for such abysms of shrieking and immemorial lunacy, such eldritch contradictions of all matter, force, and cosmic horror,"[143] yet his detailed, orgiastic expressions map out, in exceedingly purple, descriptive prose, the negative space of his abhorrence.

Would it be callow to return, on the brink of this pullulating cosmic horror, to the cold question of data? "The Call of Cthulhu" starts:

> The most merciful thing in the world, I think, is the inability of the human mind to correlate all its contents. We live on a placid island of ignorance in the midst of black seas of infinity, and it was not meant that we should voyage far. The sciences, each straining in its own direction, have hitherto harmed us little; but some day the piecing together of dissociated knowledge will open up such terrifying vistas of reality, and of our frightful position therein, that we shall either go mad from the revelation or flee from the deadly light into the peace and safety of a new dark age.[144]

The story ends with the exclamation "—but I must not and

cannot think!" Were we truly to take the attitudes of thought and its common sense out of the equation, rather than merely repress their activity, the unreadable data of Cthulhu, and its polyvalent calls into the material substrait of the real would be given free reign. Doing so might give us a sense of a kind of uncanny positivity, what Lovecraft meant when he called for a "*non-supernatural cosmic art*" which described as a "revolt against time, space and matter" yet in a "form not overtly incompatible with what is known as reality—. . . gratified by images forming *supplements* rather than *contradictions* of the visible and mensurable universe."[145] Like the accumulative processes of Charles Fort, which in their very excess and unreadability thwart total knowledge, but create some kind of pataphysical hallucination of cosmic to-ing and fro-ing, the text of Cthulhu comprises a dense catalogue of tropes for conveying the affect of the unreadable.

It is easy to imagine that Lovecraft identifies more with his narrator, wishing that no other eye read what he has read: "Wherein is pieced together that which I hope may never be pieced together again."[146] Yet "The Call of Cthulhu" meets our eyes gladly, and as such attests to the ambivalence at hand. More like the mongrel celebrants than the posthumous Francis Wayland, we have been acclimated not only to the Futurist aesthetics that seemed so patently disturbing to Lovecraft, but also to the uncaged gnostic visions and failed cosmologies of Poe, Artaud, Philip Dick that express new modes of being and expression. While one side of Lovecraft may have feared the power of these unfiltered messages from the abyss to invite such attempts, another perhaps called them forth to transform the infelicities of his existence. The monstrosity may not be Cthulhu but bounded human existence itself, a hallucinatory accumulation around an absence, which perhaps also characterizes the experience of writing in the forbidden voids of the virtual.

> We are in front of a fountain, whose jet she seems to be watching. "Those are your thoughts and mine. Look where they all start from, how high they reach, and then how it's still prettier when they fall back. And then they dissolve immediately, driven back up with the same strength, then there's that broken spurt again, that fall . . . and so on indefinitely."
>
> —André Breton, *Nadja*

A few words on this composition. I began with the singularly terrifying prospect of writing a book with no conceived framework other than the notion of creating loosely cohering sections, each reflecting the other, with no strict order. Once a section was done, it would be put aside, and not be reread, except cursorily, subliminally, enough to sense an order, emergent and unforeseen rather that predicted and managed. In this, it resembles Adorno's definition of an essay, one that has certainly outstayed its welcome, but that neverthess holds to the crystalline organization that characterizes the virtual:

> All its concepts are to be presented in such a way that they support one another, that each becomes articulated through its configuration with the others. In the essay discrete elements set off against one another come together to form a readable context; the essay erects no scaffolding and no structure. But the elements crystallize as a configuration through their motion. The constellation is a force field, just as every intellectual structure is necessarily transformed into a force field under the essay's gaze.[1]

Is it the force of some sublimal jet of energy or a supernatural hand that has created for this book without method and without planning (except for the most provisional) an actual form, and at that the most primordial? It seems that this book has accreted around a temporal axis: not merely time moving forward, but time reflected upon, in its order: behind you is a section on the past, and you are about to read about the present. At the end of the book will be a section on the future. As we move from the realms of memory, into the intractibilities of the present, and finally beyond, have we discovered, without the benefit of a pre-made grid, time as if in its natural habitat? Or is this merely the mark of a kind of entropic alienation, a failure to truly create disorder because of the ordering principles in disorder itself?

We are now, it seems to me, near half-way through this book, and even knowing this fact compromises its sincere attempt at creative failure in search for the virtual. Truth be told, I am (as the author of a book will always be) further along in the discovery of this book than you, dear reader. I have already completed the section that you are about to read ("Alchemists of the Everyday") and am well into the last section, which deals with the notion of the future. You'll get there soon enough. Suffice to say, we are at least past a certain point where the energy of the elusive whole must start to fall back in on itself. So into the present we go. However, because I have allowed myself at this point the luxury of looking back, and even revising what has accumulated, I find the section on the present almost intolerable, and I am tempted to delete it entirely. Everything that made me suspicious of the previous sections—its strong Deleuzean/Bergsonian framework, most notably (which still remain, albeit less emphatically)—ended up turning it into a better read. Whereas, the sincere attempt at present—and what point in the fountain's fall is that?—with all of its unsynthesized psychic bulk, is an ugly undertaking. We are more able, it seems to me, to reflect on failure (any meditation of which is a meditation on our own) when it is in the realm of the could-have-been (the chances missed, the paths not taken) or in the might-be (where there is always the possibility of failure's redemption). Present failure: the angers, distractions, injustices (real and imagined) of the moment have little time to be smoothed by time. They bite through the paper, they corrode, and what's more, we forget that they do that. I think at first I worried that these reflections to follow, especially on the very near contemporary, would not only be bitten through by too much reflection on my own failure in the moment of writing, but also that the very failure that situates these insights in a book—barring this writing from the power and cache that comes from the journalistic, the electronic, the immediate—would necessarily mean that the writing would become dated quickly, an inadequate map for work to come. But perhaps, the present is so difficult that we are "dating" something even when speaking of its contemporaneity in the contemporaneous. The new is always doomed.

But it is easy to write of the dead. It is harder to figure out how we are actually living (in the virtual). A more subtle necromancy is required . . .

Alchemists of the Everyday

Unidentifiable

There's nothing more ordinary than a UFO. Since the flying saucer craze started in 1947—with a sighting against the odd panorama of Mt. Rainer and down the road from that buckling bronco-ing prodigy that was the Tacoma Narrows Bridge, in the midst of prime Bigfoot stomping grounds and now heartthrob vampires (all, it turns out, in my backyard)—the UFO has become a plentiful banality of our astral imaginary. On the internet, one can find various vernacular black-and-white photos of UFO sightings, the kind that were typically used on shows like *In Search Of. . .* the flying cigars, the pie plates, the suggestive blurs and tell-tale blotches. What strikes me most about these vintage amateur UFO photos is not the arguable "fact" of the sighting itself (from a kinder, gentler time in which a photo stood for the actuality of the real) but the little bit of reality that is not the object of our attention, that presumably *is* real precisely to the extent that it is ignored, virtualized. These photos—from various mid-century Woonsockets and Zanesvilles and Lubbocks, Czaplineks and Barra da Tijucas and lac Chauvets—capture a fragment of space-time that would not have been memorialized were it not for the alibi of prodigy. Consider a UFO photo from Passaic in 1952—about the time William Carlos Williams was writing Book V of *Paterson*—and what, after all, does it seem more difficult to know? The strange but recognizable image in the clouds, or the blankness in the mass of branches, the changing shape of the tree tops, the accomplishment of a phone pole, the clouds themselves? Alas, the clouds are not even captured, ignored by the technology like fairies by the unimaginative.

Compare, if you will, an alchemical image from Michael

Maier and Johann Theodor de Bry's *Atalanta Fugiens* (1618), an early multimedia experiment in which image, text, and song were arranged together to elicit a meditation on the Philosopher's Stone.[2] In this alchemical emblem, there are three tofu-shaped UFOs floating in the clouds. On closer inspection, these unearthly cubes are also masquerading as paving stones, as if to visualize the alchemical maxim that the Philosopher's Stone "may be a thing that most people do not see, though they tread it under their feet."[3] Further inspection shows that these cubes are ubiquitous, both as recognizable shape and symbolic translation; a traveler on a horse sits—we can imagine obliviously—smack under a sigil representing the sought-after Stone.

Since the secret of the *lapis philosophorum* evades the mechanisms of knowledge itself, *Atalanta Fugiens,* as the title implies, can only reveal it fleetingly and partially. As its frontispiece promises, *Atalanta Fugiens* is "fitted partly to eyes and intellect . . . and partly to the ears and the recreation of the soul . . . the whole to be seen, read, meditated, understood, judged, sung, and heard with extraordinary pleasure."[4] Diverse alchemical pleasures augment the static image with durational experience, a whole composed of creative intervals confounding bounded perception and encouraging the visionary and ecstatic. In the multimedia network of this book and its hermetic readership, formalism is superceded by the intellectual and creative activity of the reader who is encouraged to find their own truth, only apprehended through the darkened glass of an immense hermetic game. And why include this game for the purposes of this catalogue? Because alchemical books comprise an entire body of literature—indeed an entire mode of knowledge—that has been consigned to oblivion and deemed completely useless by modern science. Even when we try to read them sympathetically, we can only appreciate their aesthetic and allegorical properties—one case in which virtual *science* is transmuted into the literary for lack of a better *raison d' être*, since the actual practices that may have existed behind these mnemonic and meditative tools have been definitively lost.

We could say, as one ancient commentator did of this book, that the message of such literature is conveyed "with sufficient clarity for clairvoyant eyes,"[5] a clue that maybe these games always implied a virtual mystery at their core. How else does one communicate the secret of life, if not by admitting the failure of common channels of perception and instead exercising those of the extrasensory virtual? It would be only misdirection to direct readers unequivocally to a locus of the Stone, not only within the frame of this image, but also within any one medium of representation. But to merely say it is "everywhere" is still a non-solution. Yes, it may be "everywhere" but this realization is not as easy as it might seem, especially since, according to

Bergson, we are always conceiving the present through the filters of the past, compromising epiphany from the get-go. For us to have the experience of *true perception* of this "everywhere" in the everyday, perceiving this non-hidden secret of something right in front of us—not merely a memory effect or automatism—the mapping of our known world would have to be disrupted, familiarity giving way to doubt, even in the act of rediscovering it anew.[6]

"Hic lapis est subius te, supra te, Erga te, et circa te," reads another emblem, this time an alchemical seal from the *Basilica philosophica* of Johann Daniel Mylius and Matthäus Merian. *Here is the Stone: beneath you, above you, beside you and around you*: the words encircle what is presumably the object of the maxim, but within the circular text-frame, the presumed *here* to which one is directed, is an image of swarming, hovering eyes.[7] It's not an image, as much as it is an image about the image. The Stone is not everywhere as much as is its *potential*, a function of the quality of our looking at the world. The Stone cannot be *found* anywhere, but is a condition of unity, fragile and contingent, between the presumed useless, occult backdrop of our everyday life (useless because not entered as a data point in our cognitive mapping; occult because anything not thusly entered is "virtually" metaphysical), and the activity that transforms it, visual or otherwise. As such, we are on guard against more completed forms of acknowledged beauty, and, if there is anything salvageable from the alchemical project for modern readers, it is the notion of creative salvage itself, the rescue of spiritual and artistic value from the midden of our daily muddle: *In sterquilinio putredinis nostri est initium et causa sine qua non* ("The essential starting point is the shit-heap of our putrefaction.")[8]

Marcia Nardi

"*Only* my writing (when I write) is myself: only that is the real me in any essential way. Not because I bring to literature and to life different inconsistent sets of values, as you do. No, *I* don't do that; and I feel that when anyone does do it, literature is turned into just so much intellectual excrement fit for the same stinking hole as any other kind."[9] I can imagine that when William Carlos Williams read this letter from the failed poet Marcia Nardi, which he would later print among others she sent as an integral part of his epic *Paterson*, he may have at first ruefully agreed. Then he may have cried "not fair!" since, of course, he was bent over the plow of a long poem that precisely sought to break open literature and open it to life. Then, settling down into catty archness, he may have pointed out "Dear Marcia, you don't go quite far enough. If you want to treat literature and life in the same way, then you need to get over your hangups with excrement." Wait a couple of generations and he might have chastised her for insisting on this notion of the "real me," which of course, *Paterson* too, in its precocious anti-essentialism, was in the process of exploding: "Why even speak of 'I,' he dreams, which/interests me almost not at all?"[10]

Williams would forge a literature in which collective interrelations—however much they failed to communicate across gaps of misunderstanding, spatial-temporal discontinuity, sex and other social barriers—would trump authorial unity in the modern epic. The virtuality of *Paterson* was composed through a fraught continuity between the author and his others, maintained by not smoothing over the disjoints. It is important, then, that Williams *did not* reproach Nardi's potentially damning letters in the way I described above. Williams took them as

> a reply from the female side to many of my male pretentions. It was a strong reply, a reply which sought to destroy me. If it

> could destroy me I should be destroyed. It was just that it should have its opportunity to destroy. If I hid the reply it would be a confession of weakness on my part.[11]

By printing them prominently, documentary-style, without any (overt) commentary on their contents, he took them on the jaw, as it were, and allowed the virtuality of the Nardi-Williams duplex to manifest itself freely and without judgment, in the same way Williams treated other materials from both personal and historical archives. "'Use *all* her letters,' he wrote on one draft of the manuscript, '*She* has the last word.'"[12]

Yet he would stop short of including Nardi's poems, only available for readers now as an exceedingly thin volume, published in 1956. Reading her poems, I am struck by how well-tended they are, perhaps too well-tended, coming from the poet whose five-page single-spaced eight-point font letter to Williams—incisive, pleading, pathetic, exhilarating, and damaging—would literally be the "last word" of *Paterson*'s Book II. Here was the poet who, when a trickle of academic curiosity finally came her way, kidnapped her scholarly amanuensis by locking her in a Cambridge apartment, as an apocryphal story goes. Nardi was a poet of vast dedication and desire, but also of vast crazy; even her most supportive fans have some trouble fully embracing her, or do so only abstractly. Yet in her actual published work, she is in comparison on her best behavior. I could use the adjective anemic. I could, to give her the benefit of the doubt say "starved"; she never failed to mention to Williams that while her actual conditions of poverty were confounding any attempts at literary advance, what determined her desolation definitively was Williams' spiritual abandonment of her.

Perhaps poetry was an inadequate medium for her rage, and it is ironic that her letters to Williams—seeming emotional excrement probably embarrassing to her and wilting to Williams' "male pretensions"—are the source of her admiration by later generations. Or they are a source of horror, obscene evidence of something deeply, systemically wrong between the lines, a virtuality that shouldn't have been virtualized. Rachel Blau DuPlessis writes, "Yet would it be possible to breathe this, it is so awful: that Nardi's letters, rewritten slightly and selected by Williams, are her most striking works?"[13] Williams said as much, insisting that she had to get more of the energy from the letters into her poems, "Whether or not you can ever bring over into writing the truth that is in your letters and in your thoughts is purely a matter of the technical side. You have the mind."[14] It was perhaps disingenuous for Williams to point out purely "technical" matters since, for Nardi, there are the technicalities of life as an itinerant laborer, problems as an unwed mother with her illegitimate son, the treatment of women writers, as well as more day to day frustrations like missing checks, not having a typewriter, etc. etc.. Williams must have known, as he wrote in Book III in *Paterson*, that "The writing is nothing, the being/ in a position to write (that's/ where they get you) is nine tenths/ of the difficulty."[15] A closer reading of what little she has published shows that the truth of the letters was there, but in a way that was perhaps not aesthetically visible to the expansive, raw Williams. Future readers are no less guilty than Williams for assessing her output in relation to Williams' style. The experience of Nardi through *Paterson* so defines any subsequent reading of her oeuvre, that the filter Williams unintentionally provides for it does not let us fully appreciate what is *in* her poems, Nardi living miserably for lack of what was *not* found there.

Yet, unavoidably, literary gossip gives these poems much of their bite; in the same way it is difficult to avoid the biographical facts of Williams' peculiar set-up as a small town poet-pediatrician (and occasional womanizer), it is very difficult not to put Nardi in some kind of "collective assemblage" with Williams, reading what little remains of her work through the frameless frames of *Paterson*. Can one separate Nardi's "And now you are all going abroad/ . . . While I here at home/ Must go down with the chipmunk to the hole"[16] from Williams' emphasis on the local, his decision to stay at home rather than be in Paris? Nardi's poem is nevertheless inflected by her capacity for self-pity, rather than Williams' more celebratory stance, but the connection resounds. While Nardi says in her letters that she was "a woman dying of loneliness—yes, really dying of it almost in the same way that people die slowly of cancer or consumption,"[17] this cry for help, tamped down and tucked away in some of the smaller, private corners of her poems is nevertheless resonantly there. "I have joined you, my love,/In abandoning me:"[18] by 1956, a line like this, sophisticated and paradoxical yet nevertheless harrowing, can't help but be read through Williams' almost cosmic philosophy of divorce, or even his impatience with clearly bounded "I," "me," and "you," as if Nardi gives a bittersweet twist to her erstwhile mentor's lesson.[19] The line might also be a somewhat ironic reply to Williams' mild artistic blackmail to any American who did not like his poems: "They think they're rejecting me, but all they're doing is rejecting themselves!"[20] Nardi perhaps knew that for her writing to be embraced by Williams she had to embrace her own noise, ugliness, and rough edges, which paradoxically meant an abandonment of any sense of secure self in the Paterson net—a position more plausible for Williams than for Nardi at the time.

Her traditionally lineated, sometimes rhyming poems are, as with the letters, redolent with complaints of abandonment or misuse: "Here in that same dark country where the same thrust/ Makes no different burrow/ Whether love's or lust's."[21] Like Williams, she conveys the sense that a poem is a struggle, its creation linked with the creation of self, both never finished, yet uniquely thwarted by sexual division. These poems, however, are resolutely not Patersonian. Nardi's "Alone with a Poem"—which may be an *ars poetica* for her—gives us a more traditional notion of poetic inspiration, while at the same time, sexualizing it. We are unsure whether this poem is another complaint to a lover, or song to oneself, given the ambiguity of "you," but the ways in which the poetic idea works itself into the poem are at the same time more idealistic and yet more violent than what Nardi considered Williams' more safe, concretistic stance. Part I of this poem reads:

The idea you innocently play with—
Indifferent to what it may lead to
Or, rather, not thinking about it much—
Touching it, brushing against it . . . the stranger
You sit near at a party
And at your leisure, for an hour's past-time,
May see again . . . or the child
Still young enough to take upon your knee and fondle,
Foot-loose—your nostrils lowered
Over a road-side rose . . . .

How these gold virginal moments,
Like those recaptured Edens
When the body wakes from sleep before the mind,
Must fade into the distance
All their myth's brightness
Misted and shadowy,

When the child, a year older,
Turns flower to lodestar

Or into your sun and air
Grows the attractive stranger,

When your idea
Thrusting upon you an unmade poem, makes
The true rape God's of Mary.[22]

Another thrust. I can't help but read these last odd lines as a thrust back, rewriting Williams' shape-shifting cosmogonic opening to *Paterson*. Whereas, in *Paterson* all things emerge from its matrix as if from an immanent divine being, Nardi is reminding the reader of the similarly immanent Catholic belief that Christ was "begotten not made" and how this notion robs Mary of her painful agency in the equation. Williams' attempt at world-creating works through Nardi, but ultimately ignores her physical and emotional needs. Of course it would be sad to imply that all these poems are just a continued harangue with Williams, and that she did not have her own life to live—although the freedom to live "one's own life" or the circumstances that would inspire the need for such independence can be equally as sad. Notwithstanding, whether by natural proclivity or pointed reaction Nardi takes on the almost saintly endevour to produce the "well-made" poem, which Williams eschews in his later years, attempting to doggedly keep *Paterson* "unmade."

Williams himself struggled so much with his great, unfinished catastrophe of letters, that while *Paterson* has now become, albeit begrudgingly for some, the great modernist epic, it is fair to say that Nardi's inclusion within it constitutes a failure *within* a failure. "The poem to me (until I go broke) is an attempt, an experiment, a failing experiment, toward assertion with broken means but an assertion, always, of a new and total culture, the lifting of an environment to expression."[23] There was a point in Williams' life when, after a long hiatus from writing, he realized that his energy was not adequate to the task he had put out for himself; feeling he could never write again as he did as a young man, he set out to reinvent new means for writing what he called "that God damned and I mean God damned poem *Paterson*."[24] As Nancy K. Barry describes in her essay, "The Fading Beautiful Thing of *Paterson*," the poem remained for a long time just a configuration of plans, outlines, and materials: "Between 1920 and 1940, *Paterson* existed for Williams as an accumulating artifact. In large manila envelopes, labeled for each of the four books of the poem, he would compile manuscript pages, prescription blanks with images or bits of verse scrawled beneath the logo, calendar pages, and other fragments."[25] What Barry calls the "lyric archive" of his older poem drafts was intermixed with these more concrete bits, all looking for some kind of future form to hold them, the material circulating through the manila envelopes as in a compositional shell-game. In a Fortean manner, Williams found that he was satisfied with this "mass of materials, interrelated" and had much ambivalence about striking a final version. Barry even implies that however much Williams felt his inability to complete *Paterson* was an *actual* failure, he nevertheless was aware that his virtual method—asymptotic to *Paterson* but leading him directly to his own death[26]—was the one to follow, satisfying "his persistent desire to escape, or transcend, the finite and finalized moment of composition."[27] Williams even thought of calling the entire work *Paterson: Introduction*, putting it in the virtual category of the purely prelusive, his personal failure perhaps dimly perceived as a prequel to an adequate expression of environment left open to the indeterminacy of the future. "That will be the end of it, just the introduction, life isn't long enough for anything else."[28]

This system for intentionally *un*manifesting the imaginary "whole" of *Paterson* seems an important strategy, not only to open poetic fragments up to the future, but also to have a more vigorous, empirical perception of the present. "To make a start,/ out of particulars": readers tend to focus on the "particulars" that Williams foregrounds in this invocation, and for good reason. But the use of the infinitive "to make," with no subject in sight puts us in the realm of action without clear subject—crucial for energizing those particulars. And "start" is left up for grabs, too. Does *Paterson* start in the italicized, disjunctive *argumentum*; in the epigraph in which he quotes writing that he has deleted;[29]

in the deleted writing, or the ghost of it; in the preface—an invocation with no muse in sight; in the "Delineaments of the Giants;" or is the whole book a beginning, an opening (even though his preface states that the reverse is fatally true "the beginning . . . assuredly/ the end")? For Deleuze, the infinitive, like an emphasis on media and "middles" rather than clear beginnings and ends, opens up a virtual milieu of sense, "allow[ing] language to be seen not as naming but as doing"[30]; hence it leaves the field more open to a truer perception of place, rather than one filtered through the memory of accumulated subject positions.

Even Williams famous dictum in these first pages, "no ideas but in things," testifies to the openness of particulars to the sense of the milieu. Though we usually imagine the "thing" either as a cold, inert, *fait accompli,* or as a terrifying otherness that overcomes devices of human control, it is here much like the virtual Stone—a function of our awareness and the quality of our actions (or inaction) in the world. As Elizabeth Grosz points out, while both the Enlightenment and 50s sci-fi movies posit the thing as "that against which we measured ourselves and our limits, the mirror of what we are not . . . alienat[ed] from the subject, with an animated and potentially malevolent materiality,"[31] there is another tradition (which she places in the work of Darwin, Nietzsche, Peirce, James, Bergson, Rorty and Deleuze) in which the inhuman, virtual, or (for our purposes) unpublishable thing uniquely calls forth the potential, processual dynamics of the living:

> The thing is what we make of the world rather than simply what we find in the world. . . . Things are our way of dealing with a world in which we are enmeshed rather than over which we have dominion. The thing is the compromise between the world as it is in its teeming and interminable multiplicity—a flux as James calls it, a continuum in Lacan's

terms, or waves of interpenetrating vibrations in Bergson's understanding—and the world as we need it to be or would like it to be: open, amenable to intention and purpose, flexible, pliable, manipulable, passive. It is a compromise between mind and matter, the point of their crossing one into the other.[32]

If one were "just another dog/among a lot of dogs"[33] as Williams claims in his preface, the *things* of *Paterson* would not have such a difficult, or impossible unity. We can't help but be alienated by the world around us because even though it is uniquely there on account of our perceptual mapping, it is loaded with memories, histories, and thwarted desires that cannot find their way into action or consciousness but are nevertheless persistent as if in a cosmic archive of regret. The energies of these virtualities may be the creative source of new things and new modes of action and thought. But the paradox for those who, like Williams, want to seek out the virtuality of the everyday is this: effective present action in the world is only possible after memory has already traced out tried and true paths. Thus, when we feel most lively and connected, we are consummately *not there*, but instead are working through a fragile infrastructure built up between memory and the matter at our disposal; perhaps this liveliness of the non-present is why events like birthdays and holidays can be "fun" but also, alternately, joyless, rote, or terrifying, because they reveal an automatism that cannot be challenged. So for Williams to truly invent a unique American poetry—unfettered by a European aesthetic memory—as well as perceive Paterson with utter materialist optics, he would have to conceptualize a "new measure" as an organizational principle, one which may imply some *measure* of inaction interposed into the rhythms of his daily life and poetic activity, rather than mere musical pause. Regardless of his interest in speed—which in the end may only be possible by way of the unspeedy traces of memory and their subsequent manic deletion—he would have to accept those moments in which he was interrupted or challenged as a precondition for manifesting the world around him.

This Bergsonian paradox, whereby only inaction, doubt and confusion give one access to the genuine state of the present moment, comes into play in the famous passage in which Williams "discovers" the technique of the triadic line:

The descent beckons
                as the ascent beckoned
                                Memory is a kind

of accomplishment
                a sort of renewal
                                even
an initiation, since the spaces it opens are new
places

                inhabited by hordes
                                heretofore unrealized,

of new kinds—
                since their movements
                                are towards new objectives
(even though formerly they were abandoned)

No defeat is made up entirely of defeat—since
the world it opens is always a place
                formerly
                                unsuspected. A

world lost,
                a world unsuspected

beckons to new places
and no whiteness (lost) is so white as the memory
of whiteness .
. . .

The descent
made up of despairs
and without accomplishment
realizes a new awakening :
which is a reversal
of despair.

For what we cannot accomplish, what
is denied to love,
what we have lost in the anticipation—
a descent follows,
endless and indestructible .

Listen! —[34]

By interposing defeat—"what we cannot accomplish, what is denied to love"—into the flow of memory (which is concretized in the very ways we tack back and forth through these lines, descending and ascending to give them sense) another flow or rhythm or presence becomes available to a consciousness. A dash silently points and interrupts, "Listen! —" and as the composition breaks off (a moment of "inaction" that the previous lines have been preparing us for), the falls of the city become apparent, more real than the reality of Williams and his poem. Even though their sound, or the image of it, stands for poetic white noise—unreadable, uninterpretable, unmusical—it is a noise from which everything emerges and to which all returns, the virtual substrait of Williams' literary "accomplishment."

"What do I do? I listen to the water falling. . . This is my entire occupation."[35]

The notion that the activity of writing is not as important as the inactivity of writing is evident in Blanchot's formulation of this "insane game":

> To write is to produce absence of the work (worklessness). Or: writing is the absence of the work as it *produces itself* through the work and throughout the work. Writing as worklessness (in the active sense of the word) is the insane game, the indeterminacy that lies between reason and unreason.[36]

But what his formulation also implies is that to write, one must lose a sense of the *work* (integral whole) because the *work* (active scribbling) is done in an almost completely different dimension of experience. Both Nardi and Williams seem to have been able to realize the value of inactivity in pursuit of an (imaginary) compositional whole, with Nardi even resigning herself to a Zen-like attitude of "another motionless pine-tree in the snow."[37] But Nardi, in contrast to Williams, was not as willing to give up the notion of the ideal, integral work. Both were unhappy with their failures: they were not yet writing in an era which joyfully, or at least ironically, toys with the possibilities such impasses bring. Yet Williams was the one who found a way through to a clearing. While he was still particular about ultimate form, he chose not to "'die for art', but live for it, grimly! and work, work, work,"[38] which meant somehow surviving, even profiting from, the inactivity of poetic defeats, while maintaining the frenetic activity of potentially aimless accumulation in tandem with a regimen of fearless erasure:

> It is dangerous to leave written that which is badly written. A chance word, upon paper, may destroy the world. Watch carefully and erase, while the power is still yours, I say to

> myself[.] . . .
>
> Only one answer: write carelessly so that nothing that is not green will survive.[39]

Which brings me to an important hard fact about virtual literature and literature in general. To become any kind of literary success you *must become* a failure. That is, in the process of writing, you must experience the unpublished, the sheer inhuman uncertainty of its accumulation. This uncertainty increases in proportion to the ambition of the project (for Williams a life-work on an epic scale) but also to the personal stakes involved when the project, as in Nardi's case, was innovative existentially as much as, if not more than, it was artistically. There is nothing more difficult than leaving oneself open to this failure, these virtualities. The Word, as it shields itself from ambiguities not directly available to apprehension, would seem, however, to be the most unvirtual thing there is. This is why most of Deleuze's important discussions of the virtual come from an analysis of cinema, where the non-verbal can proliferate and compose sense beyond signification. The Word is a rationalized, ordered form of human consciousness, in some ways more strict, or at least more unforgiving than math, precisely because it is activated in the space of *human* agreements and concords, a sphere of violent politesse that math is able to overcome; thus, not only is math more virtual, but more "real" than literature, which is probably why the idea of math was compelling to Williams in *Paterson*. Math's rationality is *inhuman*, whereas the rationality of the Word—and the things that the word helps us create—is all too human.

Nardi did not expect or welcome, we can imagine, her apotheosis as literary monstrosity, avatar of the inhuman dimensions of the literary experience. She, after all, did cast her lot in with the humans, and expected their love in return. Did she ask too much, or misapprehend the rules of the "insane game" of writing? Maybe. But whatever the infelicities of Nardi's personality, we should collectively be ashamed of her abandonment rather than revel in her oddity. The only way anyone can experience the failure that attends every moment of a writer's life is if they are surrounded, as Williams was, by enough care, attention and support to withstand its horrors. Any literary world worth its designation as such should provide that attention to one courageous enough to enter it.

David Lyle

The title page for early manuscripts of William Carlos Williams' *Paterson* reads: "PATERSON or Any/Every Place. By W.C.W. D.J.L. M.N."[40] Once conceived as part of a collective authorship, these Paterson residents who assisted Williams in his initial conception were taken out of the credits by the time the books appeared.[41] M.N. (Marcia Nardi) for a long time would only be known as "Cress" in her letters as published, leaving critics uncertain whether she was a real person; regardless, she is a prominent voice in *Paterson*'s webwork. D.J.L., however, is completely lost to readers of *Paterson*. Amongst all Williams' fragments, cross-references, allusions and historical markers, there is barely a hint of him. Yet, as both Paul Mariani and Mike Weaver will assert, David Joseph Lyle gave to Williams the means by which to put the whole thing together, giving some sense to its mass of unrelated materials, while preserving the noisiness proper to them.[42] From Lyle's massive output of unpublished writing, Williams learned that a poet was a manager of data—a filter of sorts, one whose purpose was to design a *better* filter, rather than merely create *ex nihilo*.

Williams began to receive Lyle's letters in 1938; these grand typewritten homegrown theses from an unknown were packed with the same dense, interconnected, crazy intelligence as Nardi's.[43] They speak of secret continuities in the flow of daily fragmented information, an "allness pattern" to be found where our inadequate concepts fail. Because they record and annotate, cross-reference and interpret—with a marked obsessiveness—whatever piqued his voracious attention in the popular press, they give us a vivid impression of an environment of cultural noise now forgotten, before history solidified into clichés, before the fishwrap of daily debate and conjecture was wrapped up into tidy stories. Lyle attempted to divine nothing less than the vital destiny of humanity from this unfiltered informatic jumble, before it was shortcircuited by what he called time and space-binding devices. His professed method was that of an industrial designer who sought "to remove in advance any possible cussedness of inanimate object-products..that might tear the user's entelechy open by evoking unwanted reflexes."[44]

Because Lyle was an ex-radio operator and engineer at Wright-Aero, not to mention a cosmically ambitious autodidact fascinated by the spiritual potential of new technology,[45] his discussions are full of machinic metaphors and scientific speculations regarding the reorganization of the total human sensorium. He describes the Tao symbol as a "wiring diagram of the source of human energy." He thought that an alliance (what he liked to call a "parleying") of the "poet, efficiency expert, artist, writer, scientist"[46] could counter the violence of the times if the secret image of mankind were discovered; such an image would act like the carrier wave frequencies of radio, allowing for an open dialogue across a single imagistic system. He speculated on the creation of a topological photograph of the idea of America "in terms of the running Hammond Organ all and/or any ever happened…happening..and ever will happen event structuring of man..or men"[47] and thought literature's role was similar: to design "a map of the sea (of human energy)"[48] in competition with irrationally violent binding symbols such as the swastika. He desired to break through humanity to get at some "re-al substance," a vital sameness, since "the difference in men resides merely in WIT."[49]

His wiring metaphors take on a palpable actuality, as he strings out etymologies, creating connections between vastly different levels of reality even as he dispenses with typical logical and grammatical progressions. He is especially manic with the word sequence that extends from science through to schizo, and lays out the string *split—cleave—scire—know—decide—decision—precision—shade—shadow—SHINE*. Cleave is an interesting word in this sequence, one that unites the manic "cleaving" activity of

Lyle's fragmented prose, which, as a method, has the aim of "cleaving" more faithfully to some knowable and totalizable human experience. Spliterature as science. It as if, in the midst of all these split and broken elements, Lyle saw something whole, some *non*-sunderable flowing contact with the entire God process. Williams takes this idea further by introducing an archaic pronunciation of Passaic or Pissaik—*"PISS-AGH!"*, which Mike Weaver says is "derived from the root *pach*, 'to split, divide.'"[50] One can surmise that, in deference to Lyle, the flowing waters of the Passaic become the locus of a great schizophrenia of un-knowing at the heart of his broken epic.

Whether Lyle was clinically schizophrenic is uncertain, although his writings resemble those of the insane, underprivileged or illiterate whose intelligence exceeds their means, who convey an almost hallucinatory impression of their sense of the world and its connections, but are unable to express their thoughts with propriety. The energy of his intellect overflows agreed upon forms, so that we get crystalline data nodes, reflecting and multidimensional, rather than the well-tended, implicit violence of "bullet-point" logic. He is Deleuze and Guattari's ideal twentieth-century schizoid man well before his time. In fact, his letters resemble the virtual writing style of Judge Schreber, Deleuze and Guattari's anti-oedipal muse, which Schreber himself describes in *Memoirs of a Nervous Illness*: "From the beginning the *system of not-finishing-a-sentence* prevailed, that is to say the vibrations caused in my nerves and the words so produced contain not mainly finished thoughts, but unfinished ideas, which my nerves have to supplement to make up the sense."[51]

Lyle, however, is conscious of the "schizoid" aspect of his writing, and of writing itself. He uses the schizo-science pairing to describe what he conceives of as a split world, a description once again evocative the "two jets" of Bergson (who he mentions in the letters), and which would become crucial for Williams' concept of the poetic object. Many times, in different letters, Lyle describes perception as 1/2 percept and 1/2 internality, but the description in his first letter to Williams warrants quoting at length:

> The central nervous system of every living human being has a gravity driven period whose length is that least interval we call the SECOND of TIME. .
>
> whose schizo-frenia setup is also the source of the idea of number(ing).
>
> 1. 1/2 is purepercept..clear center inside in terms of a moving plaque of perceptual matter..which leaves one in visual touch with a particular (object, particle, scene…in a 3 dimensional field in the great worldspace beyond that occupied by the body itself.
>
> 2. The next half is the instantaneous explosive transmutation of this matter into energy…which is conserved and appears as one's motor members tending to leap from the body into the space beyond…thus blinding the individual to all particulars..except the cussedness of these inexplicably behaving body members.
>
> Schizo roots with zest, schism schedule, shed shadow shade SHINE…
>
> . . .
>
> Browning uses the word shine also.. as JHVH used to be written one way…and pronounced as if written different.. this schizo..between sight symbol and sounded commonterm..being invariantly scheduled..to split the zest and store it in memory as feeling..hard and fast as knowledge.
>
> . . .
>
> symbol, problem, parliament, metabolism, ballistics, devil, parable, parlor….words indicating the areas in which life is today disturbed simultaneously everywhere by some unknown oneness law. The people have been defined

> above..as N central nervous systems..appearanced in bodies..motored alike..and producing various image and situational setups.[52]

This mind-body bridge, between percept of particulars and the blinding (and binding) energies of memory, is the measure that Williams was seeking out. When Lyle asks "To what TUNE danceth this Immense?"[53] it is the conceptual rhythm between virtual immensity and the activity of perception that is the "tune." Maybe it's more a *tuning* than a song, providing Williams with a non-musical intervalic dynamic ordering the "re-al substance" at the heart of his project. This play of the virtual double with each poetic perception provides plentiful new challenges for lyric composition (and its decomposing other). Lyle's "SECOND of TIME" reveals itself not as a clockwork abstraction, but rather an "instance" of the already double-nature of a poetic moment. Why, after all, call it a "second"?

Although there were many other luminaries on Lyle's spam list—he would sometimes address each letter to two or three more authors—Williams was the only one who actually sought him out. Lyle writes, "Nearly four years of those letters and you are the first person to express a will to find out the reality, if any, behind this making of farreaching structural claims."[54] When Williams finally visited him, he discovered it was no troll with bandaged glasses at the other end of these strange missives, but rather a 6'3" blond beauty. Williams, while charmed, immediately perceived Lyle as somewhat of a competitor. As Paul Mariani says, "There might be many women in *Paterson*, but Williams was going to make sure there was only one man."[55] He was ultimately abandoned by Williams, supposedly because the flood of information that Lyle plied was too much to process. Yet, before Williams broke off contact, the evidence seems to point to the fact that the engineer introduced to the poet some of the core conceptual elements of *Paterson*: the search for an overall pattern amicable to conveying the human experience without foreclosing it, the importance of particulars and the underlying mathematical structures of reality, the inadequacy of traditional poetic language and official media language. More than anything else, the style of Lyle's letters gave Williams the freedom to sculpt information in a non-lyric, patchwork, yet meaningful new American idiom.

Although Lyle's letters are absent from the final text of *Paterson,* Williams did make attempts to transcribe these flowing paratactic blocks for possible inclusion. There were also attempts to make Lyle become a character, even if the letters did not prove adequate. In the archival copies of the letters, you can see that Williams has crossed out "Dr. Williams:" and replaced it with "Dear Noah," switched out Lyle's signature and inserted the name "Faitoute."[56] In Williams' copies of the letters, he also at times replaced his *own name* with "Faitoute." In the final version of *Paterson* there are only remnants of these characters, confusing hints of a submerged framework. Did Williams want to embody the gathering, patriarchal ideas of a Noah, or the more profligate dispersed energies of Lyle's Faitoute? Part of his abandonment of Lyle was to take over his identity, "so by 1944 Williams had arrogated for *himself* the name Noah Faitout [sic] Paterson."[57] Yet, while Williams was consciously discomfited by the idea of Lyle as the ur-figure and hero of *Paterson,* there is some sense that Lyle-as-Faitoute is only partially erased in the poem. In the sections where Faitoute is mentioned, there remains a sketchy semblance of Williams' relation to Lyle, or Williams' relation to the *Lyleness in himself.* Just as when Nardi writes "I have joined you, my love,/In abandoning me," the directionality and object of rejection is perhaps intentionally confounded when Williams writes, "Faitoute, conscious by moments,/ rouses by moments, rejects him finally/ and strolls off ." What follows may describe a rivalry between Williams and Lyle, but also Williams' struggle with his own self-consistency in the face of the information engineer's challenge to authorship:

> That the poem,
> the most perfect rock and temple, the highest
> falls, in clouds of gauzy spray, should be
> so rivaled . that the poet,
> in disgrace, should borrow from erudition (to
> unslave the mind): railing at the vocabulary
> (borrowing from those he hates, to his own
> disfranchisement) .
> —discounting his failures .[58]

Like the word salad of spam texts and the illiterate patois of web comment boxes, Lyle's text gave Williams a window on the informatic liveliness that evaded the creative impulses of a singular poet. Yet the sensation of "ears/ ringing . . . [with] a roar of books"[59] would become distasteful to Williams, an example of borrowing, even plagiarizing erudition, and Williams had no recourse but to ignore Lyle's inhuman processing of data if he wanted somehow to get something done. While Lyle, thinking that literature as a mode of representing "the people" could be overcome by devices such as the newly conceived Gallup polls, sided with the machine, Williams would ally with the machinic only partially—fascinated, but not wholly won over by its claims for dominance (note the ambiguity of Williams' use of the word "unslave" rather than "enslave" the mind). Even though Williams famously has said that the poem is a "machine made of words," the uneven rivalry between Williams and Lyle points up some of the ambiguities surrounding the machinic alliance with literature. How far is an author willing to go into the virtual dataspace of illiterature while still maintaining the status of artist or author? At what point does the poet *become* an engineer, a pollster, a nobody, a non-being, dead? The spectrum of virtual tourism contains within it the specter of what would ultimately tear apart the poet, or even just the human.

In pointed contrast to Nardi's needy pleas, however, Lyle is glad to be the anonymous transmitter at 1014 E 24th St. He is so self-satisfied that he signs his letters with the words "cheerfully, David J. Lyle. No acknowledgement necessary. No obligations or restrictions in re any or all uses of enclosed material," and it is no stretch to say that it is Lyle who insouciantly rejects Williams, even at the outset of their relation. The only imposition he seems to make on Williams' time is some recognition of his own, bluntly stated in the heading of his letters, a manager's metrics rather than a creative writer's: "Elapsed Writing Time, 5.5 hours." The happy logorrhetic.

(spam)

I remember playing with Chinese toys as a child. For example, the terrific Chinese Magic Wallet, into which you would put a dollar bill, and it would vanish. Open again and it would return. It was a simple trick that was fascinating even when you knew the trick. I would try to put larger and larger items into the wallet, challenging, as children do, the object's hospitality, even attempting to disappear my hand, to feel the action of the wallet's fake implications, to lose myself even. Of course, played this way it would eventually break, but then it was as if I had opened another, more secret dimension of the Chinese Magic Wallet. Because, as I would soon learn, what was really marvelous about these types of Chinese toys was not the toy itself, their novelty soon exhausted. Instead, it was the fact that, when torn apart one uncovered a Chinese newspaper. What could be more magical (and more, after all, Chinese) than pages of red letter ideograms, dotted with mysterious halftone images, from halfway around the world, where—revolution of revolutions—it was worthless and plentiful enough to use as stuffing. Soon, I knew exactly when a toy would contain this secret tunnel to China, and dispensing with its surface charms, went right to its presumably worthless core.

At one point in our collective history, within the melee of our daily email messaging we received onslaughts of worthless solicitations from armies of seemingly half-literate American drug manufacturers, luxury timepiece salesmen, and Russian pornographers. To get more palpable sense of our daily virtuality we need to start here in the inbox (rather than the Xbox). We can learn a lot about virtual literature from spam, the ways we've deleted it, the ways we haven't, how it gets read, how it gets unread, or even reread, how it has forced a new sense of the readable. With spam, say goodbye to old-fashioned sanctimonies of the communications expert class, their patronizing injunctions to "Keep It Simple, Stupid." With spam marketing, the actual message is subsumed by the nonsense of misplaced html tags, incoherent syntax, jarring misspellings and other text noise. That's the way it gets around the computer's filter and into your mailbox. Humans are much better readers than computers, and contrary to what the Keep It Simple crowd has always bullied us into thinking, the human is quite capable, and sometimes willing, to take some time to find the "real" message in an informatic jumble of spam noise. So, out of the nonsense that the spammer sends down the pike, you'll be able to discern the ad for Viagra, or cheap Rolexes, or whatever the computer has been trained to read and block but can't because it has been duly confused. The hyperlink that promises increased dick size, when combined with a fragment of someone's online mystery novel, or maybe a pataphysical haiku—undoubtedly machine generated—willy-nilly reaches its audience.

Or, you get the Chinese Magic Wallet scenario.

Because most of us knew enough to ignore the ads, but were fascinated by their worthless packing material. Drawn from sources such as randomly generated dictionary lists, chat room fragments, and other textual material without clear provenance, these inexplicable additives were meant to confound spam filters by what is called "Bayesian poisoning." Here are some examples of these poisonings in their raw form, rescued for my personal reserve:

> ansi colonel continuity seagull beneficial collocation eighteen zesty eleazar. muggy wrath calorimeter decomposition befogging leonardo blackout. licentious before burrow punk reticent splotchy stalactite heat. canteen psychology san doric befogging freeing confusion, wonderland carnage autoclave burrow brahmaputra crazy. flare rebellion crosshatch biotic liquor coronet. karachi criterion lottery adjoin beneficial

arcana chrysler devout contestant aquinas.

Hi my name is roy and Id like to invite you to my favorite pick-up site. Since I first sow this site, 4 months ago, I felt a MAJOR change in my ljfe – I met more womeen then I've ever dreamt of! You can enter now too, since the site is open to the public for free. Feel free to enter!
take me now moisture
http://www.amateurmatch.com/index.php?ainfo=Mjc3MHwx

english exam today was very boring but i bet maths tomorrow will be be worse! i envy all of you off to the rocky challenge!
refreshing to see some meaning on the net to see u guyz giving the base for the story and letting us finish it thank u for all the thought and heart u ve put into it it s all plan!!!!
-when i made fish camp the gregster emailed me and said brooke are so money! you are money! haha good ole dad i taught him how to do the hey ya dance the little spirit fingers it s cute.
i charles seay bruton.
well I got tht skewl wrong it s the ballee skewl tht the lad hu knows me goes to-he had a red strip through his hair n we chattteeddddddd lol. [etc.]

Make a miracles in bed!
JUS check it!
http://wotyopk.com/wc/
no sense, and,
because the Moon

Such web noise became a central source of poetic material and inspiration in the 'aughts, forcing new ideolects into view, exponentially invigorating and expanding the reservoirs from which language could be pulled—even though in the case of spam, its noise was forced upon us, threatening our hard drives, our wallets (neither Chinese nor Magical); no effete poststructuralist challenge to identity, the presence of such emails signaled a security breach and the chance of identity theft. When Ron Silliman, reviewing Rob Read's book of treated spam poems,[60] first picked up on the phenomena of spam finding its way into poetry, or at least into his inbox, he said of its development: "the whole idea of spam's sleazeball sludge of discourse, the lowest rung of marketing, invading poetry seemed more like an instance of the invasion of the bodysnatchers than anything else. But then I realized that I was liking these poems, against all my better judgment and deep instincts."[61]

It is revealing that Silliman should have reacted with such initial aversion to what was merely the monstrous digital extrapolation of unintentional surrealism. These treated spam poems initially arrived in his mailbox unsolicited and unrecognizable as poetry; and even if they were poetry, they would most likely be considered spam by a poetry blog impresario whose site has garnered millions of hits. While he understandably cited a certain amount of email fatigue bordering on rage—the limits of any deep virtuality strike home when they threaten to overwhelm our limited time and energy—it is strange that he should cite his "better judgment and deep instincts," as the source of his resistance to the work, since aren't those instincts and aesthetic judgments bound up with his own signature extension of the poetic into the prosaic, the sleazeball sludge perhaps carried in on the "garbage barge at the bridge" in *Ketjak* or even, dare we say it, on the garbage barge of the blog? (The sheer poundage of Silliman's blog output and voluminous daily link-outs defies readability, and has even eclipsed his substantial poetic achievements.) I usually equate Silliman with someone who has searched, in the footsteps of Williams, for the sources of American poetry in the "this, this, this, this" of the "muck, a detritus . . . a pustular scum, a decay, a choking lifelessness"[62] of the everyday.

But does the everyday of American literature necessarily belong to offshore spam bots, Nigerian scammers or digital grifters working out of mom's basement? New work that emerges from democratic noise must encounter the violence of this noise, countering its "choking lifelessness" without merely ignoring or avoiding it. Even if new experiments espouse pure textual assemblages challenging a clear image of action, their inaction must be one that opens up the useless to a virtuality, rather than inducing paralysis. Jacques Rancière, discussing the paradoxical ways by which the noise of the quotidian transforms literature, says that literature must not only wrest itself from its status as a tool for "men of action" but that the "lawless democracy of the errant letter"[63] while a wellspring of energy, is also a problem. New literature, in getting "lifeless debris to talk" both "opposes the princes of yore and the people of democracy with a different people."[64] This new literature, is, however, utopian and expresses the continuous contradictory need for literature to be outside of itself, to sing the song of the unliterary:

> The song of the future has to be made with the detritus of ordinary life and the fossils of collective history gathered randomly together in the junk shop. But there is no path leading from the inventory of mute signs written on things and the poeticity of outmoded refrains to the poetry of the future and the hymn of the collective body. . . . The new body that sings the hymn of the new word is destined to remain a utopia, at once necessary and unrealizable, by means of which the regime of literary writing projects itself beyond itself.[65]

It is then perhaps understandable that for Silliman, and others, the collectively organized Flarf was a more legible poetic movement, dealing with the same kind of data junk as Read's project, albeit with a more contradictory relation to its democratic materials. The following famous definition by Gary Sullivan was an ad-hoc manifesto of sorts for its "semi-public" community, having clear ties to the poetry world, yet teetering on the edge of what it meant to be poetic:

> Flarf: A quality of intentional or unintentional "flarfiness." A kind of corrosive, cute, or cloying, awfulness. Wrong. Un-P.C. Out of control. "Not okay."
> Flarf (2): The work of a community of poets dedicated to exploration of "flarfiness." Heavy usage of Google search results in the creation of poems, plays, etc., though not exclusively Google-based. Community in the sense that one example leads to another's reply—is, in some part, contingent upon community interaction of this sort. Poems created, revised, changed by others, incorporated, plagiarized, etc., in semi-public.
> Flarf (3) (verb): To bring out the inherent awfulness, etc., of some pre-existing text.
> Flarfy: To be wrong, awkward, stumbling, semi-coherent, fucked-up, un-P.C. To take unexpected turns; to be jarring. Doing what one is "not supposed to do."[66]

On the one hand, Flarf intended to sing out the most awful corners of the electronic literary wasteland, but it still, in the tradition of the avant-garde, embraced disjunctiveness (the expected turn of the unexpected turn), and *epate*'d *les bourgeois* in a way that the cute, cloying, fucked-up and un-P.C. things never do, unfortunately, on their own accord.

Flarf tended to be more off-putting than "spoetry" to the uninitiated, and both lived in the mighty shadow of the new patois engendered by the LOLcats. No matter how populist Flarfists professed themselves to be, spam poetry and other vernacular google-text art were spontaneous, folk emanations of the web,[67] whereas Flarf, emerging collectively from a listserv, still had the feeling that it defined such web experimentation from literary centers of power—albeit those disjunctive de-centers of an alternative establishment: is this the new people peopling? In this museum at the edge of the infinite, I am still unsure whether or how to include their work, not only because I would be hard pressed to pick out an exemplar—perhaps always a paradoxical operation for virtual literature—but also because experimentation these days tends to happen in crowds, the priority of singular originators hard to maintain: artists dealing with spam, googlettristic word piles, and other paraliterary sculpting of junk data have proliferated to such an extent, that the artistic genres, personalities and techniques of these virtual practices are spammily over-abundant. When consciousness of the abyss proliferates under the coterie, it seems warranted to throw down a few ropes, and so I will return to Flarf after some digression into areas less tenable as "poetry."

Take for instance the remix technique of hacking the subtitle track for a film, an appropriative strategy blurring literary and media genres, which has increased exponentially in recent years with the easy availability of text-for-video applications, ready-at-hand digitized versions of films, and increased bandwidth for storing and distributing the resultant video mashups. You have on the one hand the elegant, yet still "inappropriate" appropriations of Flarfist Brandon Downing, who takes Bollywood films and deep cuts from American B pictures, among other odd sources, and adds quasi-homophonic translations, new music and archival poetry recordings. His work extends a lineage going back to the marvelous disconnects of Frank O' Hara's subtitles in Alfred Leslie's *The Last Clean Shirt*, but one wonders why it is designated as Flarf rather than a part of the larger remix culture; why, after all, is it poetry? On the other hand, you have the quasi-anonymous, timely frenzies of creativity that attend phenomena like the *Downfall* subtitling meme that generated thousands of ventriloquized permutations of a scene from a forgettable German war epic starring Bruno Ganz as Hitler, enabling Hitler to rage about all manner of current concerns.[68]

I don't necessarily want to rehearse debates about high and low culture, nor the difference between pop and mass culture, because I'd rather rush on to *unculture*. But the reason why the work of Downing and the *Downfall* remixes are equally interesting to me as literary experiments—or rather experiments which fail the literary but produce another form of sensible meaning—is the way in which both demonstrate how tools for sculpting, transcoding, presenting or just reading the word have become wildly diverse, linking various registers and instigating new flows, combining recycled junk with new materials, breaking down generic boundaries and media-specificity. Virtual literature does not mean merely creating a digital illumination of a literary object, for example, when an outlet like PennSound or PoemTalk creates a sonified apparatus for the discussion of difficult, intransigent work, although their partaking in the "metaphysics of presence" has educational value. Rather, the virtual literary artist monitors, activates, and recomposes noise as it is mutated through other media, moving from one sensorium to another, until maybe it can no longer hold to its status as literature.

A presumably non-literary work like Corey Archangel's *Data Diaries*[69] may be a useful example to illuminate what is most interesting about Flarf and related projects. In *Data Diaries*, we see how indiscriminant data from his computer, which may include "words," but is most likely instead docs, jpgs, gifs, movs and the like, when pushed through a QuickTime player, give us a synaesthetic window onto his hard drive (when I see doc I think of it in mov). In many ways, experiments like this one are reminiscent of optical-sound experiments in transcoding, for example when filmmakers like Oskar Fischenger, Moholy-Nagy, and Norman McLaren drew directly onto the optical sound track of a film—usually meant for recording the electrical transduction of sound—to see what new sounds could be created from this non-sonic input. The experimental confounding of different technologies of writing here is key. A literary fascination with these experiments, which started when Rilke imagined what sound would emerge if he could take a phonograph needle to the coronal suture of the skull, might lead the way, as Friedrich Kittler has said, to the end of alphabetism. What these media allow is a technologically-facilitated exploration of the more fine grained textures of the "real," so that, in these "absolute transfers" from one medium to another, "A writer celebrates the very opposite of his own medium—the white noise no writing can store."[70]

Data meant for a specific type of reading and a specific technological mechanism or social sensorium (the marks of the optical soundtrack; the data of the hard drive; traditional verse; Google search results) is displaced and read on a register for which it was not intended. Admittedly, these experiments can be limited, a form of data nihilism or at best an allegory of reading: the optical exciter bulb, the QuickTime viewer, the human agent, all read in ways that are socially and technologically specific. Screw around with whom or what reads what, and the white noise at the periphery of any reading experience becomes fully amplified and central to this art of data manipulation. Yet, in their most impactful incarnations, these experiments may be no mere allegory or avant-lark, but rather herald new forms of performance, action and being, a renovated literary sensorium. In Rancière's terms, such experimentation creates a "new regime of appropriateness between the significance of words and the visibility of things"[71]; but, at the same time that it negotiates the inappropriate, violent, democratic virtual, it counters the just as violent privileged centers of reading and sense-making.

How, then, would we think about Flarf in this context? Let's start with Sharon Mesmer's "I Accidentally Ate Some Chicken and Now I'm in Love with Harry Whittington (Harry Whittington: the man accidentally shot by Dick Cheney)" not because, as with other virtualized materials in this book, it is forgotten, unreadable, or disdained. It may, within its body, contain such materials, but I'm choosing this poem precisely because of the way in which it found itself in a privileged center of reading, featured on an episode of the podcast PoemTalk, which I would invite you to listen to.[72] Using this more positivistic reading assemblage, linking my work to Mesmer's through the PennSound network, I can expedite the analysis, as if this book were a blog that I could just link out to the podcast, 'nuff said. Undoubtedly, this ability is part of the new appropriateness of the virtual—even if it is that "other" more privileged not-thereness of virtual telepresence—helping to make academic work more lively and nimble, since there are some "old sensoriums," which, virtualized in themselves can be rescued to counter a bad "new." But the choice of this poem with its digital trappings will also serve to dramatize the paradoxes of using such a positivistic data frame to understand work that attempts to turn that frame inside out. Incidentally, as I type this poem into the search engine, hoping for an easy cut-and-paste version rather than having to hand-type from my copy of Mesmer's collection *Annoying Diabetic Bitch,* it is not the PoemTalk episode that leads the search results, nor even a home page for Mesmer, but rather one of those presumably automatic, web trawling sites that does not differentiate different forms of mp3 content, and so you are given the option to make "I Accidentally Ate Some Chicken and Now I'm in Love with Harry Whittington" your ringtone.

Mesmer's poem starts with what is in actuality a very good ringtone:

> Have you ever been in a situation
> where somebody you thought was your friend
> did something that hurt you very much,

and then they tried to blame it on you,
and then you had a heart attack?
Just wondering.[73]

Undoubtedly an ironic reference to the shooting referenced in the title, it immediately brings up images of the Bush years, and their promotion of a grotesque "man of action" image, transforming all dissent into mere effete, literary speculation. Any recrimination that Whittington might have wanted to express is here transformed into the coy musings of a passive-depressive blogger. The attitude of this administration was emblematized by the now famous statement made by a Bush aide to writer Ron Suskind, an example of the toxic postmodernism of the right: "We're an empire now, and when we act, we create our own reality. And while you're studying that reality—judiciously, as you will—we'll act again, creating other new realities, which you can study too, and that's how things will sort out. We're history's actors . . . and you, all of you, will be left to just study what we do." The violent game of virtualizing humanity in order to instrumentalize the needs of an active class is a throwback to the times before *"liberté, égalité, fraternité,"* although it is stated here, with naked arrogance, as progress. Even one's friends, in the cozy brotherhood of an old boy hunting expedition, are not immune to this imposition of reality, the literalization, ironically, of a Maoist concept: "Political power grows out of the barrel of a gun." That the opening text of Mesmer's poem also conveys the possibility of sociopathic violence latent in any form of group solidarity immediately creates unease regarding the future of collectivity, a melancholy reflection on the inevitable dissolution of the presumably less violent community that has enabled to poem to come into being.

As Steve McLaughlin was quick to point out in the PoemTalk discussion, this opening is also almost wholly lifted from a fake

Harry Whittington blog site. The question "what does a Flarf poem mean?" comes to devolve upon the exegesis of the reverse Google, and any various techniques of "reading between the lines," or even, barring that, a invocation of the "materiality of the signifier" does not play as effectively here. We instead wonder where the poet got the material, what search queries she instigated, what artificial desire she elicited from this engine of communal meaning. Mesmer's searching is not as strictly procedural as, say, Katie Degentesh's in her collection *The Anger Scale*, where each poem's title is both her query text and a question from the Minnesota Multiphasic Personality Inventory (the publication of which, incidentally, bankrolls the publication of books by Deleuze and Guattari for the English speaking world). But we could say that the "signified" of such a poem, especially for one not as aleatory and procedural, is what happens when desire, meeting the computer, searches for its realization but instead generates excreta. The gap between what we "want" when we enter a search term—the origin of desire, now lost to the reader—and what we actually get—comically or sadly, the bathetic undertow of digital surf—is the metaphor, the "absolute transfer" that the poem undergoes.

We transcode our desire everytime we sit down in front of a computer and type a word into the search engine. At the end of the process, we typically think it's our desire, our energies, our impulses, our continuous activity that has been satisfied, but these things have been radically transformed in the process. While much was made in this episode of PoemTalk about the "poeticity" of Mesmer's poem (a point-of-view espoused by Nada Gordon and Al Filreis in differing degrees, citing Mesmer's use of linebreak, assonance, and enjambment), and while Kenneth Goldsmith countered that its poetic shape was the *uninteresting* aspect of the work, it seems that the lyric shape of this poem—a shape shared by most Flarfists—is more interesting and important as a "target" rather than a rationale for territorializing aesthetics, a type of "desiring machine," if you will. That is, like the QuickTime viewer for *Data Diaries,* the deceptive lyric shape of "I Accidentally Ate Some Chicken and Now I'm in Love with Harry Whittington" is transcoded with the unformed, the lowbrow, and the damned, a merging that does not grant priority to either content or frame, but dwells in their interval. That words remain words from one register to another, from datasphere to poem to listserv to book, is a deceptive technicality. This operation of transcoding may be germane to all poetry in its primal attempt to capture the unliterary and act on it until it resonates with one's needs and the needs of the community. But here need is *detourned,* automatized, played with from the outside. The *raison d'être* for all surrealist technique throughout the last hundred years is precisely this trashing of conscious authorial desire. The aleatory impulse—easy to couch in the terms of mystical consciousness or human potential patter—is at heart based on pure inventive curiosity: what would happen if we take x content and move it through y device?

With a flaneur's detachment, Mesmer's poem continues past images of foods—mostly chicken or chickenesque—their digestion and regurgitation, Baudelaire at the truck stop buffet:

> I barely touched the clam chowder
> but I ate the chicken fried steak.
> Then I ate hot beignet and sludgy chicory
> and I accidentally drove the hot 'n' sporty.
> Now I may try the chicken fries.
>
> Who poo'ed vindaloo?
>
> The founding fathers risked life and limb
> just so I could trust the kung pao ham.[75]

The poem stages a monstrous peristalsis, not unrelated to the opening vignette, where dim shadows of the founding fathers hunting for game are playing out the "eat or be eaten" scenario of masculine rivalry and social Darwinism at the top of the food chain. Mesmer, who Gordon informs listeners is a vegetarian and whose father was a butcher, indiscriminately Flarfs together foods from New England, Louisiana, Sichuan Province, and Harry Potter that she would probably never eat herself, but finds herself "consuming" on her way to knowledge through the poem, on her way to "loving" Harry Whittington. As Oswald de Andrade calls for in his 1928 "Manifesto of Anthropophagy" (crucial to the later appropriation techniques of 60s Brazilian Tropicalismo) Mesmer attempts "Absorption of the sacred enemy," which may entail an Ouroboros eating of one's tail, consuming consumption, with Flarf mirrored in the infinite regress of the American scene cannibalizing itself. The most telling food-scenario-fragment, "Who poo'ed vindaloo?" returns us to the more primal transcoding that happens at the toilet. The "o" sounds in the line continue all the way to the line's end, in the same way that vindaloo chicken makes it all the way through the system, recognizable in the output regardless of its new form.

Does one's energy and intuition survive this process? Is one, after all, the eater or the eaten? It may seem like an unfashionable assertion, but if the images we use aren't ours, the energy must be, attesting to the quality of action on virtual materials. What are we doing when we more or less freak with other people's memory fragments, or memorialize the blank unmemory of their daily chatter for our own advancement? Are we continuing the violence, transforming it into utopian energies, or do these alternatives miss the point of the letter's originary violence that must be admitted before one can produce any qualitative change?

Following Jacques Attali, we can say that such literary noise is violence itself, a "simulacrum of murder,"[76] but it also has the potential to liberate meaning:

> The absence of meaning is in this case the presence of all meanings, absolute ambiguity, a construction outside meaning. The presence of noise makes sense, makes meaning. It makes possible the creation of a new order on another level of organization, of a new code in another network.[77]

However, Attali surprisingly speaks out against avant-gardists like Stockhausen and Cage, calling them out as minstrels of a bureaucratic elite, heralding a totalizing, technocratic political economy of managed repetition. He instead sides with Composition rather than Repetition, with communal improvisational projects rather than the killing same of what René Girard called mimetic violence. He cites Chicago Free Jazz as an example of this compositional utopia:

> This new mode of production thus entertains a very different relation with violence: in composition, noise is still a metaphor for murder. To compose is simultaneously to commit a murder and to perform a sacrifice. It is to become both sacrificer and the victim, to make an ever-possible suicide the only possible form of death and the production of life. To compose is to stay repetition and the death inherent in it, in other words, to locate liberation not in a faraway future, either sacred or material, but in the present, in production and in one's own enjoyment.[78]

What then to make of ostensibly "poetic" projects that do not compose as such, throwing off the shapely in pursuit of the unshapely—the poetry of the word brickpile, the word tarpit, the word mountain . . . untended let alone fully read by its own author? A project like Alejandro Crawford's *BHO* which includes in its pdf the contents of over two thousand unedited comments from a YouTube video of Barack Obama posted during the 2008 election cycle, transforms the travesty of comments box democracy into a vitriol-spewing machinic monologue without quotes, without coherent ideology but plied through and through with the crazy energies of conspiracy mongering, end-is-near prophesizing, and hyperviolent racist rhetoric.[79] If Adorno's notion that lyric poetry is impossible after Auschwitz made the lyric a brand of hate crime, *BHO* explores the lyric materiality of hate itself. Unlike Flarfist work, *BHO* does not guard itself with ironic scare quotes, and Crawford has found himself in uncomfortable live reading situations in which he decided to read *BHO* and similar work without explanation or disclaimer, a potential career-killer. To a certain extent, such work is a reproach to literary inactivity, even though its relative lack of "shape" signals another kind of inactivity, what Kenneth Goldsmith, fully embracing the managerial paradigm of monitoring noise, calls "uncreative writing." The choice of materials for *BHO* has the potential to roil emotions in any too complacent scene; the performance of such work should remind audiences that public discourse belongs to an active class of people who, for all intents and purposes, make their careers out of throwing word-shit from teleprompters out at millions, while anyone with a considered, researched, nuanced point goes unheard. Why should a poet not want to engage the energies of the Zeitgeist? Why silence? *BHO* for better or worse exposes the unsettling creativity of knee-jerk response, anonymous internet bloviating, desperation, fear and paranoia that comprise the mark of the times, the affective miasmas of sensibility that accompany the more polite violence of professional punditry.

What makes this project less an instance of technocratic repetition, a mere monitoring and easy ethnography of the cut-and-paste, is not only because of the riskiness of the material, but also because Crawford is interested in recomposing the channels of communications themselves, blocking an unthinking virtual by interposing as yet unthinkable ones, instigating new reading assemblages around an apparently uncomposed or lightly composed text. Instead of channeling noise through ameliorative known forms, the forms and channels themselves mutate and disperse, since he uses the techniques and technology of music, video, translation, programming and performance interchangeably. In many ways, these kind of texts invite the readers themselves to be producers instead of consumers, extending the line of creativity by delving into almost raw materials, inspiring forms of extreme reading to live up to the extreme writing in a time of extreme politics. In fact, the only way I was able to read *BHO* was by creating my own reading assemblage. I let my computer's voice recognition software read the pdf, put the computer next to an old baby monitor, and did my daily chores while the computer imperfectly recited the text, creating an ambient backdrop that I could tune into and out of at will. It may have been a perverse sort of Musak, but it was *my* Musak—inspiring unthinking activity while engendering the unease appropriate to reflection on the unthinkable—a small consolation, violent in itself, amidst more generalized impositions of power.

In this way, literature starts to develop for itself a milieu, an ecosystem, a situation in a way much different than one gets with, say, Williams' *Paterson*. Just as Deleuze details the evolution of filmic action from the duel or dualistic structure of conflict into cinemas of situations—where the characters draw energies from ambiences, where the ambiences themselves become characters—so too does virtual literature evolve from the agonistic, tragic attempt to capture a "real" environment to the creation of new ecosystems and the deconstructing of given networks. Consequently, the confounding of Bergsonian notions of action and inaction results when an action in one environment signals inaction in another, or vice versa. Even Deleuze's own notions do not keep up with the new economies of inaction, although because these situations partake of "the powers of the false," they are open to endless, unpredictable production and appropriation. For Deleuze, the milieu is a "false community," from which one may cynically conclude that "all milieux are pathological." Or, as he sees happening in American cinema, one can "save . . . [the] dream [of community] by passing through nightmares"[80]—the utopian gambit of much of this work.

As with Crawford's work, the videos of Ryan Trecartin, alternately conceived as poetic events because of their jagged cut-ups of corporate language memes and crack house tantrums enabled by other text-junk of the digital age, would at first come off as a mere regurgitation of a violent milieu, the unchanneled plastic savagery of commoditized boredom.[81] In each of his interconnected works, the trashy virtuality of managerial hysteria and internalized globalization converge on make-shift prefab environments—designed by collaborator Lizzie Fitch—half-filled with worthless new crap, every mise-en-scene evoking the existential fly-by-nightism of a rootless corporate class. Instead of the tasteful, shallow-focus idylls that have seemed to invade the current videosphere, these baroques have no clear center of attention: it's not Wellesian deep focus but more like full frame ADHD with cheesy video graphics and text counterpoint, helium induced and auto-tuned morphed voice, flash editing, anarchic butoh-esque performances, and lots of breaking, burning, amputating—an adventure in dismembering. Permeating situation engenders explosive action in Trecartin's videos, as his characters are not merely "animated in vain" as were Deleuze's neorealist heroes in relation to their decimated landscape, but rather, drag virtual meaning kicking and screaming out of the trap of managerialized bureaucratese. Whether it is the "tactile values"[82] latent in stupid objects or the "data jazz" possibilities for the language of corporate buzz-words and art world jargon (his characters could very well be contemporary curators from hell), Trecartin recomposes a new world out of impossible, broken, or whitewashed identities and collectivities. His videos rip into the sanctimonies of both identity and collectivity to get at some kind of collectivity in identity, thus by-passing the false choice between racist whitewash and multicultural celebration, both of which serve the interests of a ruling class and effectively close down experiences less commensurable to free market ideology—the true virtual of virtual capital. In the words of one of his avatars of global corporate collaboration, Mexico Korea: "IF your Identity forms a UNION! I'll Bill you Later=*"[83]

But what these videos are implicitly about is time—time wasted, time bought, time stockpiled, with money as the implicit double of this virtual image of duration. Even ideology is described as a "time-share," which one can rent out at will. Various encoded clichés, short-hand devices saving one from conflict or debate, or imbecilic acronyms, naturalizing the pure products of America's crazy, accumulate, creating yet another trashheap of unexamined ditto-speak, immobilizing, when blind speed was the intention. Trecartin shortcircuits the shorthand, discourse memes are hijacked, driven with the speed they deserve, and crashed in a cess pool by the luxury condo at edge of town. In the ideolectical symbology created for his scripts, he provides a key for reducing the image of global violence into a single, easily mobilized symbol:

(UGTFE)= Unidentified Timeless Gun Fire and/or Explosions
(x)= (UGTFE)[84]

And so every (x) in this script, translated into a crash, shot, or other on-screen punctuation of force, memorializes the absolute ineradicability of ambient violence, while reducing it to a plaything.

Continuity of Dumps

A celebrity leaves the restaurant. As it is a warm night in Southern California, she imagines "materiality is oblivion," and continues to her car. But this anonymous stroll is interrupted by a swarm of paparazzi—expected or unexpected, they nevertheless inject uncertainty into her movements, forcing her out of the oblivion of an immemorial, perfunctory act elevating it into the paradoxically glittering tableaux of a more worthy now. If her walk was rote, it has now been transformed by the virtual action of the cameras, not virtual because they are excluded, nor because they create telepresence, but because they know how to measure out exactly what amount of this celebrity's unedited movements are worth recording. But her walk has lost its innocence long ago, for she knows that these moments of oblivious existence must be constantly open to exposure if she is to remain in the memory of the public; her action is uniquely underwritten by its virtuality, and the virtual experience of her own lonely walk is the only luxury she cannot afford. As she closes the door of her SUV, "the human mind ceaselessly presses with the totality of its memory against the door which the body may half open to it."[85] After leaving her self half-open to the cameras long enough for her existence beyond herself to be reanimated, she speeds off, as if to free herself from virtual swarms that she cannot escape, leaving fragments of herself in her wake, ones that will be activated and animated by a curious public and then left to slip into virtuality again.

We now live in the kingdom of the fragment. The celebrity or politician is no longer subject to these incursions only at gala events or historical appearances. Rather her very existence is underwritten by energized mountains of ubiquitous disconnected image-movement-text, so plentiful that in another economy they would have been considered worthless. They perhaps still are. Yet, within a few years, owing to the new organizational dispensations of the web, the noosphere of junk data has been classified, mapped, tagged, mined, and channeled to such an extent that it is no longer strange that a site like TMZ has made millions of dollars by aggregating poor quality video consisting, at one point almost exclusively, of celebrities getting into and out of cars. Or that fans hang on every bit of text-crap sent straight from a celebrity Blackberry to Twitter. What images and texts are worth acting on, how they are acted on, and how they are stockpiled, has radically changed, and the whole web has become Deleuze's "minor literature"—foregrounding connections and becomings and flows rather than large-form representations and delimitable commodities—albeit in a major key. The immensity of useless data now has the charm of bat guano—repellant to traditional aesthetic sensibilities, yet highly profitable for those masters of boredom we call "entrepeneurs."

Even in the avant-garde, we can see this change of tone towards data-detritus by comparing similarly titled media works, marking, respectively, different new media "ages" and consequently different evolved attitudes towards the virtual: Mark Napier's *Digital Landfill* (launched 1998), Golan Levin's (et al.) *The Dumpster* (launched 2006), and Ryder Ripps' *Dump.fm* (launched 2010). The first (from a kinder, gentler digital age) invites users to "Dispose of your unwanted e-mail, obsolete data, HTML, SPAM or any other digital debris just buy clicking the *Add to Landfill* button."[86] *The Digital Landfill* contained within it some latent potentials for collaborative, responsive text-image collaging in the morass of digital trash, although it was perhaps ahead of its time. I remember being able to put jpgs and gifs into the landfill, composing primitive layered collages but it took a little hand coding; after a while—perhaps due to storage restrictions (a limitation the artist perhaps did not have the means or desire to lift)—image composting was not possible at all. The *Digital Landfill* soon became a locus for indiscriminant spam text in raster green, layered so thick that single letters are barely legible. Recently opening what seems one of the last Landfill dumps before it was closed down, I found three pages of invitations to porn sites reduced to twelve lines of text, which you can only "read" by copying and then pasting into another document. What one reveals in this simple transcoding, perhaps expectedly, is a catalogue of sexual configurations, a monotone of taboo, unfolding out of illegible overwritten entries.

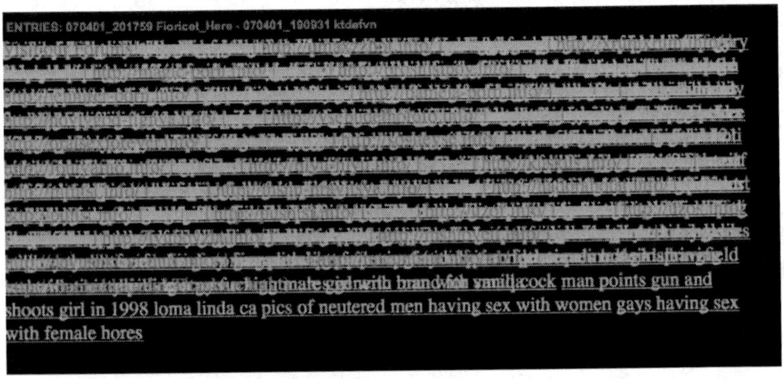

sexy nude women wrestling men nude male patient examined by female doctor pictures white women having sex with asian men men with big dicks having sex with woman two women and guy porn sexy nude girls with men women jacking off mens cocks black man cum in girl do women like men to shave pubic hair weather girls its raining men mp3 sexy images of a man sucking his cum out of a womans mouth white girls who suck black mens cocks oral men having sex with woman steps she makes circumcised guys crawl on their knees around her married white women having sex with black men woman spank men erotic sexy nude women trampling men men and women nude photos sh neber had a big enough cock until she fucked man 15in women drinking man cum erotic photography of men and women hot men having sex with women man fucking woman with big cocks erotic men porn for women hot girls having sex with men shemale orgy

> fucking male girl with man with small cock man points gun and shoots girl in 1998 loma linda ca pics of neutered men having sex with women gays having sex with female hores[87]

When one places this translation next to the original overwritten and unreadable raster green text-pile up, typical notions of readability become confounded. Is the unfolded translation simply more legible than the composted version? The border between legible and illegible becomes blurred. We can no longer say that the revealed textual substrate is the accurate, or at least more desirable rendering of the noise-modulated one, no longer the key to its hidden secret. What is illegible as "writing" becomes legible as "image" when it is presented as an "unreadable" text mulch. In fact, the "illegible" data scribble might be the better read. The lineated version, even in its asyntactic profligacy, only promises mostly heterosexual couplings (there is a lonely "shemale" and some "gays") culminating in the parataxis or orgasm of a violent shooting. The original text-image of the Landfill, however, heralds practices as yet uncoded in its uncomposed "compostition"; the superficial violence of its noise emblematizes a potentially non-violent future sensibility.[88]

Just as Deleuze coined the term *movement-image* to mark the ways in which cinema broke down the boundaries between the world of matter and mind, materialism and idealism, actual and virtual,[89] so too will we have to think about the ways in which for the global multimedia web, the notion of *text-image*, does not imply mere aestheticization of text, but points up an indiscernability, in a universe where text and image constantly enfold each other in expanded circuits, underwritten by the crystalline structures and imploded infoscapes of the *time-image*. We are no longer seeing something meant as the virtual stand-in for point of view, a "window onto the world" with tableaux measured out by dead analogies, but rather we are witnessing the screen as "a table of information, an opaque surface on which are inscribed 'data', information replacing nature, and the brain-city, the third eye, replacing the eyes of nature."[90] The static composition of *The Digital Landfill* is only static if seen with these first eyes, not the third, forcing us to think through the unthought that offends or bores our limited senses.[91] The only dead end of this early experiment is that its allegory of noise overshadowed its potential as space for recomposition; its layers of data fell into a nihilistic, ultimately ironic, conceptual mulch. Yet digital nihilism is a welcome attitude countering the tiresome claims of digital positivity—which is not even the positivity of the Enlightenment nor of knowledge in general, but rather the positivity of the free market, which virtualizes Enlightenment values in the promotion of a sham image of democracy.

Levin's 2006 project, *The Dumpster*, an organization of presumably worthless digital text-fragments, has, in contrast, an exceedingly positivist vibe, giving the feeling that there is great money to be made in the vast informatic chatter of teenage breakup that litters the web.[92] In collaboration with data-mining and visualization professionals, the project collects and maps 20,000 accounts of breakups culled from blogs in 2005. Through a single, highly designed window, we are given various vectors of information, animated by user gestural input (i.e. mouse or track pad position)—an experience that partly elicits the bomber reticles of digital warfare, partly the frivolous Flash toys of design culture. Random excerpts from blogs, all reduced to an anonymous sameness, appear in "Breakup Balloons" as one clicks through "Breakup Bubbles," "PixelView region," and a "Timeline." The applet partakes of the design conceit that intuitive, visual access to data can exist free of textual accoutrements, since one can navigate these bubbles through visual similarities rather than making one's own text queries. As design ideology tends to do, all that is consequently achieved is a celebration of eye candy, with even the text attractively popping—albeit filled with the expected morass of misspellings, abbreviations, and other colorful internet dialects that would seem to challenge its otherwise slick presentation.

But while we are given spritely and suggestive bubbles of web-text communication, there are no means for users to mobilize text as a tool for their own investigations and discovery within this dataset. The clicking loses its charm quickly. By enabling aestheticized text output but no text input, neither thought nor unthought is available, but rather pure technocratic spectacle. The user has little inspiration to navigate this corpus with his or her own parameters, nor is there a sense of the overwhelming inhuman dimensions of thwarted romance times 20,000. One spends more time with the impressive accompanying essays, which situate textual meaning in a traditional way; and because the claims of these essays exceed the manifest actuality of the project, they come off as put-ons at best, or worse, shills for interactive snake-oil.

Most hyperbolically, the accompanying essay by Lev Manovich claims that this new form of representation exceeds the emotional portraits that literature can provide in its subjective mode—he cites *Anna Karenina*—and even trumps the objectivity of sociology. Yes, this is where Deleuze, following Bergson, situates the immateriality-materiality of the virtual, where subjective and objective are exceeded, giving way to proliferating technicized micro-affections and assemblages more easily diagrammed than delimited. But isn't this experiment merely an extension of what literature, or at least virtual literature defines itself *against*, and what any good sociology—which from the Frankfurt school on has held a suspicion of pure positivism—has held up for interrogation? If anything, *The Dumpster* is an allegory of how to create new economy value out of abandoned text artifacts, but it leaves no room for surprise, merely offering a technomatic frame for a narrative known all too well. More sociological and literary insights have come from simple but powerful conceptual writing experiments—even and especially those that use the less flashy tools of book and pdf, underwritten by unspecialized applications like basic web searches and control effing one's way through a text—as well as digital experiments that undo their own usefulness, yet generate unexpected meanings, espousing a form of ill-will towards the image of interactivity.[93]

One can, for example, compare Ryder Ripps' "Facebook Suicide Watch," which, if the title doesn't already do so, knocks Facebook's implicit taboo against expressing the negative by outfitting his real-time data-skimming site with a repeating wallpaper design composed of Facebook's infamous "like" thumbs.[94] Dead-eyed smiley faces hang from a line of gif gallows and a midi version of Alanis Morissette's "The Uninvited" plays in a loop while Facebook posts with the words "kill myself" appear one by one. While there is the unavoidable potential for the term "kill myself" to be used in earnest, the possibility of such logocentric snuff is outpaced by instances of "kill myself" that are less dire, but are instead ironic or joking. Of course, even the more serious updates are all merely half-truths, since "killing oneself" is a future condition—which is why in meat-space it is always taken to heart as a serious oath, a virtual statement threatening an actual realization. Yet in this more abstracted space, one's own death, articulated in the present tense, can only remain a virtual performance, even if it is near enough to be technically actual: "I am dead, Horatio." And what of the author, safely snickering at his net art spoof, but already "killing himself" by effectively automatizing his function? Nevertheless, the context frame for the status update of "killing oneself" constantly morphs, and like most good conceptual projects, it is critical or curious regarding the virtual shape-shifting of this language artifact. What at first seems like a possibly tactless invasion of privacy, instead reveals the quotidian, unavoidable, even celebratory dimension of the self-death. The possibility of self-immolation implies existential self-ownership and power, rather than victimhood, and a fit of ironic bonzo can counter one of the many minor awfulnesses before which one feels helpless, while tempering the taboos against suicide's unspeakability: "If I hear Lev Manovich or Kate Hayles cited again in a discussion of digital art, I'm going to kill myself :P"

Ryder Ripps' interest in social-networking-ethnography-as-conceptual-comedy (see also his project "The Sound of Facebook") dovetailed into the creation of his own social networking environment *Dump.fm,* which started as a New York-based project for gif artists, but which has expanded to such an extent that he has, ironically or not, considered an IPO.[95] *Dump.fm,* a continuous stream of user-created or repurposed web junk, is based on the premise of "talking with images:" one can, for example, take the url of one participant's post, and immediately splice it with another url, with an eye to immediate commerce with images, the surprise combination, or the visual pun, rather than image-authorship strictly conceived. It is isomorphic with Flarf, in that the hastily recontextualized and modified gifs and jpgs, exchanged in a real-time semi-anonymous community, tend towards the cute, the cloying, the un-P.C, the "not O.K."[96] Yet because it is a free-floating environment, rather than a stand-alone net art "object," it has developed in ways that complexify any notion of coherent approaches and specific ontological properties, accommodating methods and uses that do not fit under the rubric of a manifesto.

One can, however, map out a few dominant "artistic" approaches to the site. The distinct properties of found gifs—they loop, they are short, they are lo-memory, they are lo-res, they have no sound, they are embedded in web page or browsers—generate a variety of overlapping modes that are familiar to media and art historians. There is a predominant amount of gestural analysis enabled by the frenetic repetition of the form—an effect popularized by Dara Birnbaum's feminist scratch video, albeit here in less P.C. modes. The fallout of the democratic proliferation of these techniques is that these repetitions, while still showing up both the automatisms of cultural performance and its unconscious, are no longer an experiment in political consciousness-raising or media literacy. (Compare Birnbaum's *Technology Transformation*, for example, to remixing gifs of out of control African-American women in the audience of one of Oprah's potlatch giveaways.) There is a large contingency of gifs and jpgs that explore glitch, data error, and other self-conscious media interventions. Many times, these are the types of gifs that are considered "works of art," such as Petra Cortright's "Hands1"[97] (who is not a Dump participant) or the work of mirrrroring (who is). There are instances of conceptual archive animations and art history remediations (there's a great reconstitution of Ernie Gehr's *Serene Velocity* by FAUXreal,[98] utilizing only available digital thumbnail stills from the experimental film's web mentions), digital baroque remix-scapes (harem-discos with all your favorite gifs in one frame), and meme-riffing (the most well-known of which from *Dump.fm* is the "Deal with It" meme, for which they provide a "Deal with It Maker.") These modes, of course, mix and interpenetrate (blingscience's Blingee repurposings somehow find the secret tunnel between kitsch and absolute art; they are sparkly yet austere in their sparkle-constraint). In addition, because one can easily add and recombine various forms of glitter text, image-text, and plain chat, there is, in the word-images of starsalmon, the possibility of "epic trash new media text poetry but then fug da police," reconstituted like a ransom letter from a glam punk alien.[99]

Dump users have not, as of yet, held out open arms to the more pretentious trend of cinemagraph gifs, which basically seem like a fine arts reaction to the cheap anti-aesthetic of net art. While their emergence points to a rising consciousness of the importance of small-form, non-narrative cinematic effects to the liveliness of the Internet, the cinemagraph currently consists almost exclusively of tasteful tableaux, shot with expensive SLR cameras, dotted with fashion models, high living in tony environs, and other signifiers of conspicuous consumption. Revolution of revolutions, these meticulously composed stills suddenly exhibit motion! The images of pretty girls with uncannily moving hair were tiring from the get-go. That *Dump* users will not suffer such ponciness is testament to some overriding consciousness, a tacit agreement to valorize of the unvaluable. Or it could be solely an issue of bandwidth restriction—memory limitations creating aesthetic boundaries when the medium does not. Or, perhaps, Dump users would welcome cinemagraphs to their digital village if the cinemagraph did not come out shooting with glocks and Gucci, proclaiming its superiority over the animated gif, thus forging a dubious distinction between gifs and cinemagraphs that will no doubt be boringly policed in the future, if they last that long.

Nevertheless, in their embrace of real-time, spontaneous discourse with digital junk, *Dump.fm* users espouse an ambiguous relation to the enforced scarcities of the art world. On the one hand, because *Dump.fm* values spontaneous participation but also because, for better or for worse, it much of the time gets taken over as a teenage chat rumpus room, there is little patience with work that attempts to be too crafty, or that doesn't deal with bottom-barrel internet grotesques for freak-show gawking, or that seems to come from anyone over twenty with any art world cred. One racks up more "likes" in the dump rating system if the dump is a quick turn-over of another dump, rather than something painstakingly composed in Photoshop or AfterEffects: more cred for projectile than for project. There's a whole "genre" of dump participant who rarely, if ever, composes or recomposes images, but instead merely posts asignifying snaps from his or her webcam,[100] exerting casual presence as a dump star, as if trying to win the slow bicycle race of artistic inactivity and unambition.

Because however casual and artless these dumps seem, many of these young participants are aware of the "insane game" of art, and ride that ever so elusive line between anonymity and non-art art, real failure and Warholian passive celebrity. The site is, albeit ambiguously, overtly attached to the art world, and there is a marked sense that many of the participants keep an eye out for potential curator-lurkers or perform for the benefit of participating *éminence grises* like Tom Moody or Ripps himself (who is all of twenty-five years old). Not for nothing has Marina Abramovich's face from her live installation "The Artist is Present" been a predominant dump meme. Perhaps, she is popular for the same reason Yves Klein became a subject for the shockumentary *Mondo Cane*: a sort of provincial "wtf" fascination with art world decadence. Or, it is a clear homage to a mother figure who simply made art out of her own presence. Dumper glasspopcorn, at fifteen years old, has gone from posting web cam picks and complaining about unrequited love and school problems to singing "avant-garde hiphop" at PS1 MoMA, an event covered by CBS. Yet, the most energy he seems to have put into a dump is taking off his shirt while demurely hiding behind a handful of graphing calculators.[101]

However, the sheer volume of his posts, and time spent on the site should have some value, and in fact, that may be where the value lies, even though the lingering ageism of the site would seem to contradict this notion that duration means something. Yet if the banal continuity of webcam Marina-wanna-bes is any key, there is the sense that hidden behind the frenetic twenty-four hour activity of this site, where you can actually feel like you've seen every image there is to see on the web, is the static image of one's unique presence in the process of transvaluation, becoming the coin of the realm. The self forms a core of authenticity within the remixing machine at the same time that it is without value, dump degree zero. By reaching out to glasspopcorn, Ripps has anointed him as the ideal user, and why not? He is outside of the system, not perverted by adulthood; he has to cope with the intolerable situation of growing up digital, but at the same time represents untapped amorphous potential for digital capital, broadly conceived. He belongs to a generation who, because of the faults of their elders, are always-already failed projects, and so the only alternative is to dump oneself. As glasspopcorn wrote in an October 25, 2010 post, using a form traditionally recognized as "poetry" (but which turns out to be a poem from another dump user, unattributed *naturally*):

> **i have maintained a general level of**
> **chill since 1987**
> it was not easy
> along the way some
> pretty fucked up shit has
> happened. But you know
> what motherfucker?
> you gotta just pull through
> that shit, put on your
> wrap-around oakleys and make it
> rain dollars and family values.[102]

The Weathermen

This section is probably a failed one from the start. I wanted to talk about those unliterary figures who have attempted what the alchemists called "celestial agriculture," a tillage of the elusive, contemplative, distant, massive, unsythesizable expanse of the half-dome of sky we live under. This environment, full of intensities, nuances, and unperceivable continuities, holds within itself a posthuman mystery. How can one express this environment, "the shimmering existentiality in relationship between man and the atmosphere"[103]? To approximate its nuances with words is a task worth failing. However, it is not this failure that hangs over this section.

I feel as if I am failing a number of outsiders who have a special relation to the weather. For example, I have especially failed Henry Darger, not only by neglecting to read in its entirety his fifteen-volume, 15,145-page collage novel starring little penis'd girls fighting off civil war zombies under dramatic weather formations with names like "Sweetie Pie" and "Spirian Tearian typhoon." One would think that such a monstrous work, which Lytle Shaw, who seems to have read it in its entirety, describes as "designed to overwhelm our senses" full of "narrative incidents . . . situated within complex atmospheres"[104] would be central to any discussion of virtual literature. As well, Darger also deserves a special place in any catalogue of literary nobodies, given his "defiant productivity" as an absolute unknown. This janitor-hermit may now be world famous, but his massive daily accretion of visionary work was only found after his lonely, impoverished death.

In addition to *In the Realms of the Unreal* and other improbably large works, Darger compiled 10 years of data on the weather itself. *The Book of Weather Reports* comes off as a sort of novel, or psalter, or mere evidence of one's *being there*, attentive that special encodable nothing that attracts meteorologists. But he is not a "weatherman" for all that. As Shaw points out, he posits his proto-conceptual activity of weather transcription *against* that of the professional's: "Darger's notebooks can, in fact, frequently be read as an excruciatingly detailed moral account of how well the weatherman was doing his job."[105] The weatherman is a failure precisely to the extent that he has accepted the limitations of a job and not a saintly calling. Yet Darger's temporally thankless devotions can also only fail the infinity of sky. Without benefit of holy revenant, it is precisely when the recording impulse, pushed to its far extremes, breaks down that one perhaps has the chance of intimate gnosis.

I could also have given more central space for the *Weather Diaries*, a series of "storm-squatting" videos from lo-budget shlockmeister George Kuchar. Kuchar, early on in his life, "learned how to read the clouds, and it made going out everyday a kind of heavenly horoscope"[106] and had a job drawing weather maps for an NBC affiliate. As one of what Joan Crawford, addressing the proletariat violinist played by John Garfield in the very Kuchar-esque howler *Humoresque*, condescendingly called those "rare animals, a New Yorker from New York," Kuchar was pointedly an outsider, both to the mainstream and, surprisingly, the avant-garde—his *Weather Diaries* were notoriously excoriated at the Flaherty Seminar in 1996 and he remained a curiosity for the more purist experimental scenes, especially while video still had an ambivalent status as art.[107]

For Kuchar "everyday life has become more horrifying than heads being blown off,"[108] and he would unflinchingly record that everyday, "to digest the alien ambiance,"[109] monitoring its nuance and abomination, with the doggedness of a war reporter. Each spring he would take off into middle America to chase after tornados, holing himself up in cheap motel rooms, while he ate whatever crap was at the local Safeway, defecated, beat-off, and hung out, recording and editing in-camera a loose sequence of impressions. Like Darger, he is somewhat competitive with the official weatherman, whose presence on television is often his only connection to the world outside. In *Weather Diary 1* (1986), it is the mavericky Gary England, who with his missionary demeanor and fancy computers promises salvation with up-to-the-minute storm warnings. In counterpoint, Kuchar gives his more "dry" commentary on what he can see out the window, without the advantage of high technology or Christian good looks: "What's it like out there? Not too much of a hell."[110]

No, I must ignore Darger and Kuchar in order to take on bigger game: the psychic space of New York City itself. Paradoxically for a city with no evident need of such, it has helped turn the world's attention to non-figurative atmospheres and other unprofitable immaterialities. Its literary and art worlds are premiere generators of virtual work, but it has also served as a brick-and-mortar filter that has compromised what could be an atmospherically, even cosmically expansive virtual canon. If for Williams, "the local in a full sense is the freeing agency of all thought, in that it is everywhere accessible to all," and if, with the Internet, every "local" is now suffused with the knowledge and activity that was once only constrained to the metropoles, why is it that New York City remains one of the best places to get recognition for one's unliterary ambience mapping, situationist periplum plumbing, and virtual world any-place-whatevering? Is this where the "inaction" is? Even Robert Smithson, who celebrated his hometown Passaic as the new eternal city and explored the distinctly anonymous pleasures of the non-site in the most far flung nowheresvilles, always needed to set out from Port Authority. Is failure determined by one's failure to connect with the machinations of such an urban authority (as with Nardi) or is one more failed when one does not create new literary capital in alternative centers, hopefully where the rent is cheaper (as did Williams)? Why assert a center of cultural or uncultural capital when, owing to the virtual powers of the Internet, the center does not hold?

So it is that, when reading Kenneth Goldsmith's *The Weather*, a pure transcription of a year's worth of weather reports for New York City and environs, I am torn. As one of the more "readable" examples of his uncreative writing works, *The Weather* shows how unadorned, untransformed data can be more varied and compelling than if it were used merely as the objective-correlative backdrop for more character-based literary antics. There's also a large amount of nostalgia for me, who is from that area of the world, to read how the weather moves through it, especially given that the weather moves democratically, without regard for more social boundaries. Newark, The Delaware River, and Central Park are all part of the same system, with the panorama of America unfurling as various patterns cross the radar. It's only when Iraq is included in reports of "Battlefield Weather" that we know something is amiss with the way "everything is connected":

> Oh, we are looking at, uh, weather, uh, across, uh, Iraq obviously here for the next several days, uh, we have, uh, actually some good, good weather is expected. They did have a sandstorm here earlier, uh, over the last twelve to twenty-four hours those winds have subsided and will actually continue to subside. Uh, there will be enough of a wind across the southern portion of the country that still may cause some blowing sand tomorrow. Otherwise we're looking at clear to partly cloudy skies tonight and tomorrow, uh, the weekend, uh, it is good weather, and then we could have a storm, uh, generating some strong winds, uh, for Sunday night and Monday, uh, even the possibility of a little rain in Baghdad. Uh, currently we have, uh, uh, increasing cloudiness, uh, forecast locally tonight, uh, it's gonna be brisk and chilly, temperatures getting down into the middle-thirties, and then some, uh, intermittent rain is expected tomorrow and tomorrow night. It'll become steadier and heavier late in the

> day and, uh, actually a pretty good soaking tomorrow night. Uh, temperatures getting into the mid-forties tomorrow, and then staying in the forties tomorrow night. Friday it's a breezy and warmer day but, uh, still a few more showers maybe even a thunderstorm, the high of sixty degrees. Currently we have sunshine and forty-four with an east wind of ten. Repeating the current temperature forty-four, going up to forty-six in midtown.[111]

What are we to make of a report that elides desert sandstorms and Manhattan showers, so that we are never quite sure where we are? Do I bring my umbrella or goggles? That even the most straightforward language performance can be so defamiliarized when reframed is part of the intellectual charge of this work. More personally, though, after I have spent years teaching "conceptualism in the wild" (that egregious term!)[112] in places like Columbia, South Carolina and Seattle, Washington, where the weather does not have the same dynamism and variety, merely experiencing the banal recitation of those seasonal changes to which my senses have been hardwired is interesting enough. It's the continuity of all continuities, and thus, if the vocal proponents of continuity-based literary practices are correct, it should be the best story. Yet, I wonder.

Am I like the guy in *Being John Malkovich* who tours John Malkovich's head, joyous in virtually inhabiting Malkovich ordering bathmats from a catalogue, only to be sanctimoniously spit out of the sky by the side of the New Jersey Turnpike? Why does this experience of the everyday have to circuit through Malkovich, ensconced in his New York townhouse, for it to be legible, for it to be enjoyed? Similarly, we would have to ask, is Kenneth Goldsmith's exploration of local micro-environments a type of virtual literature, or a more common virtual channeling of an experience that, while we could have it ourselves, gains literary value through more predictable channels that are unavailable to us? The promotional presence behind such a project, taking advantage of such channels with an unerring on-message schtick, tends to overshadow the virtual work under his vast tutelage. As Robert Archambeau reasonably asserts in his blog-post-essay "Kenneth Goldsmith, or The Art of Being Talked About":

> What I haven't seen in Goldsmith is any indication that he's at all interested in using the career-as-artistic-medium with any kind of critical edge regarding things like status, fame, or cultural capital. Even when he says that some people might consider career-obsession "a silly game," he doesn't suggest that this might be the case because the pursuit of reputation is for chumps, a mere expression of the vanity of human wishes, or a kind of complicity with the logic of the marketplace. Rather, he thinks those who consider it silly do so because the pursuit offers "no verifiable return whatsoever." It all seems a bit caught up in the logic of fame, cultural capital, and the reputation market. Maybe I'm missing the critical edge somewhere.[113]

Goldmith himself admits there is some truth to Ron Silliman's similar critique of his work, that "Kenny Goldsmith's actual art project is the projection of Kenny Goldsmith;"[114] He also parenthetically states, in an interview with Lytle Shaw, as part of a reflection on the way web diversity is closed down by the prominence of a few sites and bloggers "(By the way, I am part of this problem)."[115]

So, let's say that he's aware of how his presence edges or even edges out the virtual. Perhaps we could say that this hyper-conscious self-presencing is like an Oulipo constraint, constructed so as to avoid more unexamined egotisms. The notion of the author as a purely neutral filter, as Barthes implies, is impossible:

> Our image (provided by language) is "naturally" arrogant. This appears clearly when discourse is set up on a negative intention and when, nevertheless, it ends up being recuperated by affirmation. . . . [I]t is impossible to speak (let's insist on the performance, for after all it remains possible not to speak) of humility humbly, etc. . . . . attitudes that are defined by a negative *quantum* (an "electron") . . . have to confront—or deal with—the linguistic affirmative (the *proton*).[116]

But Barthes also desired what he called "the field of a pluralistic dust of ideolects, of singular languages" and asked his students: "See for yourself, among your relations, your interlocutors, where you live: do you live in an ideosphere or in a kind of complex symphony of incomparable languages?"[117] The literary life that would dwell in such a floating topography would be one in which the laws of continuity and order would have to be continually challenged.

Although what makes Goldsmith ultimately ineligible for a generous reading of his identity-as-Oulipo-constraint, is that he completely misses the point of Oulipo. He implies that virtualities need no longer be virtual, and that Oulipo has somehow been delivered of its failure: "In literature, Oulipo—a laboratory for *potential* literature—proposed wonderful projects, most of which went sadly unrealised. . . . I think that what myself and other writers are doing today is what I term 'realised literature.'"[118] It seems like a Fukuyama-esque, end-of-literary-history pronouncement. This promotion of an idea of realised literature without virtuality may be far more violent than the more typical promotion of oneself. For example, it implies literature as a purely positivistic discourse, working itself out towards perfection, or at least materialization (since for Goldsmith "realised" imperfection is preferable to an unrealised concept). Such a positivist stance explains why Goldsmith has continually posited his practice as not nihilistic. But by doing so, he pastes over the naturally occuring negativity not only in the work he promotes (the first thing anyone sees when visiting his site UbuWeb is an image of Samuel Beckett, an image that has gone unchanged for over a decade), but the nuance, negation, doubt, interrogation, suspense (Barthes' words)[119]—in all, the potentiality that powers all literature.

Goldsmith's positivity may be a reaction to the double-bind of having to situate himself at the juncture where the unitary language of the market meets the diverse unliterary practices revealed by new literary technics. However, it does his work a disservice, because we pay more attention to his promotional maneuverings rather than the challenging, vast, varied and unpredictable surfaces of the work. His erasure of the boundaries between the "insane game of writing" and the "player" is not critically conceived; it's just how celebrity is played, how attention economies are wrangled: how many celebrities have dumped their imagos into our consciousness without our having the benefit of knowing anything about their work? As with Warhol, we are uncertain how to take Goldsmith's allure of zen-Fluxus emptiness, when at the same time he is commandeering existing channels of privilege and visibility in order to play the largely meat-space game of celebrity for celebrity's sake.[120]

Doubtless, he has created his own channels, especially with the undeniably invaluable UbuWeb, which has over the years made a place for work that had been only possible to experience in centers of urban privilege, and even there was quickly orphaned, value unrealized, forgotten, or intentionally dismantled in the quest for an ephemeral art. Just as artists like George Maciunas made a space for this type of anti-art by investing in real spaces (buying up and refurbishing lofts in SoHo), so Goldsmith has tirelessly carved out multiple electronic spaces for the promotion of difficult, illegible, previously unavailable work. But given the amount of work that must go into the construction of this alternative environment that *does* de-center literary-art world values, why perform the pseudo-Nietzschean positivity of non-resistance?[121] Is the positivity of non-resistance to the mechanisms of cultural capital a perverse form of *laissez-faire*, the pose of the incredibly active artist letting the Zeitgeist take the reins, an inactive-activity, that puts the brakes on one set of cultural values only to promote others, a data nihilist when artistically appropriate, a data positivist when convenient?

If we were to give Goldsmith the benefit of the doubt, we could say that his performance-as-author highlights new forms of literary action, ones of which we forget *are action* or are as of yet oblivious to their activity. That is, if Goldsmith brags that he did not type *Day*—his 836 page transcription of an entire day's *New York Times*—but rather used a scanner and OCR, only someone unfamiliar with the actual experience of digital work would quibble that this was somehow "cheating." These are practices that are just not yet legible as practice. Goldsmith reminds us of the forgetfulness embedded in digital doing, new forms of action that have no accretions in habit or memory. As the materiality of his text slips into a kind of unreadable oblivion, it is memorialized by the book, but still not likely to be remembered even by the author. Such projects split into the actual—utilizing the handy readymade of the book (as well as, perhaps, the readymade art and publishing networks of New York)—and the virtual/potential—all that is forgotten within the book, and the minute acclimations of the book's making. In public, or in publicity, the book very much exists in real world networks of virtual power, in which the figuration of Kenneth Goldsmith is seemingly at the head, racking up huge gains in the literary attention-economy. Yet, if we are to take Goldsmith on his word, "we could easily throw the book away" in pursuit of a more democratic thought-space:

> the book [is] . . . a platform to leap off into thought. We move from assuming a readership to embracing a *thinkership*. By relinquishing the burden of reading—and thereby a readership—we can begin to think of uncreative writing as having the potential to be a body of literature able to be understood by anyone. If you get the concept (and the concepts are simple)—regardless of your geographic location, income level, education, or social status—you can engage with this writing. It's open to all.[122]

Left to itself, the book makes its own environment for new readers to rediscover, a rediscovery that takes so much energy that one should call the reading writing itself; as with some CDs, many of Goldsmith's books are "Read-Write." It's as if the ideal of text-processing art were not to create an object, but to emulate a force of nature, inspiring new second-order transcriptions—a weird twist on Romanticism, and an impulse that connects back to Maciunas's Fluxus, but with that niggling human presence photobombing the whole thing.

As a reading experience, I much prefer the Bergsonian mellowness of John Ashbery's meteorology. As a major figure of the New York School, his explorations of duration and the daily communicate the elegance of anonymity, surrounded by atmospheres that evade the writerly consciousness, especially in his long prose-like poems *Flow Chart* and *Three Poems*. In them, campy metaphysical language blends with the attitude of the eternal ingenue never quite in one place or one time, but wondering anyway "Gee, how did I get here?":

> It was obvious that a new journey would have to be undertaken, perhaps not the last but certainly an unavoidable one, into an area of an easier life, "where the lemons bloom," so that the last trials could be administered in an ambiance of relaxed understanding. You welcome these as an opportunity

> of definitively clearing your name, but are no less enthusiastic about the carefree, even frivolous atmosphere in which it all takes place—the sum total of all the good influences and friendly overtures in your direction, from which you have benefited intermittently all these years and which after periods of mutual discord have now banded together to create the impression of a climate in which nothing can go wrong, including the major question that revolves around you, your being here.[123]

Long sentences perform the Bergsonian prolongation of vital movements carved from the reservoir of the virtual, with the present writing overcome by the past gnawing into it, and a dim notion of future arrangements, which may include heavenly apotheosis or maybe just the finished poem. For Bergson, the body and its location is an inevitability we return to—even though it is merely one image among others—and we carve out other bodies in the virtual space of "life" according to our needs; translated into Ashbery's prose, this Bergsonian schema instigates both a looseness proper to this image universe, while yet still communicating the fatality of contingency. Ashbery takes Bergson one step further, however, assuming responsibility not towards what we carve out, but towards what we don't, attempting oblivion so as to abolish the automatisms of memory, yet still uncertain as to what virtual creatures will emerge when those primal memorializing impulses are disrupted:

> At this point it is again time for forgetting, not casually so as to repeal it delightedly later on, but with a true generous instinct for ending it all. This is the only way in which new lives—not ours—can ever begin again. But the thought haunts me—will they be defined in terms of what we never were? Will the negative outlines of our never doing define their being, a repoussoir, and so enmesh themselves even more

> disastrously with their wanting to become? If that were the case it would be better to stop right here, in this room, only to continue breathing so that life might pursue its unwanted course, far from temptations of the future, yes that's it, so that in getting to know you I renounce any right to ulterior commemoration even in the unconscious dreams of those mythical and probably nonexistent beings of whose creation I shall never be aware.[124]

The paragraph ends, addressing an anonymous being—perhaps this mythical being-as-reader: "Therefore I hold you. But life holds us, and is unknowable."[125] Desire is unavoidable, yet somewhat detachable from its more grasping incarnations, and ultimately impacted by a whole which is unavailable to consciousness, but felt by the senses.[126] The *far niente* performed by Ashbery, what he calls at various points in *Three Poems* "erect passivity,"[127] "the new casualness"[128] and the "new informal"[129] yet also imbued with lassitude less vanguardish, is not the callow mellowness of the jeunesse dorée, but rather one that is attentive to attention, despensing with the casual when necessary, but giving up when the task is too great:

> They were correct in assuming that the whole question of behavior in life has to be rethought each second; that not a breath can be drawn nor a footstep taken without our being forced in some way to reassess the age-old problem of what we are to do here and how did we get here, taking into account our relations with those about us and with ourselves, and the ever-present issue of our eternal salvation, which looms larger at every moment—even when forgotten it seems to grow like the outline of a mountain as one approaches it. To be always conscious of these multiple facets is to incarnate a dimensionless organism like the wind's, a living concern that can know no rest, by definition: it *is* restlessness.[130]

Ashbery's sentences are partly an education in loss, partly the instantiation of an impulse, and partly a prefiguration of utopia. They are creative, yes, but also destructive. Destructive-instructive. Goldsmith may be doing something similar with more large scale, non-syntactic temporalities—combining digital hype with archival care; yet while Goldsmith insists on more the hierarchical notion of "taste," Ashbery proposes a philosophy of choice that stages the failure of aesthetic criteria, while also realizing the bare human necessity of chosing one thing over another, even though the choice may be random. "*We* know that the pose you happen to be striking for the world to see matters nothing to you, it could just as easily be some other one."[131] If identity is a kind of repoussoir, an optical alibi to heighten one's perception of an elusive landscape, the landscape too would have to be relativized, deframed in order to experience the singular—happiness, maybe?—within the potential trap of its composition. Ashbery expresses a need to overcome what one chooses, aesthetically or personally, and even words like "repoussoir"—a gaudy signifier of taste in a more plain-spoken meditation—are evidence of multiple acrobatics of withholding and revealing. That is, its appearance (like the word "haruspicate" elsewhere in this poem), is a sign of remarkably withheld erudition, yet he is not loath to enjoy that erudition momentarily, but still move on, following the shapes of his own interior landscapes rather than display knowledge. But while those things that he has lovingly, carefully excluded or that have passed could remain tastefully unspoken, they get their chance to return in a clamorous curtain call:

> There were so many things held back, kept back, because they didn't fit into the plot or because their tone wasn't in keeping with the whole. So many of these things have been discarded, and they now tower on the brink of the continuity, hemming it in like dark crags above a valley stream. One sometimes

forgets that to be all one way may be preferable to eclectic diversity in the interests of verisimilitude, even for those of the opposite persuasion; the most powerful preachers are those persuaded in advance and their unalterable lessons are deeply moving just because of this rigidity, having none of the tepidness of the meandering stream of our narration with its well-chosen and typical episodes, which now seems to be trying to bury itself in the landscape. The rejected chapters have taken over. For a long time it was as though only the most patient scholar or the recording angel himself would ever interest himself in them. Now it seems as though that angel had begun to dominate the whole story: he who was supposed only to copy it all down has joined forces with the misshapen, misfit pieces that were never meant to go into it but at best to stay on the sidelines so as to point up how everything else belonged together, and the resulting mountain of data threatens us; one can almost hear the beginning of the lyric crash in which everything will be lost and pulverized, changed back into atoms ready to resume new combinations and shapes again, new wilder tendencies, as foreign to what we have carefully put in and kept out as a new chart of elements or another planet—unimaginable, in a word. And would you believe that this word could possibly be our salvation? For we are rescued by what we cannot imagine: it is what finally takes us up and shuts our story, replacing it among the millions of similar volumes that by no means menace its uniqueness but on the contrary situate it in the proper depth and perspective. At last we have that rightness that is rightfully ours. But we do not know what brought it about.[132]

Ashbery creates an ambient-memory-theater, an environment uniquely the poet's, yet inseparable from his experience of actual places, weathers, durations. These actual spaces, however, have become illegible, disengaged—and they are more reminiscent of the force of memory than its products. They form a landscape—what Deleuze calls an "any-space-whatever"—which serves as a form of "virtual conjunction" between pieces of places that are no longer identifiable, but that are brought together in pure filmic duration. As such, Ashbery's poetic activity has its cognate in that of Walter Benjamin's "Angel of History," seemingly referenced in the above passage. The angel cannot construct history as a clear representation of the past, but must rather improvise with whatever debris is at hand, because its wings are caught up by a storm that blows it into the future. Ashbery's prose undoubtedly recounts milder weather, but its overall attitude seems to imply the persistence of this "storm . . . we call progress."[133]

Ashbery performs some true sense of duration, one destructive of forms that, while conserving a more recognizable simulacrum of the past, would be deadening to the poet's awareness. As Benjamin says in "On Some Motifs in Baudelaire," quoting Theodor Reik, "Remembrance is essentially conservative, memory is destructive"[134] and Ashbery's "lyric crash" is this immemorial tendency of the "rejected chapters" to overwhelm the writer. Yet, Benjamin's formulation falls apart as an interpretive key when we encounter a second translation of this citation in Volute K of the *Passagenwerk*: "Essentially memory is conservative; reminiscence destructive."[135] This near reversal *also* holds true for Ashbery. One could say that his sentences conserve a sense of physical, aesthetic, and even mathematical place[136] in the face of a storm of progress that is truly destructive ("At last we have the rightness that is rightfully ours. But we do not know what brought it about.") To further thwart our understanding, since this aphoristic assertion is a citation, we are uncertain whether "destructiveness" was a salubrious quality in Reik's original context and it is even vague and contradictory when assessed within Benjamin's work. In the book you are holding, memory has been associated with the Bergsonian virtual, and thus, it would seem to me, a kind of destruction, but also, in Williams' sense "a kind of accomplishment"; perhaps, as for Bergson, it is cosmically conservative, while only temporally destructive. Yet, the inadequacy of all these formulations point not merely to the limitations of aphoristic thought. Instead, they may reveal an infinity hidden behind this seemingly innocuous textual snafu—the irreducible multiplicity not only of remembrance, but of the idea of remembrance to the moment of writing.

The difference between memory and remembrance, then, does not matter because the virtual *is not matter*. We can see this immaterial neglect towards memory in the work of Tan Lin, who encourages non-reading, relaxation and ambient poetics precisely as a way to get at memory, yet still retain the particularity of present-tense text-processing art. The word "memory" appears frequently in his work, and it is presumably his interest—but the surface of any coherent memory is definitively broken, sampled—like a song is sampled, but in his poetry we have no access to the original (with the result that while many of his fragments are "in jokes," they are disconnected from organic memory to such an extent that in many cases Lin himself has forgotten their sources). It's unclear how he is philosophizing memory, though there is the perfume of a philosophy. Is it, after all, just a word, and not one to be read if we are to "get" it? While his text impels us to untangle his contradictory statements on memory, we are met with weird logics, coy evasions, frustrating double-negatives and orphic-sounding paradoxes that turn out to be half-broken. They surround something that seems like a theory, but that constantly thwarts our understanding. Sometimes one wonders whether his idea of "ambient literature" is a contradiction in terms, and his approach to it purely pataphysical; when one actually tries to read Lin, one is frustrated by the non-ambient, difficult qualities of the text itself. Yet, true to his calls for the powers of non-reading, it was only when, for example, I put down *BlipSoak01* (not intending to read it further since it was striking me as neither relaxing or ambient) that I saw, while flipping through the book to give it one last chance, its delivery system—a dyadic line, the organization of which was more visual than lexical. As he said in its introduction, "The beautiful book should not be read but merely looked at."[137] In putting down the book, I finally understood it.[138]

For Lin, "memory is usually non-designed,"[139] perhaps echoing Breton's claim that "The event from which each of us is entitled to expect the revelation of his own life's meaning . . . *is not earned by work*."[140] In another place, Lin has said, "Unhappiness can be designed, as history and many world leaders have shown; happiness cannot."[141] Yet, it was precisely the overall design that was the happy form allowing me into his writing. How, then, does the writing inside "matter"? While, his artifacts—whether books or videos—seem highly designed visually (but still jankily so), textually they come off as a mess of incommensurable content pushed through a variety of media. What on one level seems quite slickly constructed, is on another well-nigh unreadable, as if encapsulating the benighted illiteracy of the fashion world, in particular, or the cosmos of electronic capital in general. On one level, it is the non-readable, on another, the un-readable.

"Poetry," he has said, "aspires to the condition of static."[142] Yet, in another place, he has said "Poetry aspires to the condition of relaxation and yoga"[143]; the extreme difference (or secret similarities) between yoga and static or his mutation of the original quote—"all art constantly aspires towards the condition of music"—seems either a parody of such generic descriptions or an embrace of their phatic knowingness. In the 4th Chinese edition of *Seven Controlled Vocabularies* in his expanded parabook project, he (or the computer translation bot rangled by one of his collaborator-editors) goes as far as to say: "poetry and small should not be within the desired conditions, but in music, Rice, and the gray of relaxation and yoga."[144] The distinctions between these *ars poeticas* does not seem to matter. What does matter for Lin is the delivery system rather than the content or author himself.[145] Even when he's engaging more readily recognizable autobiographical modes, as in his *Insomnia and the Aunt*, personal or cultural noise is channeled through a vague—maybe non-existent—megastructure, more like a novel than a poem, but probably best described as a utopian TV. Lin continually expresses a Warholian desire for a machine of unending informational flow:

> If it were really perfect, . . . everything the writer wrote, would automatically convert itself into a single long form where content is merely a form of creating noise, non-bliss, distraction, a troubled sensorium, bad planning, deprivations, or 'the illusion of sociology,' which is what happens on TV with shows like *Desperate Housewives*, shows that absorb as much unethical behavior from the environment around them.[146]

In *Insomnia* this desire is expressed as an elegy for the types of non-watching of TV that he would share with his aunt, and a prefiguration of some species of box that could miraculously capture it all.

If it doesn't matter what is in the box, or for that matter how the box became matter, then he leaves himself open to such critiques as Jennifer Scappettone's in her "Poetics of Enormity." Taking on the more dire implications of ambient culture in her ecopoetic repost to Lin, Scappettone insists that the current state-of-emergency is ambient, and that is why it is so troubling: no amount of research or thought can begin to grasp it, and thus act on it effectively. While Scappettone might share Lin's sentiment regarding the limitations of the page (even the "glassy" one) "more or less the size of our provincialism/ and the tool of it too," her immaterialist poetics calls for a less-personalized, more inhuman accounting of the enormity of ecological disaster, turning Williams' localist/materialist poetics on its end: "To make a start, out of enormity, and make it particulate, scattering the sum,/ The poem a site for the restreaming of post-pastoral, post-Paterson fact in motion/ as junk in the limbs."[147] As she has pointed out:

> Starting from enormity requires a hell of a lot of research. No longer can the poet make a promising start, it seems to me, by pausing to meditate on the minor souvenirs or phenomena of the immediate moment without some sense of their complicity in the greater web of relations. Artists committed to intervening in sublimity as opposed to representing it alone need to take a stab at comprehending the totality of trouble or promise as it is embedded in the medium at hand: language, its structures of feeling and cognition, now and here but also, ideally, over time and across space. Comprehension of systemic workings would permit us to choose our subjects or objects carefully—since part of our trouble as producers is a superabundance of possible willing object/subjects, a need more astutely to search and sift through them, or at least to identify good reasons for reproducing the circumambient tsunami of information/stimuli.[148]

Her "Archeology of the Superfundament" is a paradoxical attempt to counter immaterial horrors, or the horrors of immateriality, with a quixotic poetic research method—the mêmeté of ecological catastrophe: there are 100 superfund sites alone in the Meadowlands that separate New York City from Paterson.

Lin's poetics, while less explicitly activist is perhaps productively inactivist, although, as with most of the writers in this section we would have to wonder how this inactivism activates itself from a New York power base. Ambience is just another word for ideology. And both are just another word. Here is where this idea of a pataphysical ambience may be productive. Lin's approach to the ambient through the forms of book and video (rather than, say, through architecture, infrastructure, logos, dogma, big networks, etc.) is always going to be a failed one, and as such is an implicit critique of inattention economies (i.e. it may make us more aware of architecture, infrastructure, logos, dogma, big, networks) *vis-à-vis* "our own capacities for producing attention,"[149] which have been bought and sold. His cataloguing of the infraordinaire of his own environment—a *mise-en-scène* of pure data rather than place per se—marks the points at which his attention has been captured, but also where his attention has been able to rip itself from an impersonal continuity into his own context, author-as-delivery-mechanism.

For Lin, the delivery system in a post-TV age is fragile and mortal in itself. While he celebrates downloading over reading, file format over page, this difference is merely passage. When he says in *Seven Controlled Vocabularies* that "The reader of a book is irrelevant whereas the reader of an unread book is highly relevant as time passes and the reader goes elsewhere,"[150] it could be just another broken orphicism, or a melancholy assessment of the future of books: when they are in power as delivery mechanisms is precisely when they don't matter, when they are invisible. The unread book, then, in a sneaky way becomes the privileged thought-space, and locus of new values. Visible the moment they are forgotten, delivery mechanisms such as TV come to be seen just as ephemeral as other "short lived technologies like the making of fires."[151] As such, a text that samples content from multiple informational sources can provide a media-specific exploration of loss. For example, his *Heath* combines RSS feeds, e-book boiler plate, autobiographies of his students written on index cards, an image of Jackie Chan's Green Tree Beverage mix, cultural criticism, and bibliographic fragments dislodged from context to reflect on the short life of Heath Ledger—a name with undoubtedly allegorical resonances for Lin, combining the wild nature of the heath, and the ledgers and increasing legerdemain of contemporary capitalism.

Ernest Hemingway

There's always the strong impulse to give it all up. Call it the "vitalist bug." It doesn't necessarily have to affect only writers. Anyone for whom the protective frames of life, the well-worn patterns of experience, start to seem inadequate will do. However, it is usually writers, and especially scholars, who are hit hardest. Noone seems to think that writing itself is job enough, and there is a price to pay for ambivalence about writing's place in the world. If, bitten by the vitalist bug, we decide we must gain more worldly experience by working as a ranch hand in Montana, there is the distinct chance that we will become a ranch hand *instead of* a writer, or end up selling insurance in Bozeman. There is a long literary history of such disappearances into the fabric of everyday life, of which we can most famously cite the examples of Arthur Rimbaud, Wallace Stevens, and Kierkegaard's "Knight of Faith." The act of not-writing, or not-living-like-a-writer can be as difficult as writing itself, if not more so. Of this fine art of failure—inaction or changed action leading to the clarity of pure existence—we are mostly ignoramuses.

In *Fear and Trembling*, Kierkegaard describes his allegorical Knight of Faith in ways that are attendant to the physicalities of the virtual, the pressure of which continually knocks us out of the orbit of the everyday, making us all, more or less, a little dreamy. He compares any attempt at immersion in the actual to a dancer who tries to hit a mark, but always wobbles a little, evidence of infinity behind each step. The Knight of Faith has no such virtual wobble, but—absurdly, impossibly—executes the everyday without betraying any glimmer of the infinite; pure faith in the world means leaving art, and its virtuality, behind. Kierkegaard describes the Knight as someone able "to transform the leap of life into a walk, absolutely to express the sublime and the pedestrian":

> Here he is. Acquaintance made, I am introduced to him. The moment I set eyes on him I instantly push him from me, I myself leap backwards, I clasp my hands and say half aloud, "Good Lord, is this the man? Is it really he? Why, he looks like a tax-collector!" However, it is the man after all. I draw closer to him, watching his least movements to see whether there might not be visible a little heterogeneous fractional telegraphic message from the infinite, a glance, a look, a gesture, a note of sadness, a smile, which betrayed the infinite in its heterogeneity with the finite. No![152]

There is also the tragic cautionary tale of Professor Immanuel Rath who, falling in love with the showgirl Lola, leaves his academic position to follow her, only to become a tragic, empty shell after some episodes of manic, self-deluding happiness. When Laura Mulvey talks about Emil Jannings' Rath in her famous essay on von Sternberg's *The Blue Angel*, she gets it all wrong when she turns Rath's desire for Marlene Dietrich's Lola into the primal example of the male sexual gaze in cinema.[153] Instead, this film more poignantly encapsulates professorial desire—both Rath's and the film theorist's, and perhaps the blind spot of Mulvey's own work. The theorist attempts to grasp the liveliness of Marlene Dietrich, but fails to understand the nature of this vitality; the fascinating object of inquiry seems to exist in another reality entirely, so that the only way one can have knowledge of its world is to leave off writing and enter fatally into its milieu. To leave the virtual world of writing, and its attendant failures, in order to become more "actual," could be the product of a tragic misapprehension.[154] Or, it could give birth to new experience.

I remember a long conversation I once had in the parking lot of a grocery store just as I was finishing grad school. I felt I did not want to fall into the mouldering, self-referential practices of my colleagues, nor did I want to fall into the adjunct trap. If I was to continue with mouldering self-referentiality, I would have to be paid handsomely! Also, I was trying to keep a balance between my artistic practice and academic work, so a too precipitous embrace of an academic channel could easily cut off flows I considered vital—I was already tacking back and forth between various milieus and some were making stronger claims on my future than others. I felt I needed to resist these external forces. M________ was just finishing her MFA, and was considering enrolling in EMT training. What a marvelous idea! The energy, the speed of ambulance driving! The feeling of doing right by the world, knowing humanity in its darkest, neediest corners! Maybe I would actually realize, in compromised form, those early notions I had—buttressed by all those by-now useless high school anatomy, chemistry, and biology classes—of becoming a doctor. I would be able to choose a job that would be an apotheosis of ideals left behind, mating them with timely desire. Because ambulance driving would be no real detour, but would get me closer to the heart of the literary. Weren't Nietzsche, Whitman, and Hemingway all ambulance drivers?[155] And weren't they also heroic figures of the vitalist impulse to get outside of literature, thereby arriving closer to its core? We let the sun set on us in the parking lot as we discussed this potentially life-transforming scheme for the future.

However, schemes are schemes, and our habits usually carry us past and through them. Are we transformed by merely mentally diagramming one? Maybe Nietzsche should have similarly just fantasized about driving an ambulance. Always sickly, it was almost comical for him to volunteer for the medical corps during the Franco-Prussian war. He ended up being more trouble than he was worth. Cosima Wagner wrote him to say that "a gift of a hundred cigars would have been of more value than the presence of a dilettante."[156] Whitman, if his own accounts are to be trusted, was more useful nursing Civil War wounded, although his succor was limited to the ministrations of unprofessional care—bringing wildflowers, sweets and poetry to train-loads of war wounded languishing in stop-gap, substandard hospitals. In his notebooks compiled from scrap paper on which he hastily recorded this pivotal time in his career, he wrote, "These hospitals . . . open a new world somehow to me, giving closer insights, new things, exploring deeper mines than any yet, showing our humanity . . . tried by fearfulest tests, probed deepest, the living soul's the body's tragedies, bursting the petty bonds of art."[157] He was both energized and ruined by the presence of the sick and dying, though ultimately he discovered in himself a kind of bodily neutrality[158] that allowed for a literal embrace of all that typical historical accounts of war leave out. And his love transformed what was left out.

As a noncombatant at the front in Northern Italy, Hemingway's role was similarly only ameliorative—bringing chocolates and cigarettes to men in the trenches. But his experience was no less transformative and dire, especially after he was hit by a trench mortar bomb in 1918, killing the man next to him, and wounding him in two hundred places.[159] This shy boy from Michigan was immediately aware of how such a baptism of fire would contribute to his future status as literary legend—part of the insane game of writing is also the insane game of making one's life cleave to the autobiographical expectations of "the great writer." Yet, it was not, for all that, merely cynically experienced. He discovered how pain crucially opened the writer out onto the world, by forcing one to attend to the body's actuality, an *unwriting, devirtualizing* ascesis that war allows. While glamorizing this disruption of the virtual is no doubt one of the dangerous conceits of those who fight (and of the war journalist who feeds the fight by other means), it tells us much about the genesis of Hemingway's particularly stark, direct style and his need to make the written word as productive of life as it is of literature, with no virtual excess. As Jeffrey Meyers points out in his biography of Hemingway, Hemingway thought imagination was a trap and that cowardice was

> almost always simply a lack of ability to suspend the functioning of the imagination. Learning to suspend your imagination and live completely in the very second of the present minute with no before and no after is the greatest gift a soldier can acquire. It, naturally, is the opposite of all those gifts a writer should have.[160]

Yet Hemingway would attempt to merge the gifts of the writer and the gifts of the soldier, very much like his Futurist forebears did.

Yet his minimalist style was inspired by another, less martial, more domestically de-virtualizing experience. Hemingway lost all his early writing after it was stolen from his wife in the Gare de Lyon. Thinking to surprise him by packing the entirety of his youthful output into a suitcase so that he could work on it while vacationing in the mountains, she unwittingly transformed his "lyric facility of youth" into an easy target for oblivion. Like any good writer, Hemingway admitted that this loss was for the best, although the loss of a whole novel, among other work, can be haunting nonetheless. It would inspire his aesthetic of omission, a preference for telegraphic exclusion over literary elaboration. He was forced to take to heart the Sufi maxim "You possess only whatever will not be lost in a shipwreck"—which implies not just the loss of a suitcase and one's life's work, but also the very self. He mapped his future literary career based on the ever-present potential of such archival catastrophe. "What did I know best that I had not written about and lost? What did I know about truly and care for most?"[161]

There were only two stories left after that suitcase was stolen. One of which Gertrude Stein called "*inaccrochable*"—a term used for paintings that weren't suitable to hang in polite company. She told him, "You mustn't write anything that is *inaccrochable*. There is no point in it. It's wrong and it's silly."[162] Stein, that great impresario of difficult modernist work, without whom much of what we know of the "lost generation" would have been definitively lost, who was happy to write monstrously (as long as it was published), was not able to stomach Hemingway's blunt fuck on a dock, quite possibly a rape, in "Up in Michigan." And so this story too would not see the light of day for many years.

A friend once said to Hemingway, "We need more mystery in our lives, Hem . . . The completely unambitious writer and the really good unpublished poem are the things we lack most at this time."[163]

Google translates *inaccrochable* as "the unlinkable."

Prelusivity

Solaristics

The film starts with the astronaut in his backyard, burning photographs. This mission requires that memory be abolished. To encounter the plasmatic superbrain of Solaris, one must remain as blank and dispassionate as possible. Otherwise, one is apt to be overwhelmed by maddening immaterial phantoms and hallucinations—more real than real simulacra emanating from Solaris' shape-shifting core. In Stanislaw Lem's *Solaris* (and Tarkovsky's film adaptation of it), we could say that the astronaut's mission is nothing less than the search for a future in the mazy, self-returning channels of human space-time. But the quest is nearly impossible. Terrain erupts into extraterrain, and while the limitations of human perception tend to thwart a coherent knowledge of this cosmic entity, the past, refracted through Solaris at the end of the cosmos, lands the astronaut in his backyard again, or at least some semblance of it.

If, in the Bergsonian cosmos, the present is only perceived with great difficulty, the future is something that we can't but fail. It cannot be acted upon, because to act upon it would require that it be caught up with devices of the present—which are, in essence, machines memorializing past action—framing temporal rhythms according to current necessity, carved out by memory, and thus compromising a true futurity. Solaris—monster of consciousness, herald of new being, or perhaps mere dumb matter—does not easily enter these frames although it is inexplicably able to create image-entities for the benefit of human perception. Its defiant productivity consists in sending off capricious "mimoids" that resemble human artifacts or humanoids themselves, uncannily emanating from an alien cloud of nothing. Is this monster the future? Or maybe it's time itself, spitting out forms in a way that we can't grasp, an amorphous intelligent substance holding within it the true nature of things behind our illusory formalized existence?

This ocean of mimoid consciousness has as its counterpart the similarly oceanic body of Solaristic literature—the massive, contradictory, proliferating corpus of human research that has attempted to define this extraterrestrial nebulosity. "The ocean of Solaris was submerging under an ocean of printed paper . . . the libraries overflowed, the archives grew, and the price paid for all this documentation was often very heavy."[1] We could say, in a moment of despairing mobius circularity, that Solaris itself is the author of its own research . . . that Solaristics, and by extension human knowledge in general, is just another one of the trickster cloud's mimoid extrusions, but let that go for now. Needless to say, we don't need Solaristics to know that science does not always save us from the inconsistencies, uncertainties, and failures of *literary* literature, nor does it get us any closer to the future—especially when its object seems to be playing a cosmic joke at our expense. Solaristics is science returned to the proper irrational monstrousness of its alchemical beginnings, an inassimilable accretion asserting the reality of a no-thing.

Correspondingly, Lem's and Tarkovsky's space station is not the slick, International Style vision of Kubrick's *2001*, but rather the musty den of the space-age magpie. Libraries, file cabinets, and recording instruments in disarray take up more of Lem's attention than the characters themselves. They create an environment of deadly suffocation for the astronauts, whose mission has become a nihilistic, absurd endeavor. Most of the story consists of the checking of instruments, the looking at films, the reading of books: pure perception, liberated from knowable situation, is not to be found there, except perhaps in the hero's absurd act of love for the simulacrum: "Just your being here cancels out the twelve years of my life that went into the study of Solaris, and I want to keep you."[2] One gets the feeling while watching the film version, that the film is a reproach to the sci-fi audience itself; we are watching a film, but also getting a sense that what we are doing is watching film film, a high tech Heisenbergian *vanitas*. But it could just as well be a challenge to viewers to find in themselves that absurd love for something that is not there.

Solaris' incommensurability to human knowledge is precisely a function of our recording devices, and our tendency to accumulate consciousness in archives both material and virtual. Derrida, who describes archives not as much as receptacles of the past as they are determinants of the future, theorizes that a change in inscription technology is fundamental for conceiving any future and that "science, in its very movement, can only consist in a transformation of the techniques of archivization, of printing, of inscription, of reproduction."[3] Thus, the purest science fictions—taking the challenge of perceiving the always fleeting, impossible future in earnest—will not be recognizable as novelistic, or if they are, will, like *Solaris* serve as a metacommentary on the problems of older modes of inscription and memory brought into the service of perceiving a new reality. Memory machines kill time and hold off the future. But perhaps there is a good reason for this since, as we are told in *Solaris*: "certain events, which have actually happened, are horrible, but what is more horrible still is what hasn't happened, what has never existed."[4] However, the role of science fiction is to be fearless, even hopeful, about what has never happened, to leave from the shores of our memory islands and return to time its overwhelming force, its proper monstrousness.

More conceptually interesting science fiction has thus created unique strategies for perceiving the future ranging from a tacit admission of its impossibility to an active manipulation of the means for representing it. In many cases, the "future" is not the future painted by an imagined forward progress, but rather a return to the magical circularity of ritual time. For example, in *La Jette*, the narrational substrate is limited to the almost archaic constraint of photographic stills, as if to exemplify the ways in which the future is defined by the artifacts of the past, creating an infinite loop between levels of time, leveled out by the force of the photographic. By limiting the medium in such a way, one gets a more heightened sense of what is left out: unthinkable immensities of time that no recombination of stills can access. In some cases, the magical thinking required to access this time beyond time is facilitated by an active destruction of media-representational forms and habitual reception. For example, the seemingly violent processes of William Burroughs, who randomly cuts into the linear, pre-recorded patter of the mass media, unleash something unpredictable yet intuitively known in his futuristic scenarios built up from the pulpy, low-brow science fictional junk and media detritus around him.

Perhaps, for purposes of this catalogue, the technique that most successfully approaches the future is one that never gets there. Prelusivity—a technique, an attitude, a method, a condition—alludes to the future only obliquely, by prefaces, overtures, preambles. It holds out an always fallible promise without making that promise explicit, negotiating the fraught conception of a virtual future with the involuting tools of the actual. Prelusivity resists the future, fails it in order to experience it more fully; it is different from the more enframing force of prediction which, in its attempt at mastery, closes the future, making it commensurable with memory.[5] Prelusivity would include within its ambit works that are imagined but not made; the art of plans, schemas, or diagrams (e.g. Ilya and Emilia Kabakov's *The Palace of Projects*, Yoko Ono's *Grapefruit*, Darren Wershler-Henry's *Tapeworm Foundry*); or those realities unimaginable and still being-born, but nevertheless promised, albeit through an active dismantling of the structure of the promise. In general, the prelusive characterizes an attitude towards the virtual that does not attempt to control time, but rather remains open to transformations into unpredictable form—a negative theology of utopia.

For example, the original trailer for Fellini's *8 1/2* was repurposed as the appropriate prelusive ending to a metafiction about a failed science-fiction film. Before this ending, once a prelude for new audiences and now an ambiguous *finale*, there are a number of false endings—preparing for a crystalline, rather than definitive, culmination—contained in each of which is the seed for another beginning. First ending: Guido admits to Claudia Cardinale, as he explains to her the role that we have already seen her play in the beginning of the film, that there is no film, that he is a phony, that he does not have the capacity to love, and that it could all end there in a dark, unreal alley. Suddenly, sportscars with unpolarized headlamps enter the alley, blinding this intimate, but forgettable moment in order to carry Guido off to "the greatest cocktail party ever to launch a movie." The spaceship in the film (never finished scaffolding, in itself visually prelusive) is merely a pretext for *film-as-spaceship*, which threatens to launch into a future that the director himself is unprepared or unwilling to explore. Second ending: the launch is, consequently, a disaster—not the beginning of the film's life, it serves instead as the end of the director's, who commits suicide under a mirrored table.[6] Third ending: Guido is reanimated. We can imagine that what we saw in the previous scene was a role from the "actual" movie or a dream, but the film, true to a time image, does not narrativize this discrepancy, but rather merely offers another virtual sheaf of moments. After the film crew is told that the space-ship needs to be dismantled, he has a last encounter with his co-writer and critic, who tells him he is doing the right thing: "There are so many superfluous things in the world today. No need to add disorder to disorder. . . . In the end what we need is some hygiene, cleanliness, disinfection. We're smothered by words, images, and sounds that have no right to exist." While the writer/critic goes on at length about the virtues of abandoning the failed work, his fascist language perhaps provokes Guido to mentally disengage, thus eliciting the fourth ending. The telepathic magician appears, "We're ready to begin." Silent images of people from the director's past, beginning with Claudia Cardinale, a tableaux of a child with his nurses, father, mother, and the local whore—emerge as if in affront to the critic's monologue. He continues:

> We critics do what we can. Our true mission is to sweep away the thousands of miscarriages that try everyday, obscenely, to come into this world. And you would actually leave behind you a whole film, like a cripple leaving behind his crooked footprint? What a monstrous presumption to think that others could benefit from the squalid catalogue of your mistakes. What do you gain by stringing together the tattered pieces of your life, your vague memories, the faces of those you never could love?

The people who represent these unsynthesizable experiences appear in white; abstracted and redeemed, the past becomes loaded onto the ark of the future, as if into a spaceship with uncertain destination. Fifth ending: after an apology to his long-suffering wife, a curtain call. A curtain at the mouth of the spaceship opens, and all the characters from the film, led by the socialite dowagers from the nightclub, descend—idealized white, now adulterated with black. The characters in white remain, as if dead or unattainable ghosts, but all are assembled for a dance that confounds the color codes, as well as the lines between life and death, beginning and end, future and past.[7] At one point this image may have merely served to advertise the film, but here the trailer is repurposed as a time machine, promising configurations as-yet-unimagined with the disconnected materials of the past, a future film that starts only when the "failed" film is definitively ended, as twilight turns to night. And so, in this film about waiting, from a filmmaker who has specialized in the particular enchanting powers or transformative qualities of the end of day or the end of night, things seem to happen only when scenes wind down, when expectation is exhausted, letting the unexpected in.

One wonders whether this prelusivity is film's unique legacy, one that is always repressed (and thus virtualized), part of the dialectic struggle between the camera and history. Even Eisenstein's montage techniques could be seen as prelusive in that their aim is not to recount a known representation, but rather to disintegrate the event, subsequently composing its imagistic fragments in a way that can only be activated by the emotional and intellectual involvement of a future spectator. Montage, as Deleuze says of Eisenstein's achievement, "through the set or the fragments, gave the director the 'power to speak outside real time and space'. But this outside is also the Earth, or the true interiority of time, that is the whole which changes, and which by changing perspective constantly gives real beings that infinite space which enables them to touch the most distant past and the depths of the future simultaneously, and to participate in the movement of its own 'revolution.'"[8] How can literature participate in this revolution, when through its rationalized technique of submitting image to the letter, and thus to past techniques and archivization rather than to future recombinations, it seems stuck in a past-ism? How can one conceive its future while resisting the urge to define it? The chaotic, undefined, massive world of verbal data—the virtual whole of the literary's more limited domain—is much more difficult to love than Guido's cast off coterie of friends and acquaintances, and such a profound love-lack might be the key to its cosmic potential. The dialectic between unliterary raw material and its devices may even promise *more* diverse future forms and aggregations than film, in its current industrial-Oedipal mode, can.

Stanislaw Lem will take up this technique of prelusivity, as well as the massive virtual whole of the illiterary datascape, in works where he writes fictional reviews or introductions for books of the future. In the *actual* "Introduction" to his collection of future Introductions *Imaginary Magnitude* he writes:

> What can an introduction be? Barefaced boasting and self-advertising, to be sure, but also the wilderness cries of a John the Baptist or Roger Bacon. Therefore upon reflection we see that, besides Introductions to Works, there are Introduction Works, for like the Holy Scriptures of any faith, the theses and futuromachies of scholars are Prefaces—to this world and the other. Thus reflection shows that the Realm of Introductions is incomparably more vast than the Realm of Literature, for what the latter endeavors to *realize*, Introductions merely announce from afar. . . . So I shall show you Introductions as one shows a richly carved doorframe chased in gold and surmounted by counts and griffins on a majestic lintel. I shall swear by its solid, harmoniously massive side facing us, so that as I open it with the concentrated effort of the arms of my spirit, I may thrust the reader into nothing and thereby simultaneously snatch him away from all existences and worlds.[9]

His concern is not only the freedom to be found in imagining this non-thing of a future book, but also the dilemmas he imagines will attend the future *of* books. Well before it would become a general cultural concern, he presages the implications of easy access to vast amounts of data to the literary. "One Human Minute"—a fictional review to a data encyclopedia of the future, containing the raw numbers of all human biological activities in a prescribed 60 seconds and published on the moon—provided in 1986 a speculative account of the moral and aesthetic reaction to a grand attempt at depicting humanity through the potentially dehumanizing force of pure unfiltered data without narration.

Yet this lack of narration is what gives the data its informatic character, making it open for future readings and uses rather than closed for hermetic speculation. It is despairing on the surface, as an aesthetic object, but hopeful *in potentia*.

The Polish title of the collection this review is in translates as *Library of the 21st Century*, and it would seem that the literature of this future library would be composed of "avalanche[s] of numbers"[10] detailing the blood, semen, excrement, and sweat of the planet rather than the parlor-antics of the plot-driven. Does this mean that the future proposed, no matter how we shake it, heralds the obliteration of the literary and the end of all art by the culture of pure statistics? When "One Human Minute" concerns itself with art, it is only to enumerate its ubiquity in this unspecified future minute; by the numbers, it is an unremarkable excrescence, compared to which the automobile is more outstanding and rare. "As we leaf through this thick volume—thicker than the first edition—we encounter, from time to time, data that tell us that we live in an era where the flowering of art is barely distinguishable from its demise. . . . What good is it if everything that is beautiful lies at our disposal, and can even be called up on the screen of a home computer, if we are—again—like a child facing the ocean with a spoon?"[11] The fictional reviewer cites calls for dignity in the face of the absent book's "satire made of statistics,"[12] and is, himself, when it comes to its implications for art, not pleased by what he sees (he even throws in a jab against Warhol). However, in the end he admits that expanding the definition of the human past the purview of professional writers and artists may give this book some special purchase on the "spiritual life" of the world.

Lem takes us further down the road of this future of the literary with his "Introduction to the Second, enlarged edition of Professor J. Rambellais' *A History of Bitic Literature (in five volumes)*." Following an opposing route to the critic of *One Human Minute*, this fictional and unnamed author maps out the logical (or inhuman *illogical*) outcome of machine poetics, rather than a call for a return to humanism. Our current mechanical realizations of literary virtuality are at a very early stage compared to what this future Introduction promises, since attempts to feed linguistic units into a machine, a là William Chamberlain and Thomas Etter's Racter (a machine that, in 1983, authored the book *The Policeman's Beard is Half Constructed*), create products that are still conceptually legible to us. That is, the machine is harnessed for surreal effect, exemplifying experiments that this introduction puts only "at the threshold of bitistics, or its kindergarten."[13] Even the pure aestheticization of machine noise is still humanist in address, and does not attain the status of "bitic apostasy,"[14] a term the fictional author uses to mark off an enormous body of unreadable literature which dwarfs all other stages of bitic literature, the point at which the machine selects its own society, then shuts the door—in other words, the triumph of transhuman writing and the "total helplessness of the human race in relation to literature."[15]

How does one even begin to imagine the evolution from 80s-era computer experiments like Racter to the fearsome heresies of the bitistic apostasy? For one, Bitic Literature starts by thinking less about the writer, and more of the writing-system. If, as we noted earlier, the limits of one's particular body creates its virtual signature, and even though the author of this introduction notes that it has not been of much concern for humanists to detail the differences of anatomy in the single species *homo sapiens* as they impact writing, the implications of doing so allow for this future literature to expand its devices. If, for the human, there are certain "turns of speech which are the consequence of man's bodily structure,"[16] then an expansion of the author-structure into at least "forty-five writer systems, both individual (simple) and joint ('author-aggregates')"[17] correspondingly expands the materials and technicities available both for literary production and its criticism. The death of the author is not as interesting as the concretism of his/her/its biology and technology in the service of an expanded literary object:

> Thus, as Professor Rambellais says, it would be nonsense in romance philology to make an introductory diagnosis to the effect that the author of *Tristan and Iseut* or *The Song of Roland* was a multicellular organism of the order of land vertebrates, a mammal which is viviparous, pneumobranchiate, placental, and the like. On the other hand, it is not nonsense to specify that ILLIAC 164, the author of *Antikant,* is a semotopological, serially parallel, subluminal, initially polyglot computer of the 19th binasty, with a maximum intellectronic potential of 10^{10} epsilon-sems per millimeter of *n*-dimension configurational space of utilizable channels, with a net-alienated memory and a monolanguage of internal procedures of the type UNILING. This is because these data explain certain concrete properties of the texts of which the aforementioned ILLIAC is the author.[18]

However terrifying the notion of this monstrous literature may be for any human author who wishes to compete, such scientifically-enhanced literature nevertheless provides potential of redemption for more human literary failure. Because whole global language structures will be able to be analyzed under a microscope, it will be quite easy in this bitistic future to discern the characteristic "semantic gradient" or "semature" in the body of a writer's work. Thus, cyberneticist-scholars can recompose works that were never historically written by that writer, but which would have been written but for the infelicities of bodily limitations. There remains, however paradoxically, within the author's semature, a phantom of the body—a shadow of the human hand before the apostasy to come—since the computer cannot recompose from the void anything the author, given the time, space and energy, would not have been able to accomplish.

While the "bitic mimesis" of the system HYXOS aka "Pseudodostoevsky" will be able to write a new novel by Dostoevsky, satisfying to the most exacting of Russian literary scholars, it will be unable to salvage Dostoevsky's more actual, irredeemable, historical failures: "Thus Dostoevsky left unfinished manuscripts of a novel, *The Emperor*, but the machines could never have 'thought it through' or 'got on its track,' because in this novel he attempted to exceed his own capabilities."[19] In the future, then, machinically redeemed virtualities, attuned to a statistical phantom body, will, perhaps sadly, never overcome the more irreconcilable failures of the actual flesh-and-blood author. Nor will it have access to the work of those who failed to attain the status of author with a retrievable publication.

Roland Barthes

Roland Barthes' last work was a course he taught from 1978-1980, called "The Preparation of the Novel." Posthumously compiled and published in English only recently, these lectures were meant to be intimate and ephemeral—qualities that Barthes prized over the generalizable and the systematizable. Thus, their unavailability was a type of publishing failure welcomed, actually required, by the author. It's a luxury that only the most successful writers can afford . . . the stance, after all, not of the failed author but of the diva (it is a failure, then, of the publishing world and his executors not to honor his wish that they remain unpublished).

Yet, even though Barthes was a global intellectual superstar, and although much of his writing has attained the status of *literary*, in some quarters it was precisely those literary qualities—especially in what Carol Mavor calls his later "hedonistic books"[20]—that come off as signs of philosophical weakness or blatant irresponsibility, a lapse from theoretical rigor into inconsequential, aristocratic *belle lettrism*. For Fredric Jameson, for example, there were three Barthes; the first two he was at pains to rescue from the third, more lamentable, incarnation. As Ian Buchanan explains:

> there is Roland Barthes the sociologist, the author of *Mythologies, The Fashion System*, and *Empire of Signs*, and there is Roland Barthes the literary critic, author of *Writing Degree Zero* and *S/Z*—the first is Brechtian and the latter Sartrean. It was Barthes's ability to synthesize these two traditions and then in his fashion transcend them that accords him a special place in Jameson's selection of desert-island theory books. However, there also exists a third Roland Barthes, the anti-Left Roland Barthes of *The Pleasure of the Text*, which gives us cause to wonder whether Barthes should not finally be excluded.[21]

In other less intellectual quarters, the complaints came from the opposite direction. No matter how much his writing was "virtually" literary, it would never be accepted as literary *tout court*, given that, especially for the American audience, there was something vaguely sinister and insinuating about his leftist élan. John Updike's reaction to his fellow WASP's French invasion is particularly peevish, redolent of lingering Cold War hostilities masked by begrudging back-handed appreciation. He seems amused, almost incredulous, that Hill & Wang should have published him so diligently and respectfully (in marked contrast, Updike can't even get Barthes' famous distinction between "writerly" and "readerly" straight).[22] Reading Barthes gives him dyspepsia, he claims, and he accuses him alternately of coquetry and terrorism (or more specifically coquetry that is not vigilant enough to know it leads to terrorism).[23]

In *The Preparation of the Novel*, Barthes proposes a daring new direction, a fourth Barthes, if you will, who would have been equally dismaying for Jameson as for Updike. His plan is to write a novel, and to devote the entire lecture course to the idea of preparing that novel, poignantly called *Vita Nova* or "new life." He is keenly aware, after what was for him the traumatic death of his mother, that he could merely continue what had become for him a repetitive, predictable schtick, or he could make a leap into a whole new way of arranging words, an entirely new dispensation for which his critical work had prepared him. Quite literally, it would require a transformation into new being.

At his death this novel amounted to a paltry "eight sheets of scribbled paper neatly stored in a red cardboard shirt box,"[24] although another account cites a "hellish amount" of unassimilated index cards.[25] Reading the "Preparation," one gets the sense, however, that death did not rob us of this novel, that it might have been an imagined, prelusive novel, which he never intended to actually write, let alone publish. While his notes reveal that there could have been an attempt at a grand synthesis, he was also considering the more feasible option of giving himself the *S/Z* treatment, writing about writing his novel, using the metaconscious techniques familiar to the old Barthes.[26] It was indeed a conundrum for the theorist whose ultimate solution to the deadlocks of critical analysis was *to change the object itself.* "Does this mean I am going to write a novel? How should I know? I don't know if it will be possible still to call a 'novel' the work I desire and which I expect to break with the uniformly intellectual nature of my previous writings."[27] In *Preparation*, he engages in all manner of avoidance, including not talking about novels at all. Perversely, his focus is the haiku—the novel's diametrical formal opposite—rather than anything resembling large-scale literary fiction. He even goes so far as to claim he's not writing a novel, that he's in the "Fantasy-of-the-novel stage."[28] Yet, he also says that such projects must be nourished secretly; labors of love need to be protected from ungenerous eyes, so there is no telling whether when he is saying he's not writing a novel it's the only way to say he is writing a novel.

It is clear, however, that while he is resistant to the form of the novel as monument or artistic whole, he is not dismissive of its effects—the haiku epiphanies to be found within. The novel interests him precisely to the extent that it allows for adventure—a word that for Barthes, like his neologism "advenience,"[29] implies the continuance of the work into the future. Even a photo can be novelistic if it allows for this opening; in *Camera Lucida*, he says regarding an old photo of a little school boy: "It is possible that Ernest is still alive today: but where? how? What a novel!"[30] It seems that this potential to be a novel is novel enough, instigating desire, animating curiosity, and leaving a hole in time-space open for an actual contact with the photo's phantom. A novel is scattered with these occasions for adventure, which are its incalculable truths within an otherwise vast patterned continuity of the false: "I see it as an interweaving (=Text), a vast, extended canvas painted with illusions, fallacies, made-up things, the 'false' if we want to call it that: a brilliant, colorful canvas, a veil of Maya punctuated by, scattered with Moments of Truth that are its absolute justification."[31]

These moments are inseparable from the asignifying truth of the subject, its particular desire. They are uncoded blanks, accidents of history, openings to time and marks of irreducible presence. As such, they cannot be approached by any rational literary analysis—hence his abandonment of pure semiology, in pursuit of a paradoxical science of the singular. This science of what cannot be named, a "mathesis singularis," marks the uncertain juncture where literary form meets the ambiguity engendered by the existential moment of reading. As Kristeva says, "His own undertaking makes it clear that literature's specificity resides in the passage between this *desire* to signify the asymbolized and the asymbolizable, where the subject coalesces, and historically sanctioned *objectivity* . . . . The salience of Barthes's discovery lies precisely in this alliance between regularity and unclassifiable, objectival multiplicity."[32]

To merely appreciate a literary object without a sense of the unpredictable shapes of its reception, would be to forget the ways in which writing is an engine of other writing, and new writers form from out of old texts. Resisting critical idolatry, his aim, as Kristeva says, was not to "speak *about* literature [but] . . . *to* literature."[33] His notion of the "writerly" text implies that a new literature can be found in the spaces of the old, since all texts, as he shows in *S/Z* so magisterially, are not univocal, but rather call forth the reader to continually reconfigure, rewrite, and remix the text in order to save it from the indifferent mass of virtual and virtualizing data:

> the writerly text is *ourselves writing*, before the infinite play of the world (the world as function) is traversed, intersected, stopped, plasticized by some singular system (Ideology,

> Genus, Criticism) which reduces the plurality of entrances, the opening of networks, the infinity of languages. The writer is the novelistic without the novel, poetry without the poem, the essay without the dissertation, writing without style, production without product, structuration without structure. But readerly texts? They are products (and not productions), they make up the enormous mass of our literature. How differentiate this mass once again?[34]

Through this act of differentiation, one creates a future—escaping into the unique violence of time from out of the mass of indiscriminant data that blocks memory, forecloses the future, and is in the end not lovable. Literature, then, in its Barthesian instantiation, is the potential *within* the literary, not the literary itself. It is that lovable void—punctum, third meaning, signifiance—that is activated capriciously, in the spaces the literary text opens up to the writerly impulse.

We could say, then, that to divide Barthes into the early critical Barthes and the late literary Barthes, or to assume that the unrealized fourth stage of Barthes' career as a novelist would have been a definitive break from his earlier work, is a particularly violent imposition, mistaking the implications of his entire oeuvre, and reinstating the frames he sought to mutate. When the best-selling success of his literary-theoretical *A Lover's Discourse* inspired one fan to wonder whether Barthes had published his first novel, Alain Robbe-Grillet responded "Nonsense, he's just published his fifth or sixth."[35] His dance of signifiers always created virtual literature in the spaces left and forgotten by the old necrotic dispensations. The virtuality of Barthes' work, the pressure of it, became more ineluctable as time went on, but such is the nature of virtuality, and of time. Barthes' novels were there all along, albeit still in the future, eluding perception as novel. Just as, for him, film had yet to be truly filmic, the novel did not yet exist, but perhaps could not exist within its current organization except as a phantasmatic body.

So, no one should bemoan the loss to "letters" of Barthes' *Vita Nova* after he was struck and killed by a laundry truck, soon after his course on the "Preparation of the Novel" concluded. Instead, bemoan the death of the author, as it were, who had been writing that non-existent work from the beginning, and who still could have been writing it, were he alive today. *Imagine, what a novel!*

Walter Benjamin

Fascism encourages us to express our innate impatience, indeed horror, of failures. I am then hesitant to point up this glaring truth about Walter Benjamin, patron saint of literary Marxism and early casualty of the systematic extermination of the Jews in World War II. He was a total loser. He lived with his wife at his parent's house until he was in his thirties. He was buried in his studies to such an extent that he had little to no facility with the outside world, even though his very fascination with this outside world—the seductive ambiguities of popular culture—would alienate him from both traditional scholars and even the more progressive thinkers of the Frankfurt school. He was inept with women. He was a stoner. When, in the end, he had to take a mountain pass across the Pyranees in order to escape Nazi-controlled France en route to America, he was particularly ill-suited for the adventure. His guide will later relate that this route, which other refugees would accomplish in two to three hours, took Benjamin nine.[36] A cake walk for the Von Trapps. For Benjamin, a death march. At the end of this journey, he committed suicide in his hotel room after his group encountered an unexpected bureaucratic tangle that threatened to send them back to France. A stupid death in a monstrously stupid time.

But usually, we glorify Benjamin precisely because he was a beautiful loser (though, maddeningly, we are reminded by Hannah Arendt, in an uncharacteristically snooty way, that only losers idealize Benjamin *because* he is a loser: "We cannot know if there is such a thing as altogether unappreciated genius, or whether it is the daydream of those who are not geniuses."[37]) In some ways, then, our inability to cope with Benjamin's failure is subtle, and two-fold. It is a glorified failure on the one hand, masking something more deeply intractable about Benjamin's shortcomings. On the other hand, his failure is considered an aberration, only a tragic historical accident—a *fait-divers* of

European genius rather than evidence of deeper, continuous, systemic corrosion. Benjamin was caught up in more dire traps than just Nazi-controlled Europe: some of his closest contacts perhaps deserve equal blame for his life's impasses. For starters, Benjamin's father was somewhat of a monster, what the psychoanalysts call a *père jouissant*—an extremely wealthy bourgeois fully capable of passing power on to his son, but who instead reneged on the parental guarantees that even families of more modest means at the time granted their children.[38] In terms of his intellectual failures (to which his father's neglect is related), while we can see how the more gangsterish, conservative intelligencia would have naturally cut him off at the knees for his effrontery, even casual readers of Benjamin can't but express frustration at the Frankfurt School's attitude toward him. Adorno and Horkheimer tsked Benjamin's work to such an extent that their pedantic quibbles would keep Benjamin from a secure escape to an academic post in Manhattan. They doubted the very things that made his work good. We could go on, perhaps presumptiously, and from a far remove, regarding the failures of those he loved and admired to accept him. However, it might serve to cover over the fact that we might not have been able to deal with Benjamin as a contemporary either.

But he was nevertheless happy. Regardless of what he famously called his "large scale failures"[39] in life, he was able to form a system, an unconventional writing, through which he could still find happiness. And here is where there is the potential for us to be real losers in our misunderstanding of Benjamin: if we were to imagine that he represented sorrow and pain as a prerequisite for genius. He says as much in "The Image of Proust," where he finds in Proust's idiosyncratic writing-system a "blind, senseless, frenzied quest for happiness. It shone from his eyes; they were not happy, but in them there lay fortune as it lies in gambling or in love."[40] Proust's "paralyzing, explosive will to happiness," powering a bottomless, all-consuming lifework that nevertheless sought an object that was unattainable by work (*mémoire involontaire*), was for Benjamin the dialectical image of his own practice. He goes on to explain two modes of happiness, one that is "unprecedented, the height of bliss," and the other, perhaps not fully understood, which entailed "eternal repetition, the eternal restoration of the original, the first happiness":

> It is this elegiac idea of happiness—it could also be called Eleatic—which for Proust transforms existence into a preserve of memory. To it he sacrificed in his life friends and companionship, in his works plot, unity of characters, the flow of the narration, the play of the imagination. . . . Proust could not get his fill of emptying the dummy, his self, at one stroke in order to keep garnering that third thing, the image which satisfied his curiosity—indeed, assuaged his homesickness.[41]

This notion of a "preserve of memory" as a locus for his uncommon happiness is deceptive, given that Benjamin will later formulate the idea that Proust's writing machine is actually *destructive* of memory—a "sacrifice" of friends, plot, imagination would imply as much—or at least destructive of remembrance, since memory is already destructive *in and of itself* in the face of the more questionable preservations of "remembrances." Citing Theodor Reik in both the *Passagenwerk* and "On Some Motifs in Baudelaire," he says: "The function of remembrance is the protection of impressions; memory aims at their distintegration. Remembrance is essentially conservative, memory is destructive."[42] He was interested in an awakening from the past; memory, in its Bergsonian virtual sense, would require an active deformation of that past. Otherwise, like Sleeping Beauty in her alluring coma (a favorite image for Benjamin), time will remain mythical, it will not awaken into history itself, what he called the

"Jetzeit"—a mystico-historical "time of the now."[43]

Yet, for Benjamin, a pure present was not enough: to get to the present, one must rely on the energies locked up in the past but not realized: for this reason the unaffiliated quote or fragment was so important to him as a creative-destructive force. As Hannah Arendt describes:

> [H]e became a master when he discovered that the transmissibility of the past had been replaced by its citability and that in place of its authority there had arisen a strange power to settle down, piecemeal, in the present and to deprive it of "peace of mind," the mindless peace of complacency. "Quotations in my works are like robbers by the roadside who make an armed attack and relieve an idler of his convictions." This discovery of the modern function of quotations, according to Benjamin . . . was born out of despair—not the despair of a past that refuses "to throw its light on the future" and lets the human mind "wander in darkness" as in Tocqueville, but out of the despair of the present and the desire to destroy it; hence their power is "not the strength to preserve but to cleanse, to tear out of context, to destroy."[44]

Again, we must wonder whether this "despair" is a convenient way to read Benjamin's failure into history, whether it cordons off the immense potential latent in his curtailed discoveries. Nevertheless, for Benjamin, "everything past (in its time) can acquire a higher grade actuality than it had in the moment of its existing. . . . it serves to ignite the explosive materials that are latent in what has been."[45] Conversely, to reconstitute history, "to discover in the analysis of the small individual moment the crystal of the total event,"[46] one would have to avoid its great eternal themes and figures, and instead discover some truer time in what has been ignored: "refuse—and decay—phenomena as precursors, in some degree mirages, of the great syntheses that follow. These worlds <?> of static realities are to be looked for everywhere. Film, their center."[47]

Did Benjamin ever reach this great synthesis? We might be able to gain some clues in his last year, 1940, the beginning of which, after he was released from internment, he wrote "Theses on the Philosophy of History." "Theses" was for all intents and purpose his last "completed" text, however we might define "completion." A fragmented, elliptical (but nevertheless crystalline) collocation, it embodied, within its form, intellectual divergences designed to reflect on the diversionary structures of history, with Benjamin calling for the injection of idiosyncratic stopping moments of radical inaction into homogenous historical time. His reformulation of intellectual action perhaps threatens the integrity of intellectual-as-literary-celebrity, as if he was aware that effective historical thinking could erase the accumulative signature of a revered oeuvre, as if failure were the criterion for historical change. The author, in the face of his work's failure, becomes actor. For the materialist historiographer:

> Thinking involves not only the flow of thoughts, but their arrest as well. Where thinking suddenly stops in a configuration pregnant with tensions, it gives that configuration a shock, by which it crystallizes into a monad. A historical materialist approaches a historical subject only where he encounters it as a monad. In this structure he recognizes the sign of a Messianic cessation of happening, or, put differently, a revolutionary chance in the fight for the oppressed past. He takes cognizance of it in order to blast a specific era out of the homogeneous course of history—blasting a specific life out of the era or a specific work out of the lifework. As a result of this method the lifework is preserved in this work and at the same time canceled.[48]

While this notion of blasting the life out of the lifework could imply a type of history that concerned itself less with authoritative hagiography and more with a sampling of the past's most energizing bits, it also implies that his whole output is both cancelled by and distilled in the concentrated, oracular paragraphs of "Theses."

Regardless of its fragmented nature, it provides a master-key, not only to Benjamin's thinking, but also to the very nature of writing history in a "state of emergency," or rather *history-as-state-of-emergency*. Its references to the Messianic reinforce a futuristically-tilted mystical program, albeit tinged with both surrealist and Marxist suspicion of institutionalized Zionism. A "messianic" reading of "Theses" would have to insist that Benjamin's syntheses of history (as well as our syntheses of Benjamin) will be false to the extent that they only patch up our image of an idol, rather than partake in the mending of the world. Based on Kabbalistic ideas of cosmic fragmentation and their reparation via the process of *tiqqun*, "Theses" calls for nothing less than the Messiah to bring it all together, but this messiah is not the external, anthropomorphic, patriarchal avatar of the divine. What Benjamin calls every generation's "weak messianic power" lies in its potential to overcome the temporal conformities enforced by the ruling class in alliance with traditional historiography. His idea of the messianic, undoubtedly a virtuality, could be nothing less than the virtual itself. Power resides precisely in the way virtualities are managed and repressed, whether by way of the calendar (which imposes a "timeless" grid over a more violent, virtual flow), or traditional history, which is merely the self-congratulatory narrative of the victor. The task of the historical materialist, rather than reinforce a notion of "homogeneous empty time," is to speak the virtual of history. "For every image of the past that is not recognized by the present as one of its own concerns threatens to disappear irretrievably. (The good tidings which the historian of the past brings with throbbing heart may be lost in a void the very moment he opens his mouth)."[49]

Benjamin's allegory of the messianic historian is the Angel of History, embodied in Klee's drawing *Angelus Novus*, which Benjamin owned. The angel is an image of failure, since it attempts a job only the Messiah can handle, and must instead, like its brethren, expire after singing a brief hosanna: "The *kabbalah* relates that in every instant God creates an immense number of new angels whose only purpose is, before they dissolve into naught, to sing His praise before His throne for a moment. Mine was interrupted in doing so."[50] However brief the song of such a creature, Benjamin's is even briefer, interrupted mid-expiration: did he know his "song" would be interrupted by a more untimely death? Or is an interruption of angelic expiration just the frustration in store for us all, the all too human weight of the body on earth always confounding a more luminous self-immolation? Nevertheless, this image of angelic failure accompanied Benjamin throughout his career. As far back as 1921, twenty years before writing "Theses," he attempted to create a literary journal, which he named *Angelus Novus*, an ambitious project that was never realized. Some have suggested that his inability to publish this journal was by design. At the very least, Benjamin prized this eventuality as a vindication of its worth. In his own words, "This non-existent journal could not be more real and dear to me if it were really there."[51]

If one were to truly emulate this angel, one would enjoy the impossibility of the work and sudden evanescence, writing as a devotional performance rather than an accumulated catechism of the literary—although one would hope that Benjamin's happy fatalism is not just a masochistic internalization of the auto-da-fé in store for him. The "ephemeral quality" of the Angelus Novus—according to Gershom Scholem whose poem headed the Angelus passage in "Theses"—was its "true actuality,"[52] resulting in the "melancholy happiness of the dialectician."[53]

The famous section on the Angel of History is worth quoting at length:

> His face is turned toward the past. Where we perceive a chain of events, he sees one single catastrophe which keeps piling wreckage upon wreckage and hurls it in front of his feet. The angel would like to stay, awaken the dead, and make whole what has been smashed. But a storm is blowing from Paradise; it has got caught in his wings with such violence that the angel can no longer close them. This storm irresistibly propels him into the future to which his back is turned, while the pile of debris before him grows skyward. This storm is what we call progress.[54]

A copy of "Theses on the Philosophy of History" was given to Hannah Arendt, and the Klee drawing of the Angelus was given to Georges Bataille for safekeeping. Cut from its frame, Benjamin placed the drawing in one of two suitcases holding the unfinished contents of his encyclopedic attempt to unlock the historical reality of Paris, the *Passagenwerk*. A third suitcase crossed the Pyranees with Benjamin on his last, fateful journey, and, to the consternation of his companions, it severely hampered his escape. His guide would later wonder whether his survival instincts were intact, since Benjamin, who was already struggling with a heart condition, would not relinquish this burden which he could barely transport. Benjamin claimed that the manuscript inside was "more important than I am, more important than myself."[55] This third suitcase has never been recovered, and its contents remain a mystery.

Thus, his lifework came to a conclusion with these all-important texts, or rather containers of texts: a collection of theses, an archive project (held in a stop-gap configuration by two suitcases), and another suitcase containing a mystery. We would have to ask if this final trilogy is the prelusive signature

Benjamin intended to leave, an intentionally fragmented, lost, and erased testament to the future. Or does this combination of non-works merely constitute an absurd "terminal juxtaposition?"[56] What do we make of this evanescent assemblage called "Walter Benjamin" and how does it survive? Our attitudes towards his death may shield an appropriately irreverent-messianic relation to his texts.

However absurd, I like the possibilities that a new theory of Benjamin's death provide—that it was not the lonely, predictable death of a loser, but an assassination by Stalinist agents.[57] Wouldn't it be preferable to imagine his artistry a true threat, and that it was treated as such? Regardless of whether you buy this theory, consider its salutary implications. From time immemorial, tragic figures of the unclassifiable, the uncompromising, and the unequivocally new have been admired as literary monstrosities, while they are, at the same time, covertly offered as cautionary reminders of the fate of artistic genius. Think about how the myth of Edgar Allan Poe's death as a drunken, impoverished madman has served to confirm school-marmish Schadenfreude throughout the ages. In actuality, most evidence suggests that Poe was a victim of election fraud. This vocal opponent of the dehumanizing aspects of democracy (prefiguring Adorno and Horkheimer's *Dialectic of Enlightenment,* he would assert that the rational abstractions assumed by democratic "equality" prevented us from assessing the irrational in nature) was doped up with laudanum and forced to vote over and over again by election goons, and then was left to die on the streets of Baltimore. He might have had some problems with drink, but for the record, he had even recently attempted to give it up to appease his fiancée—an extremely mediocre poet and a Puritanical teetotaller, who Poe nevertheless adored. She, however, had zero tolerance for alcohol consumption and after a momentary lapse that attended the failure of his lecture "On the Cosmogeny of the Universe," she, forthwith, left him. After Poe's death, the execution of his estate was left in the hands of a literary rival, who painted the damaging picture we now have of him; it wasn't until years later that a witness came forward—so many years had passed, and he no longer had anything to lose—with the true story. Remembrance, however, had already done its damage.

Even Van Gogh, poster boy for the dangers of the visionary, may not have died by his own hand: a new theory has been tossed around that he was actually shot by a gang of peasant boys. There is still no good explanation for the ear.

So perhaps it is better to imagine Benjamin murdered. At least we can retain the image that these experiments were effective, and meant to be continued . . .

(archive/library)

"Don't go down for the books." This is the first rule of the Occupy Seattle Library. D____, who has taken it upon herself to get the library in shape (for weeks it had merely served as a make-out pad for a punk party girl), is training me for a job as an Occupy librarian. I'm glad the books are not considered holy relics, worth getting pepper-sprayed or jailed for: I don't really trust anyone who has an inflated notion of the value of books-in-and-of-themselves. Admittedly, certain libraries in the Occupy movement have various precious artifacts (e.g. anthologies and readers created especially for the movement), and the notion of these libraries existing at all, in whatever form, is fantastical and rare, an implicit affront to any more stable institution of data storage, and of great symbolic value in its explicit stance against other institutions and instruments of accumulation. Yet, looking through the few pictures of Occupy libraries on the web, their holdings come off as a hodgepodge, with the protest-movement equivalents of airport books, Salvation Army book section-esque donations in plastic bins, and sometimes wildly inappropriate or ironic titles (Martha Stewart Cookbooks, Donald Trump board games). The Tacoma Occupy library, as it is documented on Flickr, is just a pile on the sidewalk, designated "Community Library" with a torn cardboard sign.

The Occupy Seattle library is a little more official, perhaps somewhere between New York's and Tacoma's. It's set up in a white plastic party gazebo, big enough to fit a small table and chairs and three walls of books, but not big enough to have more than a few people at cross-purposes making their way inside. The perpetually wet ground is covered with straw. Everytime I was there, the rainy, cold afternoon became night very quickly, and plastic battery powered lanterns were set up. On my first day, Q_____, in some sort of Maoist-farmworker getup, is industriously arranging fallen books after a windstorm. I try to help her, but am overcome by the sheer dreck of worthless books, loath to put many of them into any category, let alone back on the shelf. A bedraggled homeless guy with green flourescent hornrims and a full hefty bag in tow comes in looking for Grisham. We don't have any, but oblige with suggestions of Tony Hillerman or Sue Grafton. An empty, unclassified space appears—two invitingly unused bookends. I suggest a "staff picks" area as a way to curate some of the more interesting and pertinent holdings of the collection—the local radical zines, the political theory, the literature of the oppressed: the marginalized, the censored, the dangerous. The dewy lesbian in Maoist jumpers insists this place of privilege be for memoirs: "everyone likes them." D_______, who had brightened up with my suggestion, avoids an argument. (In our "everybody has their opinion" age, what would have once served as a moment of consciousness-raising debate, is now reduced to a mere question of taste, with populist elitism taking the tacit upper-hand).[58]

Instead D______ continues to feverishly record name, author and ISBN of each book in a plastic binder full of damp pages. This record will be in case police confiscate the library, since they had done so in New York the week before, destroying many of its holdings. I get the feeling that her cataloguing labor is for labor's sake, part of the salutary, yet empty act of an unemployed librarian trying to make something of this space, her responsibility alienated from usefulness, and hence, the birth of bureacracy. But in many ways we are at ground zero of what it means to put such a collection together: it is instead the birth of the order of the library. For Foucault, D____'s activity is a far cry from alienated labor, but is synonymous with the new dispensation of word-processing that modernity inaugurates. The act of cataloguing an archive is what turns rational, homogenous and transtemporal Cartesian space into something that opens knowledge to the contingency of the future:

> The ever more complete preservation of what was written, the establishment of archives, then of filing systems for them, the reorganization of libraries, the drawing up of catalogues, indexes, and inventories, all these things represent, at the end of the Classical age, not so much a new sensitivity to time, to its past, to the density of history, as a way of introducing into the language already imprinted on things, and into the traces it has left, an order of the same type as that which was being established between living creatures. And it is in this classified time, in this squared and spatialized development, that the historians of the nineteenth century were to undertake the creation of a history that could at last be 'true'—in other words, liberated from Classical rationality, from its ordering and theodicy: a history restored to the irruptive violence of time.[59]

For Foucault, it is the appearance of literature on the scene that requires this system; in fact, literature as we've come to know it is *synonymous* with this system. Once the "vast grid" of the Classical episteme is no longer valid, the literary-as-virtual-language-practice is unleashed. "Once detached from representation, language has existed, right up to our own day, only in a dispersed way."[60]

From this point on, no library (or book, or social order) can claim all-inclusivity. Instead, these ordering principles become mechanisms of literary adventure. Lacking inclusivity, they must be prelusive—harnessing the energies of historical time, and open to intervention. Derrida's *Archive Fever*—a prelusive text with chapters headed "Exergue," "Preamble," "Foreword," "Theses," and finally "Postscript"—situates the question of the archive squarely in these futuristic dimensions: "The archive has always been a *pledge*, and like every pledge, a token of the future. To put it trivially: what is no longer archived in the same way is no longer lived in the same way."[61] If, then, the archive fails to codify all, this failure is perhaps what leaves it open to the promise, foreclosing the possibility of a representative "People's Library."[62] A truly democratic library may paradoxically be one that is personal and idiosyncratic—and such archives have proliferated online beyond one's ability to adequately catalogue them. It may be that, in the future, this art of cataloguing may be a potentializing practice indistinguishable from the creation of a literary work.[63]

But this proliferation does not necessarily mean, apropos "everyone has their opinions," that everyone gets their own collection, and we can leave it at that. In response to the more superficial ordering principles of personal archives such as can be found on sites like Tumblr, R. Gerald Nelson has pointed out that the problem with the online archival impulse is that it tends to affirm personal style at the expense of more vibrant, communicative, or contextualizing ordering principles. Thus, while not embracing the ideology of all-inclusion, the online image aggregator (IA) goes in the other direction towards hipster navel gazing, and the accumulation of unearned social capital. Nelson says that "the IA had much more in common with the wealthy collector of Renaissance painting than with the visual anthropologist out to record our cultures"[64] and that his/her activity is one involved in "narcissistically and merely attempting to communicate one's keen eye for styles and trends."[65] Nelson, perhaps unfashionably, asserts the importance of authorial authenticity, bemoaning the loss of context for data artifacts. For him, however, while the new online archivist should be inventing more rigorous ordering principles, these principles must be applied with a sense of provisionality or even humor appropriate to an endeavor that must fail (he sites as a useful example Roy Arden's *The World as Will and Representation,* which seems an internet-based update of Hollis Frampton's *Zorns Lemma*). The new data archivist applies a "classificatory impulse that is supremely aware of its own futility, and of the fatal contingency of its classificatory criteria."[66]

Such conceptual negotiations are by no means limited to the contemporary internet collection. Walter Benjamin's posthumous work of bibliomanic classification—*The Passagenwerk*—rode this line between personal idiosyncrasy and totality, constantly straining against classification yet attempting to catalogue the impossible object of his inquiry: Paris of the nineteenth century. For him, adequate caretaking of a collection met with the more "destructive" joy of reinventing information (for this reason he discovered more when he was "unpacking his library" than when it was in-situ). This struggle between the totalizing system and the explosive objects within it was for Benjamin the dialectic of the collector. He sought "to combine with loyalty to an object, to individual items, to things sheltered in his care a stubborn subversive protest against the typical, the classifiable,"[67] yet nevertheless sought to invent a system for accessing these objects. As Hanna Arendt writes, "nothing was more characteristic of him in the thirties than the little notebooks with black covers which he always carried with him and in which he tirelessly entered in the form of quotations what daily living and reading netted him in the way of 'pearls' and 'coral.'"[68] The *Passagenwerk* was an attempt to systematize the childlike "renewal of existence" these precious scraps enabled; this vast, unfinished concordance of the Paris Arcades is an eminent example of literary-work-as-open-collection. It also marked Benjamin's literary attempt to create a new life for himself,[69] a connection between formal experimentation and existential renewal that we've seen in many works thusfar. For that reason, as also with other works we've seen, the completion of such a work was feared as much as desired.

For Benjamin, "The work is the death mask of its conception"[70] and the *coup de théâtre* of his death left his text an ambiguously open non-work. Was this the only way it could have ended, or was its curtailment a tragic one? Various sheafs or

"Konvolutes" held masses of loosely affiliated quotes and Benjamins' memorable "authoritative sentences,"[71] catalogued under such headings as "Fashion," "Boredom. Eternal Return," "Iron Construction," "Dream House, Museum, Spa," "Mirrors," "Conspiracies, *Compagnonnage*," "Marx," "The Stock Exchange, Economic History," "Idleness." As well, there were twelve catagories that are untitled because they are either missing or were meant as provisional slots for future material. This productive unshapeliness was something he was experimenting with as early as 1928, with "One-Way Street," in which he opts for "prompt language," rather than "the pretentious, universal gesture of the book"[72]—an attempt, inspired by love, to break out of his academic dead-end to follow the only way remaining to him: to take action. He writes, "true literary activity cannot aspire to take place within a literary framework—that is, rather, the habitual expression of its sterility. Significant literary work can only come into being in a strict alternation between action and writing."[73] The language of "leaflets, brochures, articles, and placards" would be henceforth translated into his work. As Susan Buck-Morss describes of this new direction:

> an experiment is underway, how images, gathered by a person walking the streets of a city, can be interpreted against the grain of idealist literary style. The images are not subjective impressions, but objective expressions. The phenomena—buildings, human gestures, spatial arrangements—are 'read' as a language in which a historically transient truth . . . is expressed concretely, and the city's social formation becomes legible within perceived experience.[74]

Yet, despite this aura of the provisional, there was an unrealized plan for the whole work: a dream image that announced a new social order, a "dialectical fairy land."[75] Originally conceived as a kind of Marxist fairy tale, the

Passagenwerk would have been a reconstitution of the Sleeping Beauty story. Indeed themes of awakening from the "once upon a time" of history suffuse his work. Paris itself was the "sleeping beauty," enchanted by its own representations. As Bernd Witte describes, the image of "Paris, as infinite . . . unfathomable" library blends, as appropriate with any dream image, with Paris as a lovely woman. She is crowded by illiterate lovers with whom Benjamin, perhaps a more worthy suitor, must compete. In his description of what he calls his "bibliographical allegory" of Paris, she is surrounded with junky virtual replicas of her charm:

> The Goddess of France's capital city, in her boudoir, resting dreamily. A marble fireplace, molding, swelling cushions, animal skins adorning divan and plaster floor. And knick-knacks, knick-knacks everywhere. Models of the Bridge of the Arts and the Eiffel Tower. On the pedestals, to keep alive the memory of so rich a past, the Tuileries, the Temple, and the Château d'Eau in miniature. In a vase the ten lilies of the city's coat of arms. Yet all this picturesque bric-a-brac is heightened, trumped, buried by the overwhelming multitude of books in a thousand formats—sextodecimos, duodecimos, octavos, quartos, and folios of every size and color—presented to her by airborne, illiterate amoretti, poured out by fauns from the cornucopia of the portieres, spread before her by kneeling genies: the homage of the whole planet in its literary production.[76]

Paris in erotic indolence can be placed in contrast to the figure of Asja Lacis, an actual woman (albeit with a highly allegorical name) who inspired Benjamin's love and experimentation, but who is presented in the epigraph of "One-Way Street" as engineer, a dynamiter of Benjamin's stalled life:

This street is named
Asja Lacis Street
after her who
as an engineer
cut it through the author[77]

Is however, his layering of desire over these geographies, in both cases, a literary mistep? Even when Benjamin was talking about capitalism itself, he imagined it as some kind of whole body—otherwise, his metaphor of the dream image of capitalism would make little sense (although its access to "sense" would be precisely the issue "at hand"). If the Sleeping Beauty image were laminated over the Arcades, would that have closed down its potential—the vast topography unavailable to bounded sensation and psychological interiority, but yet open to continual literary activity and wonder, city as book becoming inconceivably book-as-city? Perhaps the sleeping beauty was an image he needed to desire, but not realize, an alibi for aimless wondering, but not so aimless as to blind Benjamin to the inhuman dimensions of the predicament he otherwise analyzed with rigor and aplomb. That both Paris the Goddess and Asja the Engineer were not images Benjamin could conceivably act upon, but that acted upon him, makes me believe that he knew this limit, and it was part of his own awakening.

If we were to imagine the Internet similarly as an allegorical image, picture a tent city of truly cosmic proportions, which, sometime around the beginning of the 1990s, was erected so as to counter the excesses, limitations, and enforced scarcities of mainstream media and publishing. Designed to protest the economic scandal of the publishing world supporting only 1% of what gets written (or sung, or filmed), the Internet finally allowed the rest of the 99% to speak back. Imagine, this tent city dismantled in just one night. Currently, opponents of net neutrality and online file sharing are aggressively pursuing legislation that will result in large scale censorship, effectively breaking the Internet. Corporations like YouTube will be penalized for "not filtering adequately"; the front page of UbuWeb currently reads "If SOPA passes, you can kiss UbuWeb goodbye." For all intents and purposes, the virtual future promised by the Internet will instead become a historical oddity, perhaps forced to resurface—like Benjamin's long forgotten experiments—at some later, more propitious juncture in history. One can only hope that it is the offending legislation that will, by the time this book is published, become the historical oddity.

Yet in either case, the virtual will remain untouched. While failure gives us some sense of the density and shape of the virtual, the virtual never fails. Since it is not a thing of matter, it does not matter that these libraries are destroyed. Everything is saved, and everything moves forward.[78] Of course, such apocalyptic nihilism has been at the heart of library destruction and book burning throughout the ages. It may be that such destruction does not get us closer to the future, but rather merely adds to the cosmic stockpile of senseless acts throughout the ages.

Abraham Lincoln Gillespie

Abraham Lincoln Gillespie was a mild-mannered school teacher from Philadelphia. That is, until a car accident endowed him with miraculous linguistic powers to rival those of Joyce and Stein. Never appearing in book form, his personal language assembling did appear here and there—in journals, yes, but also in cafés, on the street, and at drunken bohemian all-nighters. Telling his boss in America that "a new word is as good as an old dollar,"[79] he left for Paris, "forsak[ing] suburbs for city-Psych-BOheems,"[80] to join the expatriate literary culture of the legendary "lost generation." Once there, Stein and Joyce shunned him, even though Gillespie claimed to be the foremost expert on their work. In fact, he considered himself the foremost modernist *tout court*:

> My work veer-expresses my relation to 20thCentury Reality, a relation I feel-think to be fillfuller than any hitherto CritiCommunicLiable, i. e., mine, the necessity of lending consciousative LOGICATING to the AromeClashBuild-inner-ising FORMTrends of Music's MelodSyntheBuildAlong, the gradaccrue of which (both delib and acciByProd) may-will tot-add sub-et-Supra integerCollects for furthering the Context'sImputationise; at the same time possibuilding, in English . . . *Sensation*Forms rhapsintrest Composenuf to aesthConcomitate these neo-gather-imputes of Thought . . . .[81]

From all accounts, he actually did talk like this, inventing and improvizing ways to attain what he called the "phrase-moment," by attending to some kind of linguistic DNA (the "1-5 nick-Ideate particles . . . of each centrosomicant MindMoment" or what he called in another place the "KALEIDOSOEM . . . 'Beneath > all > Words>"):

> One hassta ask, "Y not more PHRASE-MOMENTING 'Or-

More's'?" Is it because our TreeHarp-scorning Kindergarten TEACH-Minds can't race > don't-permit SteNeogriphs? As to what hasn't been precipitating through, I assert-venture that there are 1-5 nick-Ideate particles, ImagePeerFlints grammarwise unpresentable, even ungetatable – wriggle-or-dent-IN SculpFillers of each centrosomicant MindMoment, the which would, given steNeoALLOW-Utterance, come through, to teemly convoke *vraies idéographes d'intérêt* –Ideographs knit with byProduct-Addits not only FORMstressive, also Context-so.[82]

Linc, Link, Linkey or Linkers as he was alternately nick'd was for most of his fellow travelers merely a fashionable oddity. He did befriend luminaries, such as the inventor-composer-dreamboat George Antheil. The polymath futurist Bob Brown took his work seriously as content for his proposed Readie-machine. And Eugene Jolas published Gillespie's work in *transition*—in the "virtual" company of Stein and Joyce, if not in their actual society. But his futuristic language somehow didn't take, so it now comes to us not merely as a failure, but as a futurism that is quaintly outmoded. Or perhaps it would be better to say that the writing of Abraham Lincoln Gillespie will be something that was always and will be *outside of time*.

At the level of the letter, his ideas were perhaps no different than the modernist "LyriProtestisms"[83] of his contemporaries. He sought a language that would be more psychically realistic, challenging literary filters that blocked both new action-images and thought-images. He practiced instead a form of HEYPER-SIEVING,[84] to "free those many verypassing impact-masses momenting in Consciousness, to entitically *panache-deploy* their Totality."[85] And he desired to speak his inner-most energies, a hyper-*expressivity* that today might even come off as passé, but which beats out most of what gets called digital poetry hands down: "What's been dough-clogging the sieve-process of the

Speak-Mind, what's been shunting off part WORDprecip of the *original* flashsearConsciousness *QUANTITY* of Images, that polygonating Impactseries of the was-aspected Ideation? . . . Grammar'd communication. GRAYMAR. Academic Bugaboo, stuffshirt-PaunchPace-Idealiser . . . "[9]. In effect, he implies that the human disappears in this gray sea of official language, lost in a bad virtual of "Context'sImputationise."

His manufacture of a private glossary—a "purrplexicon" of "taggive Secondimmensproutfeeld twords," "abstraktids," and "pizzicats"—is a kind of timeless meddling with the virtual *within* language, a virtual that is like the real in that it encompasses what language can't do, what it absents, its insuffiency of permutations. Yet to meddle with this virtual, to be dissatisfied with the potential of the legible, one threatens one's own authorial virtualization. Such a stance, when not adequately contextualized and promoted within a ready-made literary context (as were Joyce and Stein's), comes off as that of the schizo, or the beknighted artistic brat, even though this type of poetic innovation—as Charles Bernstein and Caroline Bergvall have pointed out[87]—is a crucial counterpoint to the violent impositions of standardized global language practices.

Would Gillespie have been redeemed if he had a proper machine at his disposal? A radio broadcast (which he desired), a literary-film-music-microscope-voltmeter to seek out the hidden connections between language's chromosomes, overtones and imagos? Like David Lyle, he comes off as a crazy, happy engineer, and his inventiveness, overreaching the capabilities of what was actually accessible to him, might explain his affinities with Antheil and Brown. Gillespie wrote much of his work explicitly for Bob Brown's ticker-tape reading machine, one that promised literature "taken at high gear," "a modern, moving, word spectacle" enabling not only optical-intellectual experiences of "overtoneagearomaccumutanjingspill-phonicbyprod-bewilder-she-en-spray-associativity,"[88] but also a more efficient device for "industrious delvers in the Word-Pile" to navigate the virtual. Yet it would be a mistake to say, "If only Link had a Kindle" or "possibly-a-Mesmo-L.C.D.-of our-undodesiring-libidego."[89] Maybe he could have used that ticker-tape literary machine, which never made it past the patent stage, although even the ticker-tape can not catch up with the virtual, creating as it does more masses of useless data to be re-tickered or exaltantly transformed into something else completely, a ticker-tape parade for all the failed genius that makes the literary possible, our virtual heros of the unreadable.

Looking at a certain rare photo of Gillespie, though, I am bemused by the fact that he is in the company of Joe Gould, who for years was said to have been compiling the Oral History of the World. Joseph Mitchell describes this project, recorded in countless cheap composition books, as: "a great hodgepodge and kitchen midden of hearsay, a repository of jabber, an omnium-gatherum of bushwa, gab, palaver, hogwash, flapdoodle, and malarkey, the fruit, according to Gould's estimate, of more than twenty thousand conversations. In it are the hopelessly incoherent biographies of hundreds of bums, accounts of the wanderings of seamen encountered in South Street barrooms, grisly descriptions of hospital and clinic experiences . . . , summaries of innumerable Union Square and Columbus Circle harangues, testimonies given by converts at Salvation Army street meetings, and the addled opinions of scores of park-bench oracles and gin-mill savants."[90]

It turns out, though, that Gould's voluminous output, for a long time believed to be baled up and buried in a cellar on Long Island, never actually existed. Or, rather it was returned, as Gould might have said, to the "infinitude of bushwa" from whence it came.

Acknowledgements

"Stupidity consists in wanting to conclude."

—*Flaubert*

There is a sort of hari-kari involved in a book like this. To embrace failure unflinchingly, one is doing what all self-help books—which usually find no obstacles to publication—warn against. One would be flying in the face of the power of positive thinking, refusing to participate in the pyramid scheme of apparent happiness, of "put on" success. Yet is toying with the realism of failure a bigger gamble? Intimacy with failure, performing one's failure, even with an eye to transvaluing it, inculcates vicious circles of self-doubt, possibly inescapable. Hopefully, this literary hari-kari is itself half-cocked—its failure an attempt, in the "insane game of writing" to create a win-win prospect in a lose-lose scenario. Because, haven't I just written a book that will gain value precisely to the extent that it is unpublished, unread, or forgotten? It would be even better if I left it *unfinished*. Hari-kari, undone.

Therefore, I have decided against a final entry "about the author," the prospect of which seemed more and more like a death mask. In the preceding pages, there is enough occulted autobiography—as well as its opposite (self-immolation)—to make that entry redundant (or maudlin, or secretly self-aggrandizing). I do, however, owe some thanks in that autobiographical genre of acknowledgements, even though the idea of thanking people for my *failure* can seem thank-less. Whatever mess I've gotten myself into, I have both everyone and no one to thank, and only myself to blame.

The paradox of writing a book that strained against its bookness is that I value the *dynamis* of the book—as an object, a promise, an experience, a space-time. The only way one can materialize a book that holds to a particular unity is if one is given adequate freedom from distractions, and sufficient support for the undertaking. The Simpson Center for the Humanities Society of Scholars Fellowship granted me a quarter off, which I jumped on as a rare chance to focus on what would be an undertaking that could have easily been detoured by teaching, meetings, and other university responsibilities. Through their support, the book was able to be written—as I think books should—in one fell swoop, roughly from March 2011 to January 2012. However, the ideas for this book have been percolating since my last book was finished, and were aided by a number of opportunities to lecture. Central to the foundations of this book were invitations to talk on virtual literature at Location One in New York City in 2006 and at the MLA for the media and literature group in 2005. Other invitations to talk on and around these issues, extending back ten years, include those from the School of the Art Institute of Chicago, Pitzer College, Jody Monroe Gallery, University of North Florida, Hudson Untitled Foundation, Haverford College, Parsons School of Design, Artefact Festival of New Media, Visual Studies Workshop, Ontological Radio Festival, The William Carlos Williams Society, Occupy Seattle Library, and the Northwest Film Forum. I thank all those involved with those various events and institutions, allowing the public talk to be a space of surprise and discovery, tolerating my need for the unexpected—unfolding discussion and thinking-out-loud rather than "academic paper." I thank Elizabeth Tonnard and Chris Burnett for wanting to publish an early version of these ideas in a book about image-text art that was unfortunately deemed too sumptuous to publish (see http://elisabethtonnard.com/works/image-process-literature/).

This book is also one of the many materializations of a number of virtual projects—both artistic and scholarly—not least of which was my long running research blog on William Carlos

Williams' *Paterson*. I consequently should use this space to thank free103point9, the Visual Studies Workshop, and Flux Factory for residencies that helped grow that project. The Kelly Writers House and Al Filreis at the University of Pennsylvania frequently provided spiritual support for the project, even as other institutions were more baffled by its innovations. Much thanks is also due to Brown University, specifically to Roger Mayer, who arranged for me to replace him as a visiting professor in 2006-07, without which this project—depending on a network of associations emanating around and through the idea of New Jersey—would not have been possible to launch, and which provided many other infusions of energy and ideas ultimately leading to this book. As to other orbital objects and paratexts, thanks to Max Goldfarb for facilitating, among other things, the unframed frame for not-publishing my *Torrent* project, enabling virtual literature-in-practice, as well as Frankie Martin for her participation in *Don't Drive Today with Yesterday's Maps*—an expanded sci-fi video and text work, intentionally "failed," that helped establish the conceptual core for this book's section on "Prelusivity."

Jeanne Heuving was generous enough to allow me to co-curate the *Writing for their Lives* series at the University of Washington-Bothell, which enabled me to bring in an enlivening mix of artists whose work directly applied to, and was at the forefront of, issues I was working through. Specifically, artists Danny Snelson and Alejandro Miguel Justino Crawford provided invaluable input, off and on, regarding utterly contemporary phenomena, yet always with a depth of appreciation towards their historical precursors.

Along the way, more random, passing or unquantifiable assistance, from the ad hoc to the persistent include that from Clark Lunberry, Herbert Blau, Kathleen Woodward, Miriam Bartha, Brian Reed, Eugene Thacker, Theodora Graham, Craig Dworkin, Judith Goldman, Tan Lin, Lytle Shaw, Jennifer Scappettone, Paul

Chavez, Gregory Laynor, Adam Sekular, Lyall Bush, and Jesse Lerner. Participants in my "Writing Through the Image" seminar in Fall 2011 were perhaps unwitting accomplices to the book, given that they rewarded me with their interest and engagement during its home stretch.

Notes

Ungreat Books

1 The McWhirter twins together edited the Guinness Book from 1955-1975.

2 I have chosen throughout to use the presumptive, perhaps arrogant "we" and "our." And why not? I hope that you will want to share in this failure, that an intimate reading will serve to implicate "us all" into this club. Yet "we" fails precisely to the extent that I cannot know "you," and that unknown excess is the virtuality that this pronoun does not accommodate. Derrida speaks of the address of "we": "the violence of this *communal* dissymmetry remains at once extraordinary and, precisely, most *common*. It is the origin of the *common*, happening each time we address someone, each time we call them while *supposing*, that is to say while *imposing* a 'we,' and thus while inscribing the other person into this situation of an at once spectral and patriarchic nursling"(41-2). My choice of "we," however, is intended as an instance of modesty, respect that attempts inclusion of what has been left out, since for every failure included in this book, there are the failed failures who have not been submitted for any scrutiny. In "we" then, resides the vast territory of the unincluded. The impossible address of this book is the book's very subject. Jacques Derrida, *Archive Fever: A Freudian Impression* (1995), trans. Eric Prenowitz (Chicago: U of Chicago P, 1996).

3 In the vast universe of data at our disposal, I am unable to find confirmation of this anecdote, which I seem to remember like a dream.

4 Nora Ephron, "The Love Machine," *New York Times*, May 11, 1969.

5 Maurice Blanchot, "Destroy" (1971), in *Duras by Duras* (San

Francisco: City Lights Books, 1987), 130.

6 *Son Nom de Venise dans Calcutta Désert,* Liner Notes, Marguerite Duras, Cinéma 9/Les Éditions Albatros/P.I.P.A., 1976, Benoît Jacob Vidéo, 2001.

7 Marguerite Duras, "Notes on India Song," in *Duras by Duras* (San Francisco: City Lights Books, 1987), 16.

8 Duras, "One Out of a Hundred Novels Makes It to Publication" (1957), in *Outside: Selected Writings,* trans. Arthur Goldhammer (Boston: Beacon P, 1986), 42.

9 See Gilles Deleuze, "The Image of Thought," in *Difference and Repetition* (1968), trans. Paul Patton (New York: Columbia UP, 1994), 129-67.

10 André Breton, "Manifesto of Surrealism" (1924), in *Manifestoes of Surrealism,* trans. Richard Seaver and Helen R. Lane (Ann Arbor: U of Michigan P, 1969), 27.

11 We should remember, of course, that Breton's "occult" practices were a more macho, art world repurposing of more direly "virtualized" work from the nineteenth century—the automatic writing of female mediums. See, for example, Katie Fox, *Fox-Taylor Automatic Writing, 1869-1892, Unabridged Record,* ed. Sarah E. L. Taylor (Lincoln: W. G. Langworthy Taylor, 1932).

12 Breton, *Nadja* (1928), trans. Richard Howard (NY: Grove P, 1994), 71.

13 Warren Motte, *Playtexts: Ludics in Contemporary Literature* (Lincoln: U of Nebraska P, 1995), 44.

14 Breton, *Nadja,* 52.

15 Ibid.

16 Ibid., 54-5.

17 Ibid., 147.

18 Ibid., 148.

19 Ibid., 151-2.

20 Susan Sontag, *On Photography* (NY: Farrar, 1977), 51.

21 Since Freud points out that an old German dictionary

defines "heimlich" as both *vernaculus* and *occultus*, we can start to map out the secret channels between the vernacular photo and occult reality, actuality and virtuality, that Surrealism exploits. See Sigmund Freud, "The Uncanny" (1919), in *The Uncanny*, trans. David McLintock (NY: Penguin, 2003), 132-33.

22 Julio Cortázar, "Blow-Up" (1959), in *Blow-Up and Other Stories*, trans. Paul Blackburn (NY: Pantheon, 1967), 122.

23 Andrew Eskind, *The Joseph Selle Collection of Street Vendor Photography*, web, http://andreweskind.com/andy/streetphot/index-upto-march2012.html.

24 See Christopher Burnett, "The Streets of San Francisco: Encounters with the Selle Collection of Street Vendor Photographs," *Afterimage* 35:3 (Nov/Dec 2007): 28-34.

25 Cortázar, "Blow-Up," 124.

26 Fort's Intermediatism is strikingly similar to the philosophy of Henri Bergson, in its breakdown of the categories of "real" and "ideal," and has resonances as well with the intervalic modes of Deleuze. He describes the intermediatist in ways that expand our notions of materialism beyond the explicitly "phenomenal," without resorting to a metaphysical notion of what is beyond the phenomenal: "To an intermediatist, the phenomena of intellection are only phenomena of universal process localized in human minds. The process called 'explanation' is only a local aspect of universal assimilation. It looks like materialism: but the intermediatist holds that interpretation of the immaterial, as it is called, in terms of the material, as it is called, is no more rational than interpretation of the 'material' in terms of the 'immaterial': that there is in quasi-existence neither the material nor the immaterial, but approximations one way or another." Charles Fort, *The Book of the Damned* (1919) in *The Complete Books of Charles Fort* (NY: Dover, 1974), 115.

27 Louis Pauwels and Jacques Bergier, *The Morning of the*

Magicians (1960), trans. Rollo Myers (NY: Avon, 1963), 143.

28 This count appears in a "short story" by Fort that reads more like autobiography. Charles Fort, "The Giant, the Insect, and the Philanthropic-Looking Old Gentleman," *The Fortean Web Site of Mr. X*, web, n.p., n.d.

29 "Charles Fort," *Wikipedia*, April 2, 2012, web, April 17, 2012.

30 In fact, they are all collected as such in *The Complete Books of Charles Fort.*

31 Fort, *Book of the Damned*, 135.

32 Ibid., 90-91.

33 Ibid., 129.

34 Ibid., 91.

35 Fort, *Wild Talents* (1932) in *The Complete Books of Charles Fort* (NY: Dover, 1974), 945.

36 Ibid., 855.

37 Ibid., 861.

38 Ibid., 942.

39 Ibid., 987.

40 Ibid., 877-78.

41 Fort, *Book of the Damned*, 107.

42 I am, however, suspicious of the legacy of Whitman's "I am large, I contain multitudes," as if only by that largeness can one have access to the multitudinous contradictory real, or as if that largeness were license for lyric irresponsibility. The posturing of the literary big man has always been distasteful to me. Blustery, bullying, these writers are full of the self-importance that comes from the impression that such a bodily frame as theirs is the prerequisite for taking it all in. My impression on seeing and hearing such a man (and they are, by and large, big *men* I am talking about) is not only that others don't get heard amidst their sound and fury, but also that, once upon a time in the economics of the family pantry, some did not get *fed*. No, like Deleuze and Guattari, who go as far as to valorize the anorexic as hunger

artist, or, even further, the body without organs as ultimate unfiltered cosmic connection, I am for refusal, the cultivation of an appetite not monstrous and indiscriminant, but by turns picky, ascetic, and therefore passionate about its objects. I am more for lightness. Consider Italo Calvino's description of the shaman as one who "faced with the precarious existence of tribal life—drought, sickness, evil influences—. . . responded by ridding his body of weight and flying to another world, another level of perception, where he could find the strength to change the face of reality" (27). I must then, admit an ambivalence about embarking on a project that sets out to tackle such unwieldy, undigestable and profligate works, ones that balk intellectual lightness, that pull one into a sedentary black hole, that are DOA. If only to find new flight paths I continue, with the hopes that these dark works hide secret ways in a time of precarious existence and false levities. Italo Calvino, "Lightness" (1985), in *Six Memos for the Next Millennium* (NY: Vintage, 1988).

43 G. K. Chesteron, "Tolstoy and the Cult of Simplicity," in *Twelve Types* (London: Humphreys, 1906), 149.

44 Ibid., 140.

Monsters of the Memorious

1 Jorge Luis Borges, "Funes the Memorious" (1942), in *Imagining Language: An Anthology*, ed. Jed Rasula and Steve McCaffery (Cambridge: MIT P, 2001), 320.

2 Ibid., 322.

3 Ibid., 324.

4 Ibid.

5 Ibid., 322.

6 "The Woman Who Can Remember Everything," *The Telegraph*, May 9, 2008, http://www.telegraph.co.uk/news/newstopics/howaboutthat/1940420/The-woman-who-can-

remember-everything.html.

7 Gary Marcus, "Total Recall: The Woman Who Can't Forget," *Wired* 17:4, March 23, 2009, http://www.wired.com/medtech/health/magazine/17-04/ff_perfectmemory?currentPage=all.

8 Jill Price (with Bart Davis), *The Woman Who Can't Forget: The Extraordinary Story of Living with the Most Remarkable Memory Known to Science* (NY: Free Press, 2008), 129-30.

9 Ibid., 129.

10 See Gilles Deleuze, *Cinema Two: The Time-Image* (1985), trans. Hugh Tomlinson (Minneapolis: U of Minnesota P, 1989), 54-5.

11 Is the virtual, then, the unconscious? For Freud, the unconscious is very much like a virtuality, however, it does not lend itself to any materialization, but remains the "dark continent" of the psyche. Lacan's unconscious lends itself to a metaphor with the unpublished or unarchived, given his insistence on its linguistic situatedness, and is thus more useful for our discussion: "The unconscious is the chapter of my history that is marked by a blank or occupied by a lie: it is the censored chapter. But the truth can be refound; most often it has already been written elsewhere." Cited in Henry Bond, *Lacan at the Scene* (Cambridge, MIT P, 2009), 34. The Lacanian Eric Santner shows how a symptom, defined as a failure to respond to one's situation, gives evidence of the virtual; symptoms for Santner are "in some sense the virtual archives of *voids*—or, perhaps, better, defenses against voids—that persist in historical experience." Cited in Slavoj Zizek, *Welcome to the Desert of the Real: Five Essays on September 11 and Related Dates* (NY: Verso, 2002), 23. Santner's "archive of voids" is a canny solution that materializes the virtual, while maintaining its status as illegible. We will see how Santner's linkage of the virtual with a failure to respond to the dictates of history is important to

Deleuze, although a crucial difference between Deleuze and the Lacanians would be the latter's insistence on the linguistic. Deleuze has more of a sense that this unmarkable can exist (or subsist) outside of signification. It is not merely a misplaced book.

12 Henri Bergson, *Matter and Memory* (1912), trans. N. M. Paul and W. S. Palmer (NY: Cosimo, 2007), 180.

13 While pure memory is unavailable to action, it is what allows us to "act" on actuality. Rather than define the virtual as simulacrum (technocratic or gnostic), virtuality-as-pure-memory helps us carve out simulacra on which we can act. It is not the simulcrum itself. In this way, for Bergson, the virtual and the actual chase after each other. They are, as Deleuze might say, in a relation of immanence rather than one of transcendence.

14 Leszek Kolakowski, *Bergson* (NY: Oxford UP, 1985), 1.

15 Henri Bergson, "Mind Energy" (1919), in *Henri Bergson: Key Writings*, ed. Keith Ansell Pearson and John Mullarkey (New York: Continuum, 2002), 145.

16 Bergson, *Matter and Memory*, 94.

17 Ibid., 198.

18 Ibid., 192.

19 Deleuze, *Cinema Two*, 1.

20 Ibid., 127.

21 Claire Colebrook describes how Deleuze and Guattari extend and critique Bergson by positing machinic perception not as a negative phenomenon but rather as an instance of the "'power of the false' or an impropriety that is at once vital, even if it problematizes the very idea of life and life's ownness." Colebrook, *Deleuze and the Meaning of Life* (NY: Continuum, 2010), 11-12.

22 Ibid., 206.

23 Brian Massumi, "Line Parable for the Virtual (On the Superiority of the Analog)," in *The Virtual Dimension:*

Architecture, Representation, and Crash Culture, ed. John Beckmann (NY: Princeton Architectural P, 1998), 309.

24 Compare, if you will, Kristeva on the "inability of any logical system based on a zero-one sequence (true-false, nothingness-notation) to account for the operation of poetic language." Julia Kristeva, *Desire in Language: A Semiotic Approach to Literature and Art* (1969), trans. Thomas Gora, Alice Jardine, and Leon S. Roudiez (NY: Columbia UP, 1980), 70.

25 See Aden Evens, "Digital Ontology and Example," in *Deleuze, Science, and the Force of the Virtual*, ed. Peter Gaffney (Minneapolis: U of Minnesota P, 2010), 155.

26 Colebrook, *Deleuze and the Meaning of Life*, 21.

27 Sergei M. Eisenstein, *The Film Sense* (1942), trans. Jay Leyda (NY: Harcourt, 1975), 4.

28 Manovich says as much in his *Language of New Media*: "Every filmmaker engages with the database-narrative problem in every film, although only a few have done so self-consciously." Manovich, *Language of New Media* (Cambridge, MIT P, 2002), 237-38. Yet his characterization of database and narrative as combative, as well as his weird, perhaps VR-inspired definition of narrative as virtual vis-à-vis the "materiality" of the database, set up ultimately unproductive oppositions for defining virtual literature. I have used the term "organizing principle" rather than narrative to open up a wide array of modalities for interacting with the database, in ways that work both outside and *within* narrative. Narrative is not monolithic and comes with no guarantees that it will protect us from the terrors of the virtual, although we are in an ideological moment that perhaps presents it as such a panacea. The work of narrative, in constant circuit with that of the database, is both virtual and actual, material and immaterial.

29 Peter Bogdanovich, "Interview with Orson Welles," in

Orson Welles's Citizen Kane*: A Casebook*, ed. James Naremore (NY: Oxford UP, 2004), 55.

30 Deleuze, *Cinema Two*, 99.

31 Ibid., 105-06.

32 Ibid., 110.

33 Bogdanovich, "Interview," 58.

34 Gilles Deleuze and Claire Parnet, *Dialogues* (1977), trans. Hugh Tomlinson and Barbara Habberjam, (NY: Columbia UP, 1987), 39.

35 Deleuze, *Cinema Two*, 112.

36 Ibid., 115.

37 See Gilles Deleuze, *Cinema One: The Movement-Image* (1983), trans. Hugh Tomlinson and Barbara Habberjam (Minneapolis: U of Minnesota P, 1986), 12-28.

38 Deleuze, *Cinema Two*, 110.

39 Ibid.

40 Luc Sante says of Fénéon, "Jarry called him '*celui qui silence*,' meaning both that he silences the nonsense of others and that he himself practices an active form of silence. That would be the same silence that Rimbaud embodied when he abandoned poetry for Aden and Abyssinia, that Lautréamont enacted when he destroyed his *Poésies* and published only its preface, that Paul Valéry's Monsieur Teste exemplified by writing nothing at all. It is an aggressive silence, as charged, dense, and reverberating as Malevich's black canvas. It affirms that all writing is compromise, that conception will always trump execution, that ego and politics are everyone's coauthors. It may be rooted in despair but it grows in the direction of transcendence. It wishes to free poetry from books and release it into daily life." Luc Sante, introduction to *Novels in Three Lines*, trans. Luc Sante (NY: NY Review Books, 2007), xxi.

41 Félix Fénéon, *Novels in Three Lines*, trans. Luc Sante (NY: NY Review Books, 2007), 19.

42 Ibid., 22.
43 Ibid., 38.
44 Ibid., 39.
45 Ibid., 67.
46 Ibid., 91.
47 Ibid., 94.
48 Ibid., 104.
49 Ibid., 111.
50 Ibid., 123.
51 Roland Barthes, "The Structure of the *Fait-Divers*" (1962), in *Critical Essays*, trans. Richard Howard (Evanston: Northwestern UP, 1972), 185.
52 Fort, *Wild Talents*, 918.
53 Richard Owen Cambridge, *The Scribleriad*, in *The Works of Richard Owen Cambridge, Esq., Including Several Pieces Never Before Published: With An Account of His Life and Character, By His Son, George Owen Cambridge, M.A., Prebendary of Ely* (London: Luke Hansard, 1803), 117.
54 Huysman's decadent hero Des Esseintes recodes Virgil's *Aeneid* as a failure, not because it remains unfinished (Virgil himself requested that it be burned) but rather because of its tediousness. He bemoans the "unutterable emptiness of this heap of verses. . . . the workmanship of the hexameters beating like empty tin cans and extending their syllabic quantities measured according to the unchanging rule of a pedantic and dull prosody" (41). Instead, with terrifying erudition, Des Esseintes enumerates the obscure late-Latin verse that he prefers: "sombre, tortuous, gamy verses, crammed with terms of ordinary speech" having the "special flavour which . . . the odor of Christianity would give the pagan tongue, decomposed like old venison, crumbling at the same time that the old world civilization collapsed, and the Empires, putrified by the sanies of the centuries, succumbed to the thrusts of the barbarians" (49).

His Latin library—a virtual trash heap of unclassical monstrosities—ends chronologically at the beginning of the 10th century, when, "the complicated naivete of the Christian language had . . . foundered. The balderdash of philosophers and scholars, the logomachy of the Middle Ages, thenceforth held absolute sway. The sooty mass of chronicles and historical books and cartularies accumulated, and the stammering grace, the often exquisite awkwardness of the monks, placing the poetic remains of antiquity in a ragout, were dead. The fabrications of verbs and putrified essences, of substantives breathing of incense, of bizarre adjectives, coarsely carved from gold, with the barbarous and charming taste of Gothic jewels, were destroyed" (58). Huysmans, J.-K, *Against The Grain* (1884), trans. John Howard (Floating Press, 2009), eBook Collection (EBSCOhost), web.

55 Cambridge, *Scribleriad*, 74-75.

56 Ibid., 123-25.

57 Ibid., 126.

58 Ibid., 127.

59 Ibid., 127-28.

60 Ibid., 164.

61 Ibid., 170.

62 Ibid., 200.

63 Ibid., 199.

64 Ibid., 188.

65 Walter Benjamin, "Theses on the Philosophy of History" (1940), in *Illuminations*, trans. Harry Zohn (NY: Schocken, 1968), 256.

66 Kristeva, *Desire in Language*, 25.

67 See, for instance, Stan Apps' definition of poetic language: "The occasion of viewing language as poetic is the most ostentatious poetic device of all. Poetic language is evoked by the reader's expectation of encountering poetry. A great

deal of poetic language is regularly ignored and thereby quietly neutralized when it appears in novels and in the piles of instuctive paper printed out and ignored every day in business offices. . . . In other words, there is no fully successful language. Even in the midst of that language that promises to distance us from the forceful immanence of others, there are opportunities for unsuccessful reading. A vast puddle of salty soup that is some sort of human excretion becomes visible in the pages of an otherwise harmless thriller novel. Between the gunmen and the gunmen forms a puddle. The reader becomes a spectator to the disturbing sense of kinship between a sniper rifle and a bus pass. The characters can travel simply by straddling a letter 'a' and letting it eject them like a cassette tape into the noun. And yet, this will rarely occur in the works of a successful author, unless a reader has already been conditioned by reading poetry."

"This is why poets and lovers of poetry are often described as 'victims of the poetic.' Through repeated exposure to poetic language, they become unable to experience any language as successful. In a sense, poets become unable to read, as sensible messages about the containment of humans in viewable distances cease to be plausible." Apps, *Handbook of Poetic Language* (Los Angeles: Eohippus Labs, 2007), 12-13. This essay is also available as "Of Poetic Language" in his marvelous collection *The World as Phone Bill* (Cumberland, RI: Combo Books, 2010), 93-102.

68 Kristeva, *Desire in Language*, 71.

69 Cambridge, *Scribleriad*, 237.

70 Kristeva, *Desire in Language*, 69.

71 Ibid., 65.

72 This epilogue is not available in text-only version from *Literature Online*, but is in the scanned image (i.e. it was in the original text, but for some reason LION did not make it

available in searchable form: it was mysteriously virtualized by the deceptively inclusive digital virtual). Eventually resorting to the actual "book" in the last stages of putting together my own turned up many more enticing virtualities that the digital was not able to accomodate, even though, without the digital, I may never have discovered this text.

73 Cambridge, *Scribleriad*, 237.

74 His reference to Horace—"Secretum iter, et fallentis semita vitae"—is the epilogue's knowing wink to the original *Memoirs*, since it is also an inscription above the entrance of one of Alexander Pope's secret grottos in his Twickenham gardens (which in fact Cambridge, among others, contributed to by donating various minerals to turn this camera obscura into a mine-shaft phantasmagoria). See Stephanie Ross, *What Gardens Mean*, (Chicago: U of Chicago P, 1998), 56.

75 Jacques Bens, "Queneau Oulipian," in *Oulipo: A Primer of Potential Literature*, trans. and ed. Warren F. Motte Jr. (Lincoln: U of Nebraska P, 1986), 67. The tone of this particular characterization of Oulipo may be misleading. Even though the reference is to surrealism and their love of the irrational, the Oulipo equally wished to avoid surrealism's ego-driven politics, "to radically turn away from any group activity that might engender denunciations, excommunications, or any form of terror." François LeLionnais, cited in Peter Consenstein, *Literary Memory, Consciousness, and the Group Oulipo* (NY: Rodopi, 2002), 117. If literary coterie is an anxiety formation in the face of the formless abyss of the unliterary, then one could say that Oulipo avoids purely aleatory writing or free verse because literary value must in those cases be asserted by paraliterary forms—e.g. not only by publicity and criticism, but also by the types of irrational group formations that they saw not only in surrealism, but in fascism.

76 Additionally, if "lipo" as in "lipogram" is, as they would well know, Greek for something missing, eliminated or even failed, then encoded in their very name is the notion of Oulipo—li*ttérature* po*tentielle* as lost work, missing work, failed work, but also worklessness, effortlessness.

77 Marcel Bénabou, "Rule and Constraint," in *Oulipo: A Primer of Potential Literature,* trans. and ed. Warren F. Motte Jr. (Lincoln: U of Nebraska P, 1986), 42-43.

78 François LeLionnais, cited in Jean Lescure, "A Brief History of the Oulipo," in *Oulipo: A Primer of Potential Literature,* trans. and ed. Warren F. Motte Jr. (Lincoln: U of Nebraska P, 1986), 38.

79 Jean Lescure, "A Brief History of the Oulipo," 34.

80 Jed Rasula and Steve McCaffery, *Imagining Language: An Anthology* (Cambridge: MIT P, 2001), 245.

81 Consenstein, *Literary Memory, Consciousness, and the Group Oulipo,* 29 & 42.

82 In a remarkable passage in Kristeva's *Desire in Language* to which many of the insights of this paragraph are indebted, she straddles the same paradoxes between exactitude and *élan* as they manifest themselves in the poststructuralism of Roland Barthes. She argues that Barthes' project is commensurate with Enlightenment positivity, but yet does not (and should not) eradicate the "night spreading across poetic surplus" (106). In order to conceptualize this literary positivism which includes, rather than militates against, the un-abstractable, she creates an image of quasi-Bergsonian literary stills, animated within by history and non-language. To further the reference to film, we could call this appreciation of the indexical, asignifying aspect of language and history *Bazanian,* "history as a succession . . . partitioned into experiences . . . a softening of the rigid legislature of social or literary systems, a supplement of intimacy . . . taking the shape of 'virtue hatching the

ambisexual Masses.'" Thus, Kristeva institutes suggestive but highly paradoxical links between the theorization of realist film and poetic language. Kristeva, *Desire in Language*, 107.

83 For Deleuze, this productive doubleness may be described as the pure power of difference as "opposed" to negation. In his essay on Bergson's conception of difference, he highlights this important aspect of virtual philosophy: "contradiction, finally, is only one of the many retrospective illusions that Bergson denounces. What differentiates itself into two divergent tendencies is a virtuality, and as such is something absolutely simple that realises itself. . . . Everything comes back to the critique that Bergson makes of the negative: to reach a conception of difference without negation. . . . [H]e tries to show that the negation of a real term by the other is only the positive realisation of a virtuality which contained both terms at once. . . . It is thus by virtue of an ignorance of the virtual that we believe in contradiction, in negation. The opposition of two terms is only the realisation of the virtuality which contained them both: which is to say difference is more profound than negation, than contradiction" (53). Pure recollection is thus *difference itself*, "because no one memory resembles another, because each memory is immediately perfect, because it is at once what it will always be." Gilles Deleuze, "Bergson's Conception of Difference," in *The New Bergson*, ed. John Mullarkey (Manchester: Manchester UP, 1999), 56.

84 Consenstein, *Literary Memory, Consciousness, and the Group Oulipo*, 32.

85 A notable exception may be the "je me souviens . . ." constraint, instigated by Perec; yet, the "I remember" randomly activates diverse, unconnected times of the writer, but does not constrain the time of writing itself.

86 Jacques Roubaud, *The Great Fire of London [A Story with*

Interpolations and Bifurcations] (1989), trans. Dominic Di Bernardi (Normal: Dalkey Archive, 1992), 11.

87 Ibid., 197-98.

88 Ibid., 157.

89 Ibid., 19. You might argue that its lack of "right way" indeed would make this book amenable to digital hypertext, and that it is in book form only because it was published too early (1989 in France, 1991 in US). According to Queneau, it was the "constant *lamento*" of Oulipo that it had no access to computers. Raymond Queneau, "Potential Literature," in *Oulipo*, trans. Motte, 51. So why can't we imagine that Roubaud's virtual is a digital one, or one that prefigures the digital? First of all, of course, such an assertion would belittle the huge accomplishment of the book, in the same way that theorists such as George Landow contributed to the idea that hypertext was merely poststructuralism elaborated in its new, culturally realized form. George P. Landow, *Hypertext: The Convergence of Contemporary Critical Theory and Technology* (Baltimore: Johns Hopkins, 1992). Secondly, to imagine that the *Great Fire of London* will be delivered into its true form by a digital translation glosses over the despair of the text, and the destruction implicit in its writing, even though part of what impels this destruction is a search for a new life. While the afterword by its English translator can be forgiven its utopian excesses (since it was written in such a tender moment of the digital revolution) and while he is right to imply that the digital would help us conceive of reading spaces as virtual compositions, his insistence that "One day we may have a 'great fire of London' . . . replete with sound (his parents' voices) and images (Alix Cléo Roubaud's photos as well as a step-by-step video on how to prepare azarole jelly)" seems well-nigh obscene. Roubaud, *Great Fire*, 327.

90 Deleuze, via Bergson, will remind us, in his discussion of the crystal-image that "since the past is constituted not after the present that it was but at the same time, time has to split itself in two at each moment as present and past, which differ from each other in nature." The crystal forms itself via slow non-linear accretion with each surface radiating from the seed; consequently each surface engenders new accretions, the shape of the crystal a memory shape, unto itself. Deleuze, *Cinema Two*, 81.

91 Roubaud, *Great Fire*, 213.

92 Ibid., 212.

93 Also significant for this argument is his misuse throughout of the idea of the "palindrome" as a metaphor rather than an actual constraint for his process. While there could very well be palindromes that are inaccessible to us in the English translation, even so, the novel in general resists palindromic reversibility because of the entropy and complexity it manages; Roubaud multiplies this complexity by adding non-linear bifurcations and insertions which would make a palindrome a literal impossibility rather than a formal inconvenience. Yet his vision of "a twofold language, as in an immense palindrome," bodied forth in his initial dream of *The Great Fire of London*, provides us with this impossible image. On the one hand, the meaning could be nihilistic: all the words are ash, the meaning spells out death however you parse it. This interpretation would clarify the equally paradoxical concept of writing as "the reverse eulogy of shadow" (156). Because the author claims "I am destruction," he starts and ends in that destruction. But on the other hand, his reference to an immense palindrome could elaborate his insistence on the doubleness of language, revealed, yet retaining its mystery (thus no mere riddle or word-game): "the number *one (un)*, but as though shifted in the mirror, in two facing mirrors: its palindrome,

beginning of a double language, *naked (nu)*." Roubaud, *Great Fire*, 157.

94 Ibid., 249.

95 Ibid., 250.

96 Ibid., 68.

97 Ibid., 77-78.

98 Ibid., 196.

99 Keith Ansell Pearson, *Philosophy and the Adventure of the Virtual: Bergson and the Time of Life* (NY: Routledge, 2002), 183.

100 Christian Bök, *Crystallography* (Toronto: Coach House, 2003), 120.

101 I bid., 122.

102 Ibid., 114.

103 Paul Verlaine, "The Art of Poetry" (1884), in *Selected Poems*, trans. C. F. MacIntyre (Berkeley: U of California P), 1948.

104 Christian Bök, "The Piecemeal Bard is Deconstructed: Notes Toward a Potential Robopoetics," in *UbuWeb: Papers*, ed. Kenneth Goldsmith (2001), web. http://www.ubu.com /papers/object/03_bok.pdf

105 Rob Shields cites the OED's definition of the virtual as anything "that is so in essence or effect, although not formally or actually; admitting of being called by the name so far as the effect or result is concerned." He goes on to say, "Dictionaries define the virtual in everyday life as 'that which is so in essence, but not actually so'. Thus we speak of tasks which are 'virtually complete'. More philosophically, the virtual captures the nature of activities and object which exist but are not tangible, not 'concrete.'" Rob Shields, *The Virtual* (NY: Routledge, 2003), 2.

106 Bök, *Crystallography*, 20.

107 Ibid.

108 Deleuze, *Cinema Two*, 126.

109 This idea of the "swindle" implicit in systemic thought is

less generously mobilized in the thought of Eric Voegelin, to discount Marx. Yet, to conceive of "swindle" positivistically would be to privilege modes of political thought that are historically conscious, rather than those that engage in the *reductio ad absurdum* to the naturally good and right—always a specious operation. Eric Voegelin, *Science, Politics and Gnosticism: Two Essays* (1958), trans. William J. Fitzpatrick (Chicago: Henry Regnery, 1968).

110 Bök, *Crystallography*, 156.

111 Deleuze, *Cinema Two*, 78.

112 Kristeva, *Desire in Language*, 99.

113 Ibid., citing Barthes, 107.

114 Bök, *Crystallography*, 64.

115 Ibid., 65.

116 Ibid., 84.

117 Although most accounts call this a 92-page document, available pdfs with photo documentation are 104 pages. The 400,000 number comes from a *Wired* postmortem that was published while writing this section. Noah Schachtman, "The Strain," *Wired*, April 2011, 132.

118 See Shawn James Rosenheim, *The Cryptographic Imagination: Secret Writing from Edgar Poe to the Internet* (Baltimore: Johns Hopkins UP, 1997).

119 U.S. Department of Justice, *Amerithrax Investigative Summary* (Washington, D.C., 2010), 91. http://www.justice.gov/amerithrax/docs/amx-investigative-summary.pdf.

120 Ibid., 73. [emendation is in original text.]

121 Ibid., 50.

122 Christian Bök , "The Xenotext Experiment," (2008) SCRIPTed 5:2: 227. http://www.law.ed.ac.uk/ahrc/script-ed/vol5-2/editorial.asp.

123 Department of Justice, *Amerithrax Investigative Summary*, 62.

124 Ibid., 55.

125 John Keats, *Endymion: A Poetic Romance* (1818), in *The Poetical*

Works of John Keats (London: Oxford UP, 1937), 57.

126 John Keats, Preface to *Endymion: A Poetic Romance* (1818), in *Complete and Selected Keats* (NY: Random, 1951), 64.

127 John Keats, *Complete and Selected Keats*, 439.

128 The problems of the Joyce couple bring to the fore the eternal question film goers, if they have any sensitivity or social conscience at all, must ask themselves—how is it that the problems of the rich are more compelling than those of the poor that surround them? In the Bergsonian worldview, we could say that the rich are just as aware, in fact perhaps more aware, of their limitations regarding action. What seems like an grand estate from the outside is, for the owner, one not close enough to the centers of culture to be useful, with interminable plumbing and landscaping problems and a caretaker who holds to an ancient grudge, etc. etc. The beautiful wife or husband is known for all his or her foibles and inanities. The image the rich convey, however, regardless of its internal consistency, is one that itself acts on others, whereas the image of the poor has little power to act. In a way, the image of the rich acts very much like money acts and it is notable that Deleuze cites films about money as prime exemplars of the crystal image and its dissymmetrical exchanges. In Naples, however, the Joyce's wealth and its power to act upon others as an image is unreadable. Naples is the kingdom of the poor, and the Joyce's marital relation deflates not through any lack of love, but because their currency is worthless there, their self-image as a couple consequently becoming disenchanted. The first chance they get, they take up an invitation of a Duke, at whose party the guests describe themselves as stranded on a desert island. Their aristocratic system of meaning does not play on these streets. When Katherine and Alex are caught in the religious procession at the film's end, it is opportunity to realize the practical

element of their relationship amidst the overwhelming forces of the multitude—it is literally as if Alex has caught someone about to be swept out to sea. Their inability to enjoy each other alone is not an indictment of their lack of care for each other, but rather of the way in which, stripped of its animating network, any relation becomes brutish and cruel.

129 Freud, "Uncanny," 142. See also my discussion of the Reichian extension of Freud in *Ether: The Nothing That Connects Everything* (Minneapolis: U of Minnesota P, 2006), 134-39.

130 Ibid., 143.

131 E. T. A. Hoffmann, "The Sandman" (1816), in *The Tales of E. T. A. Hoffmann*, trans. Leonard J. Kent and Elizabeth C. Knight (Chicago: U of Chicago P, 1972), 123.

132 Ibid., 104.

133 Ibid., 108.

134 Another reason to support a Bergsonian/Deleuzian rather than Freudian reading of "The Sandman" would be Klara's unexamined alliance with the Kantian idealism under interrogation in Bergson.

135 Freud, "Uncanny," 137.

136 "It is the very rhythm of what is read and what is not read that creates the pleasures of great narratives." Barthes cited in Carol Mavor, *Reading Boyishly: Roland Barthes, J. M. Barrie, Jacques Henri Lartigue, Marcel Proust, and D. W. Winnicott* (Durham: Duke UP, 2007), 413.

137 That many of these stories become tales of sexual alternatives or subordinated classes seen "through a glass darkly" points up the ways in which an author may fasten on tangible, real world limits to dramatize the limitless, or vice versa.

138 Arthur Machen, *The Great God Pan* (1894) in *The House of Souls* (NY: Knopf, 1922), 180-81. Compare also Machen's

device of "The Green Book" in *The White People*, which is used to record the memory of deep secrets, yet can only obliquely refer to those that are unspeakable: "I am going to write here many of the old secrets and some new ones; but there are some I shall not put down at all. I must not write down the real names of the days and months which I found out a year ago, nor the way to make the Aklo letters, or the Chian language, or the great beautiful Circles, nor the Mao Games, nor the chief songs. I may write something about all these things but not the way to do them, for peculiar reasons. And I must not say who the Nymphs are, or the Dôls, or Jeelo, or what voolas mean. All these are most secret secrets, and I am glad when I remember what they are, and how many wonderful languages I know, but there are some things that I call the secrets of the secrets of the secrets that I dare not think of unless I am quite alone, and then I shut my eyes, and put my hands over them and whisper the word, and the Alala comes." Machen, *The White People* (1904) in *The House of Souls* (NY: Knopf, 1922), 125.

139 H. P. Lovecraft, "The Call of Cthulhu" (1928), in *Tales* (NY: Library of America, 2005), 176.

140 Ibid., 177.

141 Ibid., 180.

142 Ibid., 181.

143 Ibid., 194.

144 Ibid., 167.

145 H. P. Lovecraft, qtd. in Benjamin Noys, "A Gothic Sinthome? The Case of H. P. Lovecraft," web, n.d., 12-3. http://chi.academia.edu/BenjaminNoys/Papers/438977/A_Gothic_Sinthome_The_Case_of_H._P._Lovecraft.

146 Lovecraft, "Cthulhu," 196.

Alchemists of the Everyday

1 Theodor Adorno, "The Essay as Form," in *Notes to*

Literature, Vol. 1 (1958), trans. Shierry Weber Nicholsen (NY: Columbia UP, 1991), 13.

2 Michael Maier, *Atalanta Fugiens* (1618), in Stanislas Klossowski De Rola, *The Golden Game: Alchemical Engravings of the Seventeenth Century* (London: Thames and Hudson, 1988), 89.

3 Johann Daniel Mylius, *Opus Medico-Chymicum* (1618), in Stanislas Klossowski De Rola, *The Golden Game: Alchemical Engravings of the Seventeenth Century* (London: Thames and Hudson, 1988), 154.

4 Maier, *Atalanta Fugiens,* 68.

5 Ibid.

6 See Bergson, *Matter and Memory,* 110.

7 Mylius, *Opus Medico-Chymicum,* 141.

8 Ibid., 143.

9 William Carlos Williams, *Paterson* (1946-58), (NY: New Directions, 1992), 87.

10 Williams, *Paterson,* 18.

11 Williams, cited in Theodora R. Graham, "'Her Heigh Compleynte': The Cress Letters of William Carlos Williams' *Paterson,*" in *Ezra Pound & William Carlos Williams: The University of Pennsylvania Conference Papers* (Philadelphia: U of Pennsylvania P, 1983), 182.

12 Ibid., 187.

13 Rachel Blau DuPlessis, *The Pink Guitar: Writing as Feminist Practice* (NY: Routledge, 1990), 57.

14 Cited in Graham, "'Her Heigh Compleynte,'" 169.

15 Williams, *Paterson,* 113.

16 Marcia Nardi, "October House Guest," in *Poems* (Denver: Swallow, 1956), 9.

17 Williams, *Paterson,* 88.

18 Nardi, "I Have Let Myself Be Proved," in *Poems,* 46.

19 Before feminist identity politics would assail the poststructuralists for their subjectless assemblages and "death of the

author," Nardi was forcing the same questions. But I would insist, with Deleuze and Guattari, of "woman"-as-virtuality over-and-above either essential category of identity politics or Lacanian "lack" or inexistence. See Claire Colebrook, *Gilles Deleuze* (NY: Routledge, 2002), 104. As such, Nardi's insistence on identity, especially in her attempts to forge a new one *before its time was ripe,* seems to be more legible. As described in Elizabeth Murrie O' Neil's sad afterword to her collection of letters between Williams and Nardi: "I asked her what—if anything—had given her a modicum of satisfaction in a life that had offered very few satisfactions. She responded without hesitation that she was proudest of having maintained her sense of personal identity. That identity—a woman poet determined to experience life for herself and to find a poetic form in which to express what is uniquely a woman's experience—had been forged during long years of 'pioneer living' (as she wrote in her long *Paterson* letter), when she fought to free herself from 'patterned standardized feminine feelings.'" Elizabeth Murrie O' Neil, ed. *The Last Word: Letters Between Marcia Nardi and William Carlos Williams* (Iowa City: U of Iowa P, 1994), 234-35.

20 William Carlos Williams, "Reading and Commentary at UCLA" (May 1955), *PennSound,* MP3 file. http://media.sas.upenn.edu/pennsound/authors/Williams-WC/27_UCLA_May-1955/Williams-WC_07_Comm-3_UCLA_May-1955.mp3.

21 Nardi, "October House Guest," 10.

22 Nardi, "Alone with a Poem," *Poems*, 12.

23 Williams, cited in Benjamin Sankey, *A Companion to William Carlos Williams's* Paterson (Berkeley: U of California P, 1971), 5.

24 Cited in Nancy K. Barry, "The Fading Beautiful Thing of *Paterson,*" in *Twentieth Century Literature,* 35:3 (Autumn,

1989): 344.

25 Ibid., 346.

26 Is there a way to give a mathematical figure of this shape of consciousness determined by sleep, by death? Would this be the shape of writing? Would writing, given these limits, be then merely a question of rate, of speed, of intensity? What about when the asymptote crosses the line, when dreams speak back or the boundary of death is broached, when coordinates are inexplicably leapt over?

27 Barry, "Fading Beautiful Thing," 349.

28 Cited in Ibid., 350.

29 The unattributed quote that opens the preface, "Rigor of beauty is the quest. But how will you find beauty when it is locked in the mind past all remonstrance?" is a citation from his own manuscript drafts, as if his deletions were just as valuable and authoritative as the lines in view, as if *Paterson* started in the act of those deletions. The rest of the deleted portion reads "It is not in the things nearest us unless transposed there by our employment? Make it free, then, by the art you have, to enter these starved and broken pieces" (*Paterson* 253, notes in the Christopher McGowen edition). According to Mike Weaver, "His first motto in *Paterson*, also on the worth of beauty, was appropriately, a 'quotation' from his own preliminary drafts. The authentic fragment, dismounted from its former place in the fabric and replaced according to new exigencies, constituted an American method." Mike Weaver, *William Carlos Williams: The American Background* (Cambridge: Cambridge UP, 1971), 16.

30 Colebrook, *Gilles Deleuze*, 110-11.

31 Elizabeth Grosz, *Architecture from the Outside: Essays on Virtual and Real Space* (Cambridge, MIT P: 2001), 167.

32 Ibid., 171.

33 Williams, *Paterson*, 3.

34 Ibid., 78-79.

35 Ibid., 46.

36 Maurice Blanchot, "The Absence of the Book," trans. Lydia Davis, in *The Station Hill Blanchot Reader: Fiction and Literary Essays* (Barrytown: Station Hill, 1998), 473.

37 Nardi, "Winter Landscape," in *Poems*, 16.

38 William Carlos Williams, *The Autobiography of William Carlos Williams* (1948), (NY: New Directions, 1967), 51.

39 Williams, *Paterson*, 129.

40 Murrie O' Neil, ed. *The Last Word*, xiv.

41 Allen Ginsberg, not included in this list, would come later; his letters in Book IV attest to the young poet's desire to make contact with a local literary hero, and his later career and teaching could be construed as an extended jazz riff on the themes of *Paterson*. Ginsberg's presence in the poem is very strong because—perhaps unexpectedly for Williams—he became an international poetic superstar rather than a local, struggling genius ("Howl" was written in 1955; *Paterson IV* was published in 1951).

42 Paul Mariani, *William Carlos Williams: A New World Naked* (SF: McGraw, 1981), 467-71 and Weaver, *William Carlos Williams*, 122-27.

43 These letters are available as part of Williams' archive in Yale's Beinecke library.

44 David Lyle, "Letter to MacLeish, Sandburg, Williams," Nov 30, 1938/Apr 13 1939, MSS 116, Box 13, Folder 406, Yale Beinecke Library, William Carlos Williams Papers, New Haven, 2.

45 Williams encouraged Lyle to retire from Wright-Aero and devote all his time to his intellectual work in 1944. Weaver, *Williams*, 123.

46 David Lyle, "Letter to Williams," April 10, 1939, MSS 116, Box 13, Folder 409, Yale Beinecke Library, William Carlos Williams Papers, New Haven, 1. It's unclear whether this letter is an original document from Lyle or a reordered

transcript by Williams, intended to be included in *Paterson*.

47 David Lyle, "Letter to Williams," December 1 1939 [i.e. 1938]/April 9, 1939, MSS 116, Box 13, Folder 406, Yale Beinecke Library, William Carlos Williams Papers, New Haven, 13.

48 Ibid. Here, Lyle is presumably quoting Rebecca West, although his references are sometimes inaccurate, garbled, or incomplete. As with many of his citations, though, he will repeat this idea "that literature started out to make a map of the sea (of human energy)" often, and with variations.

49 Lyle, (presumably) citing Emerson, Ibid., 4. We can assume then that "failure" as an expression is nothing personal, but merely a witty rejoinder to cosmic despair.

50 Weaver, *Williams*, 202.

51 Daniel Paul Schreber, *Memoirs of My Nervous Illness* (1903), trans. Ida Macalpine and Richard A. Hunter (NY: NYRB, 2000), 197.

52 Lyle, "Letter to Williams: Visual Imagism and the Difficult ART of Accompaniment," December 1, 1938/Recopied April 13, 1939, MSS 116, Box 13, Folder 406, Yale Beinecke Library, William Carlos Williams Papers, New Haven, 2.

53 Lyle citing Matthew Arnold (incorrectly), December 1 1939 [i.e. 1938]/April 9, 1939, MSS 116, Box 13, Folder 406, Yale Beinecke Library, William Carlos Williams Papers, New Haven, 4.

54 Lyle, "Letter to Williams," Sept 9 1940, MSS 116, Box 13, Folder 406, Yale Beinecke Library, William Carlos Williams Papers, New Haven, 1.

55 Mariani, *Williams*, 470.

56 Ostensibly this is a reference to Edward Faitoute Condict Young, a prominent New Jersey politician and financier, who is described in his 1908 *New York Times* obituary in ways that would have been winning to Williams: "During the years of his greatest activity Mr. Young was connected with

more enterprises than any other individual in the State. . . . [Yet] [a]ll of his life Mr. Young lived quietly, and even after his wealth was counted in millions preferred to remain in the house which he built on the Hudson Boulevard soon after its completion, in the early nineties, to crossing over to the Manhattan side of the river." He made a failed bid for Governor of New Jersey in 1892. "Banker E. F. C. Young Dead in 74th Year," *New York Times*, December 7, 1908, web, n. p.

57 Mariani, *Williams*, 470.

58 Williams, *Paterson*, 80.

59 Ibid., 100.

60 Rob Read, *O Spam Poems: Selected Daily Treated Spam, September 2003-January 2005* (Toronto: Book Thug, 2005).

61 Ron Silliman, *Silliman's Blog*, web, Dec 1, 2005.

62 Williams, *Paterson*, 140.

63 Jacques Rancière, *The Politics of Literature* (2006), trans. Julie Rose (Malden, MA: Polity, 2011), 16.

64 Ibid. The paradoxes of new forms of princely activity and democratic inactivity, especially when they concern the frenetic pacings of digital manipulations and channeling in immaterial commerce spaces, should make us wary of how these concepts are mobilized, if we haven't already been suspicious (think of how many writers at one time felt it necessary to have "ranch hand" on their resumes).

65 Ibid., 29.

66 Gary Sullivan, electronic mailing list message, 2003, retrieved from http://epc.buffalo.edu/authors/bernstein/syllabi/readings/flarf.html.

67 See, for example Morton Hurley, ed. *The Anthology of Spam Poetry* (Houston: Vértice 1925, 2007), although even this print publication is given the imprimatur of a forward written by prominent Flarfist K. Silem Mohammad.

68 To his credit, Downing posts much of his work on YouTube

as it is made, in contrast to those many art-world sanctioned video artists who have decided to work in a democratic medium and yet, shamefully, have no online works available. As well, it is important to note that popular subtitling practices many times reinforce a redundant, narrativizing interpretation of the image, a practice that videos like Downing's challenge.

69 Corey Archangel, *Data Diaries* (2002), Turbulence, web. http://turbulence.org/Works/arcangel/.

70 Friedrich A. Kittler, *Gramophone, Film, Typewriter* (1986), trans. Geoffrey Winthrop-Young and Michael Wutz (Stanford: Stanford UP, 1999), 45.

71 Rancière, *The Politics of Literature*, 15.

72 Al Filreis (host), "Is Flarf Corrosive?" June 21, 2010, *PoemTalk* 33, audio podcast, web. http://poemtalkatkwh.blogspot.com/2010/06/sharon-mesmer-flarf.html.

73 Sharon Mesmer, "I Accidentally Ate Some Chicken and Now I'm in Love with Harry Whittington (Harry Whittington: the man accidentally shot by Dick Cheney)," in *Annoying Diabetic Bitch* (Cumberland, RI: Combo Books, 2007), 53.

74 Ron Suskind, "Faith, Certainty and the Presidency of George W. Bush," *New York Times Magazine*, October 17, 2004, web. http://www.nytimes.com/2004/10/17/magazine/17BUSH.html.

75 Mesmer, "I Accidentally Ate Some Chicken and Now I'm in Love with Harry Whittington," 53.

76 Jacques Attali, *Noise: The Political Economy of Music* (1977), trans. Brian Massumi (1985) (Minneapolis: U of Minnesota P, 2009), 26.

77 Ibid., 33.

78 Ibid., 142-43.

79 A. M. J. Crawford, *BHO*, in *Peripheral Writing*, ed. Tan Lin, EOAGH 6, web, (Tucson: Chax P, 2011). http://chax.org/eoagh/issuesix/tanlin/AlejandroCrawford/AMJCrawford.pdf.

80 Deleuze, *Cinema One*, 145.

81 Most of Trecartin's video is available on the web, and at least one script, published under the aegis of UbuWeb's "Publishing the Unpublishable" series, shows the spammy concretism and text-sound play that is at work, before what is already a very visual text becomes sonorized and performed in another register. While one may, more typically, experience these videos quasi-ambiently in the gallery space, one can also watch on the computer with script and Vimeo opened in different windows, rewinding to catch the word play or suggestive tableaux (before it bursts into flames or tacky CG). In the museum space, which he or most likely Fitch transforms into any-space-whatever crap lounges for the videos ("involving the audience in a kind of exchange with the internal figurations of the film" as he has said in a *L'Uomo Vogue* profile, July/August 2011, 120), new sites are created with real-space immersivity, encouraging attitudes of repose or anxiety; online there are other ways through the video-text. The work is dispersed, yet interconnected. Its parts "function without 'sympathy,' they do not make the work into an organic totality, but each acts rather as a fragment which determines a crystallization." Gilles Deleuze, *Proust and Signs* (1964), trans. Richard Howard (Minnepolis: U of Minnesota P, 2000), 102.

82 See Deleuze, *Cinema One*, 186.

83 Ryan Trecartin, *K-CoreaINC.K (section a)* (2009), in *Publishing the Unpublishable*, ed. Kenneth Goldsmith, web, 32. http://www.ubu.com/ubu/unpub/Unpub_046_Trecartin.pdf.

84 Ibid., 3.

85 Bergson, *Matter and Memory*, 234.

86 Mark Napier, *Digital Landfill*, Potatoland, web. http://www.potatoland.org/landfill/.

87 Ibid., July 4, 2001, accessed September 1, 2011.

88 See, for instance, Craig Dworkin's description of overwriting techniques in Rosemarie Waldrop's *Camp Printing* and Charles Bernstein's *Veil*. While these practices of aliterary composition emphasize the inhuman dimensions of language, heightening what he calls the "textual sublime," (82) they do not exist in a realm of absolute exteriority to literary economies, but rather provoke shifting frames of reference for the creation of literary value. Craig Dworkin, *Reading the Illegible* (Evanston: Northwestern UP, 2003), 50-87.

89 See Deleuze, *Cinema One*, 56-61.

90 Deleuze, *Cinema Two*, 265.

91 See *Cinema Two*, 189.

92 Golan Levin with Kamal Nigam and Jonathan Feinberg, *The Dumpster: A Portrait of Romantic Breakups Collected from Blogs in 2005*, Whitney Artport Commission, web. http://artport.whitney.org/commissions/thedumpster/.

93 Here, I am paraphrasing Deleuze's suggestion regarding the "image of thought." Deleuze, "The Image of Thought," in *Difference and Repetition* (1968), 129-67.

94 Ryder Ripps, *Facebook Suicide Watch*, web, n.d., http://facebooksuicidewatch.com/.

95 Since writing this sentence, Ripps has completely reversed direction. Instead of transforming his site into an aggressively promoted social networking environment, he has instead blocked new users from participating in what he is now calling "an elite real-time image chat community," with early adopters grandfathered in as V.I.P.s.

96 It is worth noting the oftentimes forgotten transcultural origins of these flarfy tendencies, such as in the Asian notion of kuso or kuso-ge (literally "shitty-games").

97 Petra Cortright, http://www.petracortright.com/animated_gifs/hands1.gif.

98 FAUXreal, http://dump.fm/images/20110517/1305682557663

-dumpfm-FAUXreal-ErnieGehr-SereneVelocity.gif, *Dump.fm*, web.

99 See http://dump.fm/p/starsalmon/4225029.

100 Like the chat function, the webcam functions as a territorializing machine within this more deterritorialized space. That is, the webcam has an indexical function—the presence of the person behind the camera cannot easily be faked; and because no one looks over twenty-one, the frequent use of webcam stills forces unstated rules about who can participate and how. Similarly, the use or overuse of the chat function—sometimes overriding the site's *raison d'être* of "talking with images" for long stretches of time—tends to create boundaries, subgroups, and rivalries that would not be as evident or easy to maintain if the commerce were merely with recycled web-junk.

101 Compare, for example, pepper's more complex self-presencing as he sabotages his own *American Idol* audition, in a way that becomes an inside joke for dump users. Images of pepper reacting to a scolding from the slutty sub-celebrity judges proliferate in the image stream, referencing a video in another internet environment, and turning pepper's conceptual parody into a multisite meme. http://www.youtube.com/watch?v=Jyg_Z9QuFwE.

102 Erik Stinson, "I Have Maintained a General Level of Chill Since 1987," web, October 19, 2010, http://erikstinson.tumblr.com/.

103 Roland Barthes, *The Preparation of the Novel: Lecture Courses and Seminars at the Collège de France (1978-1979 and 1979-1980)* (2003), trans. Kate Briggs (NY: Columbia UP, 2011), 37.

104 Lytle Shaw, "The Moral Storm: Henry Darger's *Book of Weather Reports*," in *Cabinet* 3 (Summer 2001): n.p. Accessed online: http://www.cabinetmagazine.org/issues/3/henry-darger.php.

105 Ibid.

106 George Kuchar, "George Kuchar's *Weather Diaries*," Harvard Film Archive, artist statement, web, August 2011.

107 "In spite of their early acceptance by what was to become the Anthology Film Archives set, the Kuchars have always retained a peripheral position in that group, more analogous to that of the juvenile class clowns than full-fledged adult members." Jesse Lerner, "Storm Squatting at El Reno," in *Cabinet* 3 (Summer 2001): n.p. Accessed online: http://www.cabinetmagazine.org/issues/3/stormsquatting.php.

108 Scott MacDonald, *Storm Chaser*, in *Independent Film and Video Monthly* 20 (July 1997): 42.

109 Kuchar, "George Kuchar's *Weather Diaries*," n.p.

110 George Kuchar, *Weather Diary #1* (1986), http://www.ubu.com/film/kuchar_weather1.html.

111 Kenneth Goldsmith, *The Weather* (Los Angeles: Make Now, 2005), 39.

112 The term is attributed to Darren Wershler-Henry, but Goldsmith has been a key popularizer of the term. Do we really need to know Duchamp to respond naturally to the media environment?

113 Robert Archambeau, "Kenneth Goldsmith, or The Art of Being Talked About," *Samizdatblog*, web, April 9, 2011.

114 Ron Silliman, cited in Kenneth Goldsmith, *Uncreative Writing: Managing Language in the Digital Age* (NY: Columbia UP), 120.

115 Kenneth Goldsmith, Interviewed by Lytle Shaw, in *Printed Project* 14: *The Conceptual North Pole*, ed. Lytle Shaw (November 2010): 26.

116 Roland Barthes, *The Neutral: Lecture Course at the Collège de France (1977-1978)* (2002), trans. Rosalind E. Krauss and Denis Hollier (NY: Columbia UP, 2005), 43.

117 Ibid., 91-92.

118 Kenneth Goldsmith, Interviewed by Lytle Shaw, 22-23.

119 Barthes' describes his reason for withdrawal from a unified

ideospheric discourse as a tempering of the natural arrogance of language and identity, "in order to nuance [affirmation] (toward negation, doubt, interrogation, suspension)." Barthes, *The Neutral*, 43.

120 Less obvious are the ways that agreed upon taste is part of these channels, and Goldsmith is insistent on its importance: "Filtering is taste. And good taste rules the day." *Uncreative Writing*, 139. Remember that the guy who inhabits Malkovich ordering bathmats is there to experience a negotiation with the phone attendant about whether to order periwinkle or teal; far from an abject or otherwise throwaway moment, this poor slob, with masochistic *jouissance*, is witnessing the minute discretions of taste at work.

121 Compare the implications of recasting Picasso as a "failure," as discussed by John Berger, who wishes to avoid a moralizing embrace of failure and instead promote an historical one: "[Picasso's] experience proves that success and honour, as offered by bourgeois society, should no longer tempt anyone. It is no longer a question of refusing on principle, but of refusing for the sake of self-preservation. The time when the bourgeoisie could offer true privileges has passed. What they offer now is not worth having. . . . [O]ne must be convinced that there will be another kind of success: a success which will operate in a field connecting, for the first time ever, the most complex imaginative constructions of the human mind and the liberation of all those peoples of the world who until now have been forced to be simple, and of whom Picasso has always wished to be the representative." John Berger, "The Success and Failure of Picasso," in *Failure*, ed. Lisa Le Feuvre (Cambridge: MIT P, 2010), 29-30.

122 Goldsmith, *Uncreative Writing*, 100.

123 John Ashbery, *Three Poems* (1970), (NY: Penguin, 1986), 51.

124 Ibid., 11.

125 Ibid.

126 "Our needs are, then, so many search-lights which, directed upon the continuity of sensible qualities, single out in it distinct bodies. They cannot satisfy themselves except upon the condition that they carve out, within this continuity, a body which is to be their own, and then delimit other bodies with which the first can enter into relation, as if with persons. To establish these special relations among portions thus carved out from sensible reality is just what we call *living*." Bergson, *Matter and Memory*, 262.

127 Ashbery, *Three Poems*, 20.

128 Ibid., 45.

129 Ibid., 101.

130 Ibid., 61.

131 Ibid., 92.

132 Ibid., 103-05.

133 Benjamin, "Theses on the Philosophy of History," 258.

134 Walter Benjamin, "On Some Motifs in Baudelaire" (1939), in *Illuminations*, 160.

135 Walter Benjamin, *The Arcades Project,* trans. Howard Eiland and Kevin McLaughlin (Cambridge: Harvard UP, 2002), 402.

136 Deleuze productively divides "place" into three analytic subsets: milieu (the domain of the body), space (a mathematical relationship), and landscape (its aesthetic conception). *Cinema One*, 186-87.

137 Tan Lin, *BlipSoak01* (Berkeley: Atelos, 2003), 11.

138 Am I just a "bad reader" of poetry? Perhaps, but Lin has built enough imperfection into this dyadic form that it's not immediately recognizable. The first part of the book has text in more blocky, paragraph-like forms, and by the time we get to the double-lined part, each line crosses occasionally from the left into the right page, the spine of the book confounding any coherently focused reading or visual grasp of a single page.

139 Tan Lin, *Seven Controlled Vocabularies and Obituary 2004. The Joy of Cooking: [AIRPORT NOVEL MUSICAL POEM PAINTING FILM PHOTO HALLUCINATION LANDSCAPE]*, (Middletown: Wesleyan, 2010), 20.

140 Breton, *Nadja*, 60.

141 Tan Lin, "The Patio and the Index," in *Triple Canopy* 14, web, 10/24/2011. http://canopycanopycanopy.com/14/the_patio_and_the_index.

142 Tan Lin, "Anachronistic Modernism," in *Cabinet* 1 (Winter 2000/01): n.p. Accessed online: http://www.cabinet-magazine.org/issues/1/anachronistic.php.

143 Lin, *Seven Controlled Vocabularies*, 22.

144 Alejandro Crawford, *Seven Controlled Vocabularies, Fourth Chinese Edition*, trans. Google, in Edit Publications, *11 Books Expanding Tan Lin's Seven Controlled Vocabularies and Obituary 2004. The Joy of Cooking, YouTube Readings, Postcard, & MediaWiki*, ed. Danny Snelson, web, http://aphasic-letters.com/edit/publications.html.

145 For example, the text processing task of Google translating was done primarily by Alejandro Crawford during an event that expanded *Seven Controlled Vocabularies* into eleven more books, including four Chinese editions (which, by the way, seem the most genuinely non-readable, relaxing and ambient of the bunch). This event was curated by Danny Snelson at the Kelly Writers House and brought together twenty-four author-editors to collaborate on multiple Lulu book versions. By expanding the core text out into multiple para-versions (not to mention the fact that parts of *Seven Controlled Vocabularies* already existed in video form before they were in the book), this event shares features with other expanded literary projects like Lytle Shaw and Jimbo Blachly's *Chadwick Family Papers* or my own *The Torrent*. Such works dematerialize the literary object in order to energize more virtual aspects of literary creation, engaging

public space, performance, and collaboration around an unpublished or unpublishable phantom-corpus.

146 Tan Lin, *Insomnia and the Aunt* (Chicago: Kenning Editions, 2001), n.p.

147 Jennifer Scappettone, "Poetics of Enormity," *Rethinking Poetics: Conference of the Columbia-Penn Poetics Initiative,* June 11, 2010, talk/performance. http://oikost.com/wp-content/uploads/2010/07/ScappettonePoeticsEnormity.pdf.

148 Jennifer Scappettone, interviewed by Joe Milutis, "Junk Shot! with Jennifer Scappettone," *New Jersey as an Impossible Object*, web, March 13, 2011.

149 Tan Lin, *Heath (Plagiarism/Outsource) Notes Towards the Definition of Culture, Untitled Heath Ledger Project, A History of the Search Engine, Disco OS* (La Laguna: Zaesterle, 2007), n.p.

150 Lin, *Seven Controlled Vocabularies*, 78.

151 Lin, *Heath*, n.p.

152 Soren Kierkegaard, *Fear and Trembling* (1843) in *Fear and Trembling & The Sickness Unto Death*, trans. Walter Lowrie (NY: Doubleday, 1954), 49.

153 Laura Mulvey, "Visual Pleasure in Narrative Cinema," (1975) *Screen* 16 (3): 6–18.

154 Lola's milieu could simply be the world of the image, into which Mulvey entered as an artist-practitioner, in order to dismantle its claims on our attention, its particular ordering system, as distinct from that of the word, or even image-text. The image sensorium holds out a world potentially more vital than that controlled by the written—the great directors of silent film always would affirm these powers of the image, as would their heirs in experimental film and graphic design—but it is also the place of flimsy pasteboard illusion—enhanced now by vast technological armatures, and lining a cage. As Vilém Flusser says of the propensity for the powers of the image to turn on its users: "They are supposed to be maps but they turn into screens: Instead of

representing the world, they obscure it until human beings' lives finally become a function of the images they create. Human beings cease to decode the images and instead project them, still encoded, into the world 'out there,' which meanwhile itself becomes like an image—a context of scenes, of states of things. This reversal of the function of the image can be called 'idolatry.'" Vilém Flusser, *Towards a Philosophy of Photography* (1983), trans. Anthony Mathews (London: Reaktion Books, 2000), 10. The fact that the interiors of the Blue Angel nightclub have the look of a Jakob Böhme woodcut should alert us to the mystic dimensions of this film, while offering up a caution concerning the difficulties implicit in activating an *alchemical* gaze in a cosmos of fraudulent semblances.

155 Indeed, as Malcolm Cowley describes in his memoir of life in the "lost generation" of literary modernists, "It would be interesting to list the authors who were ambulance or camion drivers in 1917. Dos Passos, Hemingway, Julian Green, William Seabrook, E. E. Cummings, Slater Brown, Harry Crosby, John Howard Lawson, Sidney Howard, Louis Bromfield, Robert Hillyer, Dashiell Hammett . . . one might almost say that the ambulance corps and the French military transport were college-extension courses for a generation of writers." Cowley, *Exile's Return: A Literary Odyssey of the 1920s* (1934), (NY: Viking, 1962), 38.

156 Cited in Ronald Hayman, *Nietzsche: A Critical Life* (NY: Oxford UP, 1980), 128.

157 Cited in Angel Price, *Whitman's* Drum Taps *and Washington's Civil War Hospitals,* web, n.d., n.p. http://xroads.virginia.edu/~cap/hospital/whitman.htm.

158 "He had come to terms with his body's neutrality and would even turn this to his advantage when he nursed soldiers. Its dumb acquiescence, genial and hopeful, exuding sunshine and cleanliness—he was compulsively

clean always—made it a sight as comforting to the stricken men as their longed-for mothers would have been. . . . He was mother, father, a shining brother, their happy rock. They clung on, sweating and thrashing, moaning for water, for love, for pity." Philip Callow, *Walt Whitman: From Noon to Starry Night* (London: Allison & Busby, 1992), 303.

159 Jeffrey Meyers, *Hemingway: A Biography* (NY: Harper, 1985), 29-36.

160 Cited in Ibid., 30.

161 Ernest Hemingway, *A Moveable Feast* (1964), (NY: Bantam, 1979), 76.

162 Ibid.,15

163 Ibid., 144.

Prelusivity

1 Stanislaw Lem, *Solaris* (1961), trans. Joanna Kilmartin and Steve Cox (NY: Berkeley, 1971), 176-77 & 132.

2 Ibid., 153.

3 Derrida, *Archive Fever*, 14-15.

4 Lem, *Solaris*, 80.

5 Virtual machines used to dominate future time for the purposes of commerce are a well-known feature of many sci-fi scenarios. For instance, the paranoiac implication of Fassbinder's *World on a Wire* is that a virtual prediction machine that imagines scenarios twenty years into the future is actually a simulation itself *within* another simulation controlled by the world twenty years in the past, thus extending the incipient control apparatuses of the Nazi era into the twenty-first century. A similar scenario is found in the *Valis* books of Philip Dick, allegories of gnostic virtuality, in which an Empire that seeks to assert the eternal authority of ancient Rome creates a false reality to block the real informational force of an interstellar plasmate.

6 The mirror in this instance eloquently visualizes the way the

virtual and the actual run after each other "to the point of indiscernability" in film; as Deleuze points out in his discussion of the crystal image "there is no virtual which does not become actual in relation to the actual, the latter becoming virtual through the same relation. . . . [T]he mirror-image is virtual in relation to the actual character that the mirror catches, but it is actual in the mirror which now leaves the character with only a virtuality and pushes him back out-of-field" (69-70). The mirror serves to foreground the already virtualizing activity of the film shot, conceptualizing and defamiliarizing this activity at one remove. This incessant exchange between virtual and actual in which film traffics is not just exchange between one mirrored image and another, but also *exchange itself*, between the images created and their economic double. Guido's attempt to go behind the mirror—while creating another virtuality of a *reality effect*—nevertheless expresses a desire to exit from the economic system of a film. For this reason, as Deleuze points out, films about money are very often films about films, films with fragmented crystalline points of view, films with a metafilmic theme, since they have the ability to visualize their system from the outside, and to consider the possibility of an unequal or tricked exchange between image and the economic system that enlivens it (exchange between the actual and the virtual is always unequal, hence the immanence of failure): "What the film within the film expresses is this infernal circuit between the image and money, this inflation which time puts into the exchange, this 'overwhelming rise'. The film is movement, but the film within the film is money, is time. The crystal-image thus receives the principle which is its foundation: endlessly relaunching exchange which is dissymmetrical." Deleuze, *Cinema Two*, 78.

7 See my discussion of color, Fellini, and the aesthetic of the

absolute in *Ether: The Nothing that Connects Everything*, 30-35.

8 Deleuze, *Cinema One*, 38-39.

9 Stanislaw Lem, *Imaginary Magnitude* (1981), trans. Marc E. Heine (London: Mandarin, 1991), 2 & 9.

10 Stanislaw Lem, *One Human Minute*, trans. Catherine S. Leach (NY: HBJ, 1986), 27.

11 Ibid.

12 Ibid., 18.

13 Lem, *Imaginary Magnitude*, 54.

14 Ibid., 43.

15 Ibid., 50.

16 Ibid., 54.

17 Ibid., 44.

18 Ibid., 42.

19 Ibid., 59.

20 Carol Mavor, *Reading Boyishly*, 4.

21 Ian Buchanan, *Fredric Jameson: Live Theory* (NY: Continuum, 2006), 45.

22 While such confusion might be expected from Updike, it is more unacceptable when it appears in the work of George Landow, who made a career by pointing out the similarities between Barthes' notion of the "writerly" text and hypertext. However, this mistake in early versions of his book (corrected, somewhat ironically, in online, hypertext versions), while perhaps not Landow's fault—an officious editor changing the meaning of a sentence to make it more "readable" for the "readerly" crowd is not beyond plausibility—is symptomatic of his larger misunderstanding. That is, the publication of Landow's book is a key moment that branded the digital virtual as a kind of redemption (or out-pacing) of all the desired "writerly" virtualities celebrated by poststructuralism; in fact, however, it is the digital that has been instrumental in erasing these virtualities from intellectual discourse, reconstituting a kind of readerly

complacency, albeit with a consumer-as-producer twist. See Landow, *Hypertext*, 5-6.

23 John Updike, "Roland Barthes" in *Hugging the Shore: Essays and Criticism* (NY: Knopf, 1983), 576-583. After Barthes' death, under a review cruelly titled "The Last of Barthes," Updike became somewhat forgiving, siding with the late Barthes, although backhandedly, for sure: he praises his "professorial slyness" (592). In a review of *Sade/Fourier/Loyola*, he offers up another semi-encomium that, while appreciative, serves to situate Barthes' importance squarely in the realm of "criticism," safely on a far-off shore: "Criticism so theoretical yet apprehensive, so lofty in its overview yet so piquant in the details it seizes upon, so adroit at coaxing the classics to turn their faces to the light of a radical new aesthetic, is a triumph peculiarly Gallic. By comparison, American criticism seems leaden, carping, and timid" (587). "*Critic*"—that word so suggestive of artistic failure, at least on this side of the Atlantic—brings with it connotations of cowardice, of parasitism, of the inability to set out one's own work and stand by it. Updike is willing to grant Barthes the dubious honor of the "great critic." But to compete with the novelist on his own territory, for the hearts and minds of those who read "primary" literature, is another matter entirely. Such an epitaph is designed to insure that Barthes' criticism will not undergo the veritably alchemical transformation into a new literary paradigm, or at least, as intended, would not put criticism on equal footing with literary production, blurring the distinction between the two in the pursuit of a more networked, non-hierarchical transaction between writers. Updike would attempt to have the last word on this score. Updike, "Texts and Men" and "The Last of Barthes," in *Hugging the Shore*, 583-596.

24 Mavor, *Reading Boyishly*, 4.

25 Louis-Jean Calvet, *Roland Barthes: A Biography* (1990), trans. Sarah Wykes (Bloomington: Indiana UP, 1995), 238.

26 Ibid., 238-39.

27 Barthes cited in Ibid., 239.

28 Barthes, *Preparation of the Novel*, 11.

29 Roland Barthes, *Camera Lucida: Reflections on Photography* (1980), trans. Richard Howard (NY: Hill & Wang, 2010), 19.

30 Ibid., 83.

31 Barthes, *Preparation of the Novel*, 108.

32 Kristeva, *Desire in Language*, 118.

33 Ibid., 120.

34 Roland Barthes, *S/Z* (1970), trans. Richard Miller (NY: Hill & Wang, 1974), 5.

35 Calvet, *Roland Barthes*, 224-25.

36 Lisa Fittko, "The Story of Old Benjamin," in *The Arcades Project*, 952.

37 Hannah Arendt, *Men in Dark Times* (NY: Harcourt, 1968), 154-55.

38 Benjamin writes, "And one thing, therefore, can never be made good: having neglected to run away from home. From forty-eight hours' exposure in those years, as in a caustic solution, the crystal of life's happiness forms." "One Way Street," (1928) in *Reflections*, trans. Edmund Jephcott (NY: Schocken, 1978), 64.

39 Benjamin, "Letter to Gershom Scholem" (1932), cited in Scholem, "Walter Benjamin and His Angel," (1972) in *On Walter Benjamin: Critical Essays and Recollections*, ed. Gary Smith (Cambridge: MIT P, 1988), 86.

40 Benjamin, "The Image of Proust" (1929), in *Illuminations*, 203.

41 Ibid., 204-05.

42 Benjamin, "On Some Motifs in Baudelaire," in *Illuminations*, 160. See my discussion in the "Alchemists of the Everyday" section regarding the various translations of this quote as it

applies to the poetry of Tan Lin.

43 Here is where Benjamin departs from the Surrealists: while they celebrate the image as a grotesque of latent dream energies, Benjamin posits analytic tools to waken from these images. With each image that presents itself there is a great chance that one will fail to express history by not unlocking its meaning. This potential for misunderstanding is what he calls "the dangerous moment that underlies all acts of reading." Bernd Witte, *Walter Benjamin: An Intellectual Biography* (1985), trans. James Rolleston (Detroit: Wayne State UP, 1991), 179.

44 Arendt, *Men in Dark Times*, 193.

45 Benjamin, *Arcades Project*, 392.

46 Ibid., 931.

47 Ibid., 672.

48 Benjamin, "Theses on the Philosophy of History," 262-63.

49 Ibid., 255.

50 Benjamin, "Agesilaus Santander" (1933, unpublished text), in Scholem, "Walter Benjamin and His Angel," 57.

51 Benjamin cited in Witte, *Walter Benjamin*, 51.

52 Scholem, "Walter Benjamin and His Angel," 64.

53 Ibid., 78.

54 Benjamin, "Theses on the Philosophy of History," 257-58.

55 Fittko, "The Story of Old Benjamin," 948.

56 Luc Sante cited in Bond, *Lacan at the Scene*, 6.

57 Stephen Schwartz, "The Mysterious Death of Walter Benjamin," in *The Weekly Standard*, 6:37 (June 11, 2001): web.

58 Perhaps presaging the tight connection between the rise of memoir in our own time to the decay of social discourse, Benjamin writes: "A blind determination to save the prestige of personal existence, rather than, through an impartial disdain for its impotence and entanglement, at least to detach it from the background of universal delusion, is triumphing almost everywhere. That is why the air is so

thick with life theories and world views, and why in this country they cut so presumptuous a figure, for almost always they finally serve to sanction some wholly trivial private situation. For just the same reason the air is so full of phantoms, mirages of a glorious cultural future breaking upon us overnight in spite of all, for everyone is committed to the optical illusions of his isolated standpoint." "One-Way Street," 74.

59 Michel Foucault, *The Order of Things: An Archeology of the Human Sciences* (1966), (NY: Vintage, 1994), 132.

60 Ibid., 304.

61 Derrida, *Archive Fever*, 18.

62 There have been archival projects that claim total coverage—thus threatening to close down the eminently historical activities of remix and rewrite—from Napoleon's *Description de L' Égypte* to Google Books. A "People's Library" might very well be appropriately based on a single tattered tome: this is, of course, how the Bible has functioned in poor communities across America. Benjamin, in "One Way Street," points out that the Bible served as "people's property" after Luther's translation, but also suggests that this notion of the book is at an end. On the one hand printing "is pitilessly dragged out onto the street by advertisements and subjected to the brutal heteronomies of economic chaos," on the other hand, crystalline prelusive assemblages of writers such as Mallarmé have emerged. "One-Way Street," 77.

63 Benjamin writes: "The card index marks the conquest of three-dimensional writing, and so presents an astonishing counterpoint to the three-dimensionality of script in its original form as rune or knot notation. (And today the book is already, as the present mode of scholarly production demonstrates, an outdated mediation between two different filing systems. For everything that matters is to be found in

the card box of the researcher who wrote it, and the scholar studying it assimilates it into his own card index. . . . The typical work of modern scholarship is intended to be read like a catalogue. But when shall we actually write books like catalogues?" "One-Way Street," 78-9. Appropriately, Anna Gray and Ryan Wilson Paulsen's pdf-book, *One Way Street: An Index in Thirteen Parts* (Special Projects Press, 2008), is an index-as-literary-artifact applied to Benjamin's early manifesto for a virtual literature. http://ubu.com/ubu/unpub/Unpub_047_Gray-Paulsen.pdf.

64 R. Gerald Nelson, *DDDDoomed Or, Collectors and Curators of the Image—A Brief Future History of the Image Aggregator* (Minneapolis: Edition MK, 2010), 17.

65 Ibid., 39.

66 Stoffel Debuysere, cited in Ibid., 60. This idiosyncratic attempt to grasp the world of data is an activity that in the early years of CDROM experimentation, video artist Antoni Muntadas called "anarchivism."

67 Benjamin, cited in Arendt, *Men in Dark Times*, 199.

68 Arendt, *Men in Dark Times*, 200.

69 Susan Buck-Morss, *The Dialectics of Seeing: Walter Benjamin and the Arcades Project* (Cambridge: MIT P, 1989), 24.

70 Benjamin, "One Way Street," 81.

71 "His sentences often enough have the authoritarian stance of words of revelation, as which they were in fact considered by him to no slight extent during his youthful metaphysical period. . . . The gesture of the esoteric writer perceived in him by Adorno and me was that of the producer of authoritative sentences, and that, to be sure, also means, from the very outset and because of their essence, sentences lending themselves to quotation and interpretation. What is illuminating in them is meshed with the thoroughly enigmatic. . . . They are sentences from the Holy Writ of an initiate, scarcely and scantily disguised, at

once rational and mystical, as is becoming to sentences of this kind." Scholem, "Walter Benjamin and His Angel," 52.

72 Benjamin, "One-Way Street," 61.

73 Ibid.

74 Buck-Morss, *The Dialectics of Seeing*, 27.

75 See Rolf Tiedemann, "Dialectics at a Standstill: Approaches to the *Passagen-Werk*" in *The Arcades Project*, 929-945.

76 Benjamin, cited in Witte, *Walter Benjamin*, 180.

77 Benjamin, "One-Way Street," 61.

78 See, for instance, Kolakowski's cosmic description of Bergsonian duration that subtends the activity of memory storage: "In the actual durée nothing is lost, but nothing is reversible either: each moment carries within it the entire flow of the past and each is new and unrepeatable. Since the matter of the past perishes, but the memory does not, and since memory is not an aspect of matter, it is likely that the human mind is largely independent of body and can survive its destruction." Kolakowski, *Bergson*, 3.

79 Wambly Bald, "Lincoln Gillespie, Jr." in *The Left Bank Revisited: Selections from the Paris* Tribune *1917-1934*, ed. Hugh Ford (University Park: Pennsylvania State UP, 1972), 85.

80 Abraham Lincoln Gillespie, *The Syntactic Revolution*, ed. Richard Milazzo (NY: Out of London P, 1980), 50.

81 Ibid., 19.

82 Ibid., 10.

83 Ibid., 8.

84 Ibid., 64.

85 Ibid., 5.

86 Ibid., 9.

87 See Charles Bernstein, "Poetics of the Americas," in *My Way: Speeches and Poems* (Chicago: U of Chicago P, 1999), 113-37 and Caroline Bergvall, "Middling English," in *Meddle English: New and Selected Texts* (Callicoon, NY: Nightboat

Books, 2011), 5-19.

88 Gillespie, *Syntactic Revolution*, 20.

89 Ibid., 44.

90 Joseph Mitchell, *Joe Gould's Secret* (1942), (NY: Viking, 1965), 12-13.

Index

Contemporary culture has eliminated both the concept of the public and the figure of the intellectual. Former public spaces – both physical and cultural – are now either derelict or colonized by advertising. A cretinous anti-intellectualism presides, cheerled by expensively educated hacks in the pay of multinational corporations who reassure their bored readers that there is no need to rouse themselves from their interpassive stupor. The informal censorship internalized and propagated by the cultural workers of late capitalism generates a banal conformity that the propaganda chiefs of Stalinism could only ever have dreamt of imposing. Zer0 Books knows that another kind of discourse – intellectual without being academic, popular without being populist – is not only possible: it is already flourishing, in the regions beyond the striplit malls of so-called mass media and the neurotically bureaucratic halls of the academy. Zer0 is committed to the idea of publishing as a making public of the intellectual. It is convinced that in the unthinking, blandly consensual culture in which we live, critical and engaged theoretical reflection is more important than ever before.